Haiti: From Revolutionary Slaves to Powerless Citizens

This title focuses on Haiti from an international perspective. Haiti has endured undue influence from successive French and US governments; its fragile democracy has been founded on subordination to and dominance of foreign powers. This book examines Haiti's position within the global economic and political order, and how the more dominant members of the international community have, in varying ways, exploited the country over the last 200 years.

Alex Dupuy is John E. Andrus Professor of Sociology at Wesleyan University in Middletown, CT, USA.

Europa Country Perspectives

The new *Europa Country Perspectives* series, from Routledge, examines a wide range of contemporary political, economic, developmental and social issues from areas around the world. Complementing the *Europa Regional Surveys of the World* series, *Europa Country Perspectives* will be a valuable resource for academics, students, researchers, policy-makers, business people and anyone with an interest in current world affairs.

While the *Europa World Year Book* and its associated Regional Surveys inform on and analyse contemporary economic, political and social developments at the national and regional level, Country Perspectives provide in-depth, country-specific volumes written or edited by specialists in their field, delving into a country's particular situation. Volumes in the series are not constrained by any particular template, but may explore a country's recent political, economic, international relations, social, defence, or other issues in order to increase understanding.

Haiti: From Revolutionary Slaves to Powerless Citizens
Essays on the politics and economics of underdevelopment, 1804–2013
Alex Dupuy

Haiti: From Revolutionary Slaves to Powerless Citizens

Essays on the politics and economics of underdevelopment, 1804–2013

Alex Dupuy

Routledge
Taylor & Francis Group

LONDON AND NEW YORK

First edition published 2014
by Routledge
2 Park Square, Milton Park, Abingdon, Oxon OX14 4RN

and by Routledge
711 Third Avenue, New York, NY 10017

Routledge is an imprint of the Taylor & Francis Group, an informa business

British Library Cataloguing in Publication Data
A catalogue record for this book is available from the British Library

Library of Congress Cataloging in Publication Data
Haiti, from revolutionary slaves to powerless citizens : essays on the politics and economics of underdevelopment, 1804-2013 / Alex Dupuy.
    pages cm. – (Europa country perspectives)
Summary: "This title focuses on Haiti from an international perspective. Haiti has endured undue influence from successive French and US governments; its fragile 'democracy' has been founded on subordination to and dominance of foreign powers. This book examines Haiti's position within the global economic and political order, and how the more dominant members of the international community have, in varying ways, exploited the country over the last 200 years"– Provided by publisher.
    Includes bibliographical references and index.
1. Haiti–Politics and government. 2. Haiti–Foreign relations. 3. Haiti–Economic conditions. 4. Economic development–Haiti. 5. Democracy–Haiti–History. 6. Failed states–Haiti. I. Title.
    F1921.D87 2014
    972.94–dc23
        2013040547

ISBN: 978-1-85743-710-2 (hbk)
ISBN: 978-0-31585-654-4 (ebk)

Typeset in Times New Roman
by Taylor & Francis Books

Editor, South America, Central America and the Caribbean: Jackie West
Editorial Assistants: Amy Welmers, Lydia de Cruz

Printed and bound in the United States of America by Edwards Brothers Malloy

Contents

Acknowledgements

First and foremost I want to express my most profound gratitute and indebtedness to Franck Laraque for his mentorship and all he has taught me over the past forty some years. No one has inspired me more than he to never give up hope and the belief that a more just and egalitarian future is possible. I am immensely grateful to Leslie Demangles for his careful reading of all the essays in this book and for his most helpful editorial comments and suggestions. I would also like to thank Robert Fatton for his comments on Chapter 1; Hilbourne Watson for his comments and suggestions on earlier drafts of Chapter 3; and Linden Lewis for his comments and suggestions on the published version of Chapter 6. I also want to thank my friends and colleagues Robert Fatton, Leslie Desmangles, Robert Maguire, Carolle Charles, François Pierre-Louis, Henry "Chip" Carey, Linden Lewis, Hilbourne Watson, Anton Allahar, and Brian Meeks. The stimulating discussions we have had and the many panels we have shared at the annual meetings of the Haitian Studies Association and/or the Caribbean Studies Association have influenced my thinking on the issues I deal with in this book.

Last but not least, I want to thank the editorial and production staff at Routledge especially Jackie West, Editor, South America, Central America and the Caribbean, Europa Country Perspective Series; Kris Wischenkämper, Copy Editor; Paola Celli, Senior eProduction Editor; and Tom Hussey, Book Cover Designer.

Chapter 4 "The transition to democracy and the demise of color politics in Haiti" is a revised version of the article: "From François Duvalier to Jean-Bertrand Aristide: The Declining Significance of Color Politics in Haiti," in Kate Quinn and Paul Sutton, eds. *Politics and Power in Haiti*, 43–63. New York: Palgrave Macmillan, 2013. Reprinted with permission from Palgrave Macmillan.

Chapter 5 "The World Bank and Haiti: abetting dictatorship, undermining democracy" is a revised version of the article "Globalization, the World Bank, and the Haitian Economy," in Franklin W. Knight and Teresita Martinez-Vergne, *Contemporary Caribbean Cultures in a Global Context*, 43–70. Chapel Hill: The University of North Carolina Press, 2005. Reprinted with permission from The University of North Carolina Press.

Chapter 6 "Class, power, sovereignty: Haiti before and after the earthquake" is a revised version of the article "Class, Power, Sovereignty: Haiti Before and After the Earthquake," in Linden Lewis, ed., *Caribbean Sovereignty, Development and Democracy in an Age of Globalization*, 17–34. New York: Routledge, 2013. Reprinted with permission from Routledge.

Acronyms

AFL-CIO	American Federation of Labor-Congress of Industrial Organizations
ALBA	Alianza Bolivariana para los Pueblos de Nuestra América (Bolivarian Alliance for the Americas)
BNC	Banque Nationale de Crédit (National Bank of Credit)
BPH	Banque Populaire Haïtienne (Haitian Popular Bank)
CARICOM	Caribbean Community
CBTPA	Caribbean Basin Trade Partnership Act
CD	Convergence Démocratique (Democratic Convergence)
CEP	Conseil Électoral Provisoire (Provisional Electoral Council)
CEPR	Center for Economic and Policy Research
CIA	Central Intelligence Agency
CTMO-HOPE	Commission Tripartite de Mise en Oeuvre de la Loi HOPE (Tripartite Commission for the Implementation of HOPE)
EERP	Emergency Economic Recovery Program
EU	European Union
FAO	Food and Agriculture Organization
FL	Fanmi Lavalas (Lavalas Family Party)
GDP	gross domestic product
GOH	Government of Haiti
GRULAC	Grupo Geopolítico de América Latina y el Caribe (Group of Latin American and Caribbean Countries)
ha	hectare
HELP	Haiti Economic Lift Program
HOPE	Haitian-Hemispheric Opportunity through Partnership Encouragement Act
HTG	Haitian Gourde
IDB	Inter-American Development Bank
IFC	International Finance Corporation
IFI	international financial institution
IGH	Interim Government of Haiti
IHRC	Interim Haiti Recovery Commission
IMF	International Monetary Fund

INGO	international non-governmental organization
INITÉ	Unity Party
LESPWA	Hope
MINUSTAH	Mission des Nations Unies pour la Stabilisation en Haïti (United Nations Stabilization Mission in Haiti)
MT	metric tons
NGO	non-governmental organization
OAS	Organization of American States
OPL	Organisation Politique Lavalas (Lavalas Political Organization)/Organisation du Peuple en Lutte (Organization of People in Struggle)
PDVSA	Petróleos de Venezuela S.A.
PM	prime minister
SME	square meter equivalents
SRI	System of Rice Intensification
US(A)	United States (of America)
USAID	United States Agency for International Development

About the author

Alex Dupuy is John E. Andrus Professor of Sociology at Wesleyan University in Middletown, CT, USA. He is an internationally recognized scholar and specialist on Haiti. He has lectured at universities and colleges across the USA and abroad, and has given many interviews and commentaries on Haitian affairs on local, national, and international radio and television networks, including the News Hour with Jim Lehrer, Toronto Public TV, Democracy Now!, WBAI, National Public Radio, Pacifica Radio, the BBC, the CBC, and the Australian Broadcasting Company. In addition to his many articles in professional journals and anthologies, he is the author of *Haiti in the World Economy: Class, Race, and Underdevelopment Since 1700* (1989); *Haiti in the New World Order: The Limits of the Democratic Revolution* (1997); and *The Prophet and Power: Jean-Bertrand Aristide, the International Community, and Haiti* (2007).

Introduction

By all measures, the Saint-Domingue Revolution of 1791–1804, also known as the Haitian Revolution, was the most radical of all the 18th century revolutions. It was indeed an epochal event. The American Revolution of 1776, and the French Revolution of 1789 fought for the principles of national self-determination, liberty, equality, and fraternity, but limited them to white European and American men only. Both of these preceding revolutions sought to maintain the system of chattel slavery and its corresponding racial stratification order by declaring that black men and women were not fully human and hence were unqualified for citizenship, equality, liberty, and self-rule. The Saint-Domingue/Haitian Revolution, fought by slaves and free people of color, also known as *affranchis*, challenged the premises of colonialism, slavery, and white supremacy, and declared once and for all that the ideals of liberty, equality, justice, and self-determination belonged to all of humanity. Thus, in many ways, the Haitian Revolution was the first truly modern revolution. For if by modernity we mean the belief in the universal equality of the human race, the right of self-determination, and the possibility of achieving it, then the Saint-Domingue Revolution was the first of the modern epoch—associated with the rise of the capitalist world-system in the 16th century—to have been fought for that purpose.

The impact of the revolution also went far beyond the borders of Saint-Domingue, which the revolutionary leaders renamed Haiti after they declared its independence from France on January 1, 1804. By destroying the wealthiest French colony in the Caribbean, the revolution also dealt a deadly blow to French imperial ambitions in the New World, just as the American Revolution had done earlier to England's. Slightly larger than the state of Maryland, Saint-Domingue's 452,000 slaves out-produced all the other French and English Caribbean sugar colonies put together, and supplied about half of the sugar and coffee consumed in Europe and the Americas at the time of the French Revolution of 1789 (Williams 1970: 238–39; Geggus 2002: 5). Fought in that part of the world where colonialism and slavery still dominated, the victory of the black slaves and free people of color of Saint-Domingue sent shock waves throughout Europe and the Americas. As Alyssa Goldstein Sepinwall put it, "It would not be an overstatement to call the Haitian Revolution's international effects cataclysmic" (Sepinwall 2009: 317). Slaveholders every-where feared that the spirit of rebellion would spread among their own slaves, and took measures to restrict immigration from Saint-Domingue. Filled with the passion for freedom fueled by the revolution, Haiti invaded neighboring Spanish San Domingo (today the Dominican Republic) to abolish slavery there, and provided direct assistance to the struggle for independence and the abolition of slavery in Venezuela in 1820. Despite this support Simón Bolívar, under pressure from the USA, refused to recognize and invite Haiti to the first hemispheric Congress of Panama in 1826 (Trouillot 1990: 52; Geggus 2002: 27–28).

The Revolution has stood since 1804 as the symbol of black freedom from slavery, racism, and colonial oppression everywhere. During the ceremony to commemorate the bicentennial of the Revolution on January 1, 2004, South African President Thabo Mbeki stated in his address that the Haitian Revo-lution must be celebrated "because it dealt a deadly blow to the slave traders who had scoured the coasts of West and East Africa for slaves and ruined the lives of millions of Africans," and because of "the heroic deeds of these Africans who single-mindedly struggled for their freedom and inspired many of us to understand that none but ourselves can defeat those who subject us to tyranny, oppression and exploitation" (Mbeki 2004). Randall Robinson, founder and former president of TransAfrica, wrote, "the revolution was fought by Haitians but won for all of us ... The blacks of St. Domingue forced the world to see both them and the millions of other Africans enslaved through-out the Americas with new eyes ... They had banished slavery from their land and proclaimed it an official refuge for escaped slaves from anywhere in the world. They had defeated the mightiest of the mighty. They had shattered the myth of European invincibility" (Robinson 2004). And C. L. R. James, author of the classic *The Black Jacobins: Toussaint Louverture and the San Domingo Revolution* first published in 1938, put it thus, "The revolt is the only suc-cessful slave revolt in history, and the odds it had to overcome are evidence of the magnitude of the interests that were involved. The transformation of slaves, trembling in hundreds before a single white man, into a people able to organise themselves and defeat the most powerful European nations of their day, is one of the great epics of revolutionary struggle and achievement" (James 1963: ix).

One hundred and eighty two years later, the Haitian people fought another but peaceful and much less earth-shattering "democratic revolution," as I called it in *Haiti in the New World Order* (Dupuy 1997), that brought down the brutal and murderous 29-year Duvalier dictatorships in 1986. From 1986 to 1990 a broad popular movement, composed of many different political, religious, civic, human rights, women's, professional, labor, peasant, and media organizations, arose and fought to prevent the military from re-establishing a dictatorship by demanding the creation of a just, egalitarian and inclusive democracy. Among the grievances they expressed and wanted redressed were those that had to do with social justice, land reform, jobs, higher wages, healthcare, education, and social services. This was, in short, a movement for what I have called a maximalist or redistributive democracy in *The Prophet and Power* (Dupuy 2007), which required at the very least the transformation of Haiti's inegalitarian and unjust class structures and the renegotiation of the country's subservience to the major powers (the USA and France in particular) and the international financial institutions (IFIs) they control, that is, the World Bank, the International Monetary Fund, and the Inter-American Development Bank, whose neoliberal (or free trade and free market) policies have ravaged the Haitian economy and impoverished the population even more.

In December 1990, Father Jean-Bertrand Aristide was elected by a landslide victory to carry out this mandate. The former liberation theologian priest who championed the people's cause equated capitalism with a "mortal sin." He called the International Monetary Fund the "International Misery Front" and demanded an end to foreign, especially US, dominance and interference in the internal affairs of Haiti. With the support of the Haitian bourgeoisie the Haitian military toppled him nine months after he took office in February 1991 and exiled him to the USA. To crush the popular movement and put an end to this experiment in participatory democracy, the military junta that toppled Aristide launched a wave of repression against his supporters and killed thousands of them. In October 1994 US President Bill Clinton author-ized a US-led multinational United Nations military force to remove the junta from power and return Aristide to office to complete the remaining 18 months of his presidential term.

However, in 1994 Aristide was a changed man. As a condition of his return he agreed to implement the neoliberal policies, including the privatization of public enterprises. Under strong popular protest he backed off doing so before he left office in February 1996. One of his last acts as president was to disband the Haitian army that had overthrown him and which since the US occupa-tion of Haiti (1915–34) had been the major power broker in the country. The USA and the IFIs cut off aid and loans to Haiti until the government of René Préval (1996–2001) resumed the implementation of the policies. Aristide was re-elected for a second and final term in November 2000 and assumed office in February 2001. This time he was committed to implementing the neo-liberal policies in the hope of winning the support of Washington and the IFIs, but to no avail. A broad opposition coalition that formed in the wake of the parliamentary and presidential elections they contested refused to recognize the legitimacy of the new government and won the backing of the major powers, principally the USA, Canada, and France. The opposition's main objective was to force Aristide out of power, and with the help of former members of the army who took up arms against him they succeeded in doing so in February 2004 and sent him into exile for the second time.

An interim government installed by the international community—again principally the USA, Canada, and France—and backed by a multinational United Nations force known as the United Nations Stabilization Mission in

Haiti (in French, Mission des Nations Unies pour la stabilisation en Haïti—MINUSTAH) "pacified" the country, that is, suppressed supporters of Aristide and his *Fanmi Lavalas* (FL—Lavalas Family) party, and prepared new parliamentary and presidential elections. René Préval won a second and final five-year presidential term in February 2006 and was succeeded five years later by Michel Martelly in 2011. Neither Préval nor Martelly challenged the neoliberal policies or the strategy for economic growth advocated since the 1970s by the USA and the IFIs, that is, the garment assembly industry that relies on Haiti's abundant and cheap labor force. In other words, since Aristide's first overthrow, the "maximalist" or "redistributive" democracy the Haitian people had demanded in 1990 had been replaced by what I have also called a "minimalist" democracy that disempowers the people to serve the interests of the tiny but wealthy Haitian business class and foreign capital.

The essays that follow analyze the various stages of this historical trajectory. The first two chapters deal with the creation of the slave colony of Saint-Domingue and its class and racial structures. Chapter 1 "The capitalist world-economy, the fetishism of commodities, and the social geography of race: a reply to Michel Foucault" serves as an overall theoretical framework for understanding the historical origins of the ideologies of race and color associated with the emergence of the capitalist world-system in the 16th century. The rise of that system was characterized by the differential incorporation of workers from different parts of the world in its global division of labor and their simultaneous ethnicization or racialization that corresponded to their rank-ordered economic roles. It suggests how the specific demographic, class, and power relations of the slave colonies of the Caribbean in general, and that of Saint-Domingue in particular, led to a more nuanced formulation of race and color ideologies than in the USA. Chapter 2 "Toussaint Louverture, the Haitian Revolution, and Negritude: a critical assessment of Aimé Césaire's interpretation" focuses specifically on the development of the class and racial conflicts of Saint-Domingue that culminated in the revolution of 1791. The essay also contextualizes the role that the divisions between the mulatto and black factions of the indigenous ruling class would play in the development of Haiti after its independence.

The remaining four chapters deal with post-colonial Haiti. Chapter 3 "From revolutionary slaves to powerless citizens" offers an overview of the economic and political history of Haiti. Since the revolution had destroyed the plantation system that made Saint-Domingue the wealthiest sugar colony in the Caribbean in the 18th century, Haiti would turn to the production of coffee for export in the nineteenth. The reason for this transformation was due to the fact that the former slaves who worked on the colonial sugar plantations fought successfully to transform themselves into a landed peasantry and resisted fiercely the attempts by the new ruling class to maintain the plantation system and proletarianize them.

Unable to proletarianize the majority of the peasantry, the Haitian bourgeoisie remained divided and weak; it derived its wealth primarily from land rents and export and import commercial enterprises, and from control of the state. Foreign capital exploited the divisions and weaknesses of the Haitian ruling class and governments to reassert its dominance in the 19th century, symbolized by the indemnity Haiti agreed to pay to France in 1825 in return for its recognition of Haiti's independence. Unable to repay the debt or to finance other government functions and initiatives, Haitian governments from 1825 onward became heavily indebted to foreign banks. The governments of these lender countries (principally France but also Germany, England, and the USA) would then use the debt as a means of pressuring Haitian governments to allow their businesses to be established in Haiti (primarily commercial and financial) and reassert their dominance. The US occupation of Haiti from 1915 to 1934 would displace France as the dominant power.

Three categories of peasants emerged during the 19th century: those who owned land, those who possessed (mostly public) land but had no legal title, and those who rented land from the government or from the large landowners who subdivided their properties. The majority of peasants were in the latter two categories. There also emerged a landless peasantry—i.e., a rural proletariat—that hired itself out as day laborers to those with land. Thus, although most peasants had access to land and could block their full proletarianization, they remained powerless economically and politically and could not block the different mechanisms of exploitation or extraction to which they were subjected, such as the rents the sharecroppers had to pay to the landowners, the direct and indirect taxes appropriated by the state, or the *corvée* labor rural state officials forced them to perform on public works projects. Thus, just as the bourgeoisie had not succeeded in expropriating the majority of the producers and exploiting them directly as wage-laborers, the peasants had not succeeded in becoming self-sufficient and avoiding subjugation and exploitation by the dominant classes. I have termed these dual processes the Pyrrhic victory of the peasantry and the stalemate of the bourgeoisie.

The US occupation of Haiti unleashed a process of proletarianization and new forms of capital investments in agriculture, mining, and garment manufacturing industries for export. The latter would become the principal source of foreign investment from the 1970s onward, based exclusively on Haiti's abundant and cheap labor force. The complete dependence of the Haitian bourgeoisie and state on foreign investment and foreign aid, respectively, has given free reign to the USA and the IFIs to shape Haiti's economic policies, the consequences of which have been to reinforce Haiti's subservience to foreign capital and exacerbate its underdevelopment and poverty.

Chapter 4 "The transition to democracy and the demise of color politics in Haiti" returns to the politics of color. Its main objective is to show how the politics of color has declined in significance since the turn to democracy in the 1990s. As I mentioned above, the divisions between the mulatto and black factions of the bourgeoisie expressed themselves as ideologies of color that each faction deployed to justify its claim to power. Thus, I argue that the ideologies of color were an expression of an "intra"-class conflict between the two factions of the dominant class rather than an "inter"-class conflict between the dominant, middle, and working classes. Put differently, the ideologies of color were not integral to the reproduction of Haiti's division of labor—as they were in Saint-Domingue—and consequently became much more transparent, and could be more easily challenged. That is what I show happened when the popular struggles for democracy brought down the 29-year Duvalier dictatorships and their "*noiriste*" ideology in 1986, and ushered in the transition to democracy with the election of Jean-Bertrand Aristide in 1990. That transition, I argue, displaced "color" as the ideological claim to power and replaced it with the question of legitimacy, that is, government by consent of the governed and whose interests the state defends regardless of the "color" of who governs.

Chapters 5 and 6 analyze the economic policies the USA and the IFIs foisted on Haiti since the 1970s and their consequences. Chapter 5 "The World Bank and Haiti: abetting dictatorship, undermining democracy" shows how the Bank (and the other IFIs) collaborated with the Duvalier dictatorships in the 1970s and 1980s, and the military regimes between 1986 and 1990, and devised the agricultural, trade, and industrial policies that have had devastating effects on Haiti's food production capacity, exacerbated its unemployment, encouraged labor migration, and deepened its poverty. Unlike its support for the dictatorships, the USA and the World Bank opposed any and all attempts at reforms by the democratically elected governments since the 1990s, including wage increases for workers in the export assembly industries, by cutting off Bank loans or grants and foreign aid until these governments complied with their dictates. Chapter 6 "Class, power, sovereignty: Haiti before and after the earthquake" expands that analysis by showing how, even after admitting the failure of the neoliberal policies, the IFIs and the Interim Haiti Recovery Commission co-chaired by former US President Bill Clinton who took charge of post-earthquake "reconstruction" continued to push for them. The last two chapters challenge the claims made by the USA and the IFIs that the policies they devised for, and the aid they provided to Haiti were meant to promote its economic development. Rather, I argue, their real objective was and is to facilitate the accumulation of capital by maintaining Haiti as a source of cheap labor for foreign investors, keeping its market open to US agricultural and other exports, and ensuring that democracy does not mean the empowerment of the Haitian people such that they can effectively determine their own agenda.

1 The capitalist world-economy, the fetishism of commodities, and the social geography of race

A reply to Michel Foucault

In this essay, I draw on Marx's theory of the fetishism of commodities to suggest a theory of the fetishism of race. I will then use that theory to offer a critique of Foucault's argument on race which he developed in *La Volonté de savoir* (1976) translated as *The History of Sexuality, Volume I: An Introduction* (1980) and in *Il faut défendre la société* (1997) translated as *Society Must Be Defended* (2004).[1]

Fetishism and "race"

For Marx, a commodity contains both use-value and exchange-value, or simply value, and under capitalism it is produced strictly for creating surplus-value or profit for the capitalist. The pre-condition for the continual and expanded production of profit is the commodification of all the means and factors of production, including and especially land, labor, and money, and the production of commodities for sale in national and world markets. However, for Marx only labor can produce surplus value or profit.[2] As he put it, "The production process, considered as a unity of the labour process and the process of creating value, is the process of production of commodities; considered as the unity of the labour process and the process of valorization,[3] it is the capitalist process of production, or the capitalist production of commodities" (Marx 1977: 304).

In *The Poverty of Philosophy* (Marx) and *The Manifesto of the Communist Party* (Marx and Engels), Marx asserts that as it struggles against the bourgeoisie, the proletariat, whose common situation constituted it as a mass that shares "common interests. ... is already a class as against capital, but not yet for itself." But in its struggle against capital, this "mass becomes united, and constitutes itself as a class for itself. The interests it defends become class interests [and] the struggle of class against class is a political struggle" (Marx 1976: 211). And the proletariat, which alone is the "really revolutionary class," and whose movement is "the self-conscious, independent movement of the immense majority, in the interest of the immense majority ... cannot stir, cannot raise itself up, without the whole superincumbent strata of official society being sprung into the air" (Marx and Engels 1976: 494–95).

Against this certitude of revolution, however, Marx offered many reasons why it might not happen. Aside from the arguments that the workers could be swayed by the dominant bourgeois ideology of freedom, equality, property, and the pursuit of self-interest, the most powerful in my view is the very opacity of the capitalist relations of exploitation whereby the production of commodities and the surplus value or profit they yield come to be seen as natural and self-determined rather than stemming from the relations between capital and labor. The theory of the fetishism of commodities does exactly that by offering a theory of knowledge or rather of consciousness based on the difference between the essence of the social relations of exploitation embedded in the capitalist production of commodities and how they are apprehended by consciousness as social relations between the commodities themselves. The commodities that workers produce through their collective labors do not belong to them, but are appropriated by the capitalists and sold in a market at a price.

Money, which assumes the universal form and expression of value, becomes the medium through which commodities are bought and sold, and individuals buy them according to their needs and their means. And since for the workers the wages they receive depend in part on their skills, efforts, or personal achievements, they compete among themselves and have an incentive to develop their skills in order to increase their wages and buy more commodities. As Marx put it, it "is the worker himself who converts the money into whatever use-value he desires; it is he who buys commodities as he wishes and, as the *owner of money*, as the buyer of goods, he stands in precisely the same relationship to the sellers of goods as any other buyer" (Marx 1977: 1033, emphasis in the original).

However, just as the values or prices of their labor (i.e., their wages) vary, so do the prices of the commodities the workers produce and buy vary in time and place. But the individuals producing or buying them do not decide these fluctuations. Rather they seem to operate according to their own laws and determine in turn whether or not individuals are able to buy them (Balibar 2007: 58). The fetishism of commodities, then, is the form in which commodities are exchanged and thus apprehended by consciousness. As Marx put it,

> The mysterious character of the commodity-form consists therefore in the fact that the commodity reflects the social characteristics of men's own labour as objective characteristics of the products of labour themselves, as the socio-natural properties of these things. Hence it also reflects the social relation of the producers to the sum total of labour as a social relation between objects, a relation which exists apart from and outside the producers.
>
> (Marx 1977: 164–65)

In other words, in the production and exchange of commodities under capitalism there appears to be no connection whatsoever between the values of commodities and their physical properties, and the social relations from which they arose. Rather,

[it] is nothing but the definite social relations between men themselves which assumes here, for them, the fantastic form of a relation between things ... In other words, the labour of the private individual manifests itself as an element of the total labour of society only through the relations which the act of exchange establishes between the products, and, through the mediation, between the producers. To the producers, therefore, the social relations between their private labours appear as what they are, i.e., they do not appear as direct social relations between persons in their work, but rather as material relations between persons and social relations between things.

(Marx 1977: 165–66)

The political implications of this fetishism are significant, since rather than questioning the social relations of commodity production and seeking to change them, the workers would seek to improve their marketability and their income in order to purchase commodities and improve their standard of living. Insofar as workers in capitalist societies come to see the commodities they buy not as the products of their collective labors and the social relations between themselves and the capitalists who employ them, and insofar as they also occupy different positions in the division of labor and their labor-power fetches different values (wages) in the labor market, they are more apt to see themselves as competitors in the market place than as sharing a collective and antagonistic relationship to the collective class of capitalist employers. Moreover, the workers came from different geographic regions, spoke different languages, practiced different religions, and had different physical characteristics such as different skin colors, facial features, or hair textures, and they would be incorporated differently and unequally in the social divisions of labor of global capitalism. It is from these divisions and the competition and conflicts they would generate among them within and between countries that their cultural and phenotypical differences would be seized upon to create ideologies of racial superiority and inferiority.

Although he did not theorize these practices as such, Marx was well aware of the social relations and conditions that produced them. In a "Confidential Communication" he wrote for The General Council of the First International in 1868–70 on the "Question of the General Council Resolution on the Irish Amnesty," Marx pointed out how the English bourgeoisie had kept the English working class down by forcing poor Irishmen to emigrate to England and giving rise to hostile divisions in the proletarian camps. As he put it,

The revolutionary fire of the Celtic worker does not go well with the nature of the Anglo-Saxon worker, solid, but slow. On the contrary, in all the *big industrial centers of England* there is profound antagonism between the Irish proletariat and the English proletariat. The average English worker hates the Irish worker as a competitor who lowers wages and the *standard of life*. He feels national and religious antipathies for him. He regards him somewhat like the *poor whites* of the Southern States of North America regard their black slaves. This antagonism among the proletarians of England is artificially nourished and supported by the bourgeoisie.

(Marx 1972: 258–59, emphases in the original)

Marx's language in this passage was referring to the simultaneous creation of two interlinked ideologies associated with the rise of capitalism, namely, nationalism or ethnocentrism, and racism as it developed in different geographic locations and incorporated different categories of workers in its social divisions of labor. The creation of the nation-state beginning in the 17th century and symbolized in the Peace of Westphalia in 1648, involved what Etienne Balibar calls a "fictive ethnicity," by which he means the constitution of the "people" of a nation into an ethnic group wherein each individual possesses one, and only one, ethnic identity. Insofar as a nation-state does not naturally possess an ethnic base, the populations included within its territory become ethnicized, that is, "represented in the past or in the future *as if* they formed a natural community, possessing of itself an identity of origins, culture and interests which transcend individuals and social conditions" (Balibar 1991: 96, emphasis in the original). This process allowed for the peoples of the world to be divided into as many ethnic groups as there are nation-states in the world-economy. In this way,

> national ideology does much more than justify the strategy employed by the state to control populations. It inscribes their demands in advance in a sense of belonging in the double sense of the term—both what it is that makes one belong to oneself and also makes one belong to other fellow human beings.
>
> (Balibar 1991: 96)

But the construction of the nation-state and of the ethnic group(s) that identified or came to identify with it was uneven and contradictory. Usually one ethnic group would become dominant in any given nation-state, and some sort of rank order would be established among the subordinate groups. One of the most important consequences of the ethnicization of the world's work force, Immanuel Wallerstein argues, was to "[encrust a] ranking of occupational/economic roles, providing an easy code for overall income distribution" (1996: 78). Moreover, ethnicization would be elaborated into what would become one of the most important pillars of historical capitalism, namely, racism: "Racism was the mode by which various segments of the work-force within the same economic structure were constrained to relate to each other. Racism was the ideological justification for the hierarchization of the work-force and its highly unequal distribution of reward" (Wallerstein 1996: 78).

However, racism would do much more than justify inequality. It would be both self-suppressive and oppressive by socializing groups to accept their position and role in the economy on the one hand, and by keeping low-ranking groups in line, on the other (Wallerstein 1996: 79). For racism to take hold in one's imagination, it could not be based exclusively on feelings of antipathy or claims of cultural superiority or inferiority. It had to be anchored in something visible and permanent. That something would be what W. E. B. DuBois (1989) called the "color line." If we define racism as claims of superiority of one group over another on the basis of genetic and/or cultural traits, the lines that separate the subordinate group from the dominant one would tend to blur over time if they both shared similar phenotypical characteristics. That is what happened to those who came to be classified as white "ethnics" in the USA, for example, as the barriers of exclusion among them broke down and they intermarried and integrated socially. However, it is an entirely different matter when the dominant group alleging to be superior and alleging the subordinate group to be inferior are separated by physical characteristics, mainly skin color. Visible phenotypical characteristics can then more easily become the signifiers of alleged innate differences between groups, and the spatial and social distances between them can be maintained through barriers of exclusion or social closure.

I want to stress that there is nothing in the facts of visible physical differences that by themselves explain racism. As Barbara Fields put it,

> Race is not an element of human biology ... nor is it an idea that can be plausibly imagined to live an eternal life of its own. Race is not an idea but an ideology. It came into existence at a discernible historical moment for rationally understandable historical reasons and is subject to change for similar reasons.
>
> (Fields 1990: 101)

In other words, there are no genes for whiteness, blackness, or other classifications, only ideological interpretations of phenotypes (Allen 1994: 22). This can be shown, for example, in the different classifications used in the Caribbean, Brazil, and South Africa to depict people in a continuum from white to black, in contrast to the USA where anyone with visible admixtures of white European and black African features would be classified as black. Put differently, and to quote Wallerstein again, "The belief that certain groups were 'superior' to others in certain characteristics relevant to performance in the economic arena always came into being after, rather than before, the location of these groups in the work-force. Racism has always been post hoc" (Wallerstein 1996: 79).

I argue then, that when societies such as those founded by colonialism involved the mixing together not only of peoples of different geographical regions and cultures but of different physical appearances as well, the biological form of racism tends to overdetermine the cultural form in such a way that people with similar physical characteristics are formed into racial groups whether or not they differ culturally. As David Roediger has shown, for example, Irish workers who emigrated to the USA before the Civil War faced intense animosity at the hands of native-born whites who often compared them unfavorably to blacks. To distinguish and distance themselves from black Americans and become accepted as white, the Irish adopted the same racist attitudes as native-born whites. As Roediger put it, the "imperative to define themselves as white came but from the particular 'public and psychological wages' whiteness offered to a desperate rural and often preindustrial Irish population coming to labor in industrializing American cities" (Roediger 1991: 137). Yet, as Mary Waters has shown, as white immigrants who initially faced discrimination from native-born whites became assimilated into the broad mainstream of white society, this did not preclude individuals from exercising what she calls "ethnic options" or "symbolic ethnicity," that is, the ability to choose one's ethnic identity, as say, English, Irish, or German, without being questioned or accused of trying to "pass" as other than what one says one is or to whom one "belongs" (Waters 1990: 18–19).

Black Americans have no such option. As John Thornton has shown, those brought to the American colonies as slaves hailed from different parts of Africa, from "dozens, if not more, independent cultures," and hence were not "homogeneous enough to constitute a single cultural block" (Thornton 1998: 183). However, once there they would be racialized and homogenized as blacks. Even centuries later, Waters writes,

> Black Americans are highly socially constrained to identify as blacks, without other options available to them, even when they believe or know that their forebears included many non-blacks ... [If] one were part Afri-can and part German, one's self-identification as German would be highly suspect and probably not accepted if one "looked" black according to the prevailing social norms.
>
> (Waters 1990: 18–19)

In other words, blacks could only have one identity and it had to be racial not ethnic.

Frantz Fanon was more categorical on the roots of this reduction:

> In the *Weltanschauung* of a colonized people there is an impurity, a flaw that outlaws any ontological explanation. Someone may object that this is the case with every individual, but such an objection merely conceals a basic problem. Ontology—once it is finally admitted as leaving existence by the wayside—does not permit us to understand the being of the black man. For not only must the black man be black; he must be black in relation to the white man. Some critics will take it upon themselves to remind us that this proposition has a converse. I say that this is false. The black man has no ontological existence in the eyes of the white man. Overnight the Negro has been given two frames of reference within which he has to place himself. His metaphysics, or less pretentiously, his customs and the sources

on which they were based, were wiped out because they were in conflict with a civilization that he did not know and that imposed itself on him.

(Fanon 1967: 109–10)

Expressed in yet another way, in a racist society blacks must forever carry what Glenn Loury calls the "stigma" of race, which he defines as "the identity unreflectively imputed to someone by observers who, not being privy to extensive idiosyncratic information, draw conclusions about a person's deeper qualities on the basis of the easily observable indicators that may lie at hand." This ascribed or imputed identity "is 'virtual' because it can diverge from the subject's actual identity; and it is 'social' because the imputation occurs within the context of the social encounter and is structured by the nature of the social relationship that obtains between the subject and the observer" (Loury 2002: 9).

It is in this sense that I argue that just as the capitalist social relations of production gave rise to a fetishized ideology of commodities that substituted social relations of production between workers and capitalists for social relations between objects, so, too, would racism, especially in its biological variant, give rise to a fetishism of race. Rather than seeing race as an ideology resulting from social relations of exclusion or differential incorporation in the division of labor, race came to be seen as determining the relations among individuals classified on the basis of phenotype. Race, then, appears to be natural and determinative of relations between human beings rather than being explained by the social relations of exploitation and exclusion that produced it as an ideology. Race, in short, becomes fetishized.

Thus, as long as this fetishization leads people to believe that "race" has its own determination, it presents itself as commodities do, endowed with different social values. Race fetishism, then, would compound the class divisions such that not only would members of the subordinate and devalued or stigmatized race be located in lower ranks in the division of labor, but even when they and members of the positively valued racial group were in the same class location, they would fetch lower exchange values (wages) in the labor market. Moreover, insofar as individuals come to identify themselves as belonging to specific races or ethnic groups, they would socialize those born into the group to so identify themselves to create bonds of social solidarity to either preserve or challenge their position in the social division of labor. Henceforth, racial or ethnic identity would function to reproduce the social relations and practices that perpetuate the ideology, much like the fetishism of commodities functions to reproduce the capitalist social relations of production. Or, to recall the point Balibar made earlier, race came to define not only who one is, but also to whom one belongs. Or, again as Fields puts it,

Nothing handed down from the past could keep race alive if we did not constantly reinvent and re-ritualize it to fit our own terrain. If race lives on today, it can do so only because we continue to create and re-create it in our social life, continue to verify it, and thus continue to need a social vocabulary that will allow us to make sense, not of what our ancestors did, but of what we ourselves choose to do now.

(Fields 1990: 118)

Foucault on "race" and racism

It is in the context of the above discussion that I now want to consider Foucault's ideas about race and racism, what he calls their discourses, and the transformations they underwent in Western Europe from the 16th to the 20th centuries. Foucault starts by making a distinction between race or race struggles and "racism" or "racist discourse" because the latter was "nothing more than a particular and localised episode in the great discourse of race war or race struggle" (Foucault 2004: 65). The distinction is important for Foucault, because whereas the concepts of race and race war fused with the idea of revolution to produce a revolutionary counter-history from the end of the 16th to the 19th centuries, racism or racist discourse converted that counter-history into a biological racism from the 19th century onward (Foucault 2004:79–81). I consider the claim of race or race war as a revolutionary counter-history that was later usurped by and converted into a racist discourse and counter-revolutionary biological racism to be Foucault's most singular contribution to the debate on race and racism. None the less, I will argue that his argument does not hold.

For Foucault, history is about the discourse of power. The race struggles and the race discourses they generated in Western Europe, principally in England and France, were part of a counter-history against the history of sovereignty or the history that was deployed in the service of sovereignty. The history of sovereignty from Roman times to its demise in the late Middle Ages sought to create a unity by identifying the people and the nation with the monarch or the sovereign. However, more than binding the people, the function of sovereignty was to enslave them. The historical eruption of the race wars would shatter the myth of unity and replace it with the principle of heterogeneity. Henceforth, difference rather than sameness would be emphasized, and the heterogeneous groups that would identify themselves as Saxons, Normans, Franks, Gauls, Celts, and so on, would come to see their history as different from the history of others, and hence that the victory of the one would mean the defeat of another. Thus, the defeat of the Saxons at the Battle of Hastings in 1066 meant a victory for the Normans and their conquest of England, or the victory of Clovis and the Franks meant the defeat of the Gallo-Romans in the late 5th century and the former's consolidation of power over Gaul or what would later become France. Thus, as Foucault puts it, the fact that all the great feudal lords possessed all the lands and demanded taxes would be seen by the defeated populations as "acts of violence, confiscations, pillage, and war taxes that are being levied through violence ... The triumph of some means the submission of others" (Foucault 2004: 70).

Henceforth, the new history or counter-history of the race struggles would be disruptive rather than unifying because it would express the silenced grievances of those who had been defeated. This counter-history, then, challenged the hitherto dominant Roman-style history by disinterring the history or the memories that it had deliberately suppressed or misrepresented. The function of this new discursive history was, Foucault argues, "to show that laws deceive, that kings wear masks, that power creates illusions, and that historians tell lies" (Foucault 2004: 72).

This new history of the race struggle had yet another function, namely, that of critiquing and attacking power, and of demanding rights that had been suppressed or denied, or declaring war against the rights that the old sovereign power had arrogated to itself by declaring new rights. It is "a biblical-style historical discourse [that] tears society apart and speaks of legitimate rights solely to declare war on laws" (Foucault 2004: 73). This new history of the race struggle spelled the death-knell of antiquity and the beginning of a new awareness of the bloody origins of Europe and its divisions into ethnic groups, peoples of different regions, rulers and subordinates, or victors and vanquished. However, it would be a mistake, Foucault insists, to see this new historical discourse as belonging only to the oppressed, the vanquished, or the people. As with all discourses, this new revolutionary discourse against a particular form of power can circulate, change, and be appropriated by different groups for different purposes. Therefore, just as it was used by English revolutionaries at the time of the 17th century English Revolution, and the French aristocracy against Louis XIV during the mid-17th century Fronde, it would be used to justify colonization in the 19th century (Foucault 2004: 71–72).

Foucault's argument takes a radical turn at this juncture with his recognition that while the new discourse of race struggle is polyvalent and does not have a biological meaning, it is also not entirely free-floating. First and foremost, it expresses a historic-political divide wherein two races can be said to exist when one group defeats and dominates another and has the power to write the history of that group with which it does not share the same language or the same religion, and the only connection between them is forged through war. Alternatively, two races can be said to exist when two groups coexist without mixing "because of the differences, dissymmetries, and barriers created by privileges, customs and rights, the distribution of wealth, or the way in which power is exercised" (Foucault 2004: 77). Thus, just as the emergence of group differences, or what he calls the race struggles, gave rise to a counter-history that challenged the hitherto prevailing history of sovereignty in the 16th century, so too, the shift to a biological racism in the 19th century would give rise to a counter-history that would displace the counter-history of race struggle that had been converted into a discourse of class struggle and revolution.

At this point the new racism rears its ugly head. This new racism no longer expresses a struggle between race groups against an unjust state monopolized by the sovereign in the name of sovereignty, but becomes a struggle to protect the purity and superiority of one race against all the foreigners and deviants who have infiltrated the society and hence threaten the survival of the superior race. Henceforth, the discourse of racial purity replaces that of race struggle, and racism becomes biologically monist. The state, therefore, must be called upon to "[protect] the integrity, the superiority, and the purity of the race. The idea of racial purity, with all its monistic, Statist, and biological implications: that is what replaces the idea of race struggle" (Foucault 2004: 81).

Put differently, the new biologically monist racism could be seen as the revenge of the old-style Roman sovereignty against those who had used the discourse of race struggle to challenge that sovereignty by raising the banner of revolutionary emancipation. Thus, racism becomes an inversion of the old revolutionary discourse, a new weapon to preserve the sovereignty of a State that could no longer guarantee its survival except by creating medico-normalizing techniques of power. As Foucault puts it,

> Thanks to the shift from law to norm, from races in the plural to race in the singular, from the emancipatory project to a concern with purity, sovereignty was able to invert or take over the discourse of race struggle and neutralize it for its own strategy. State sovereignty thus becomes the imperative to protect the race.
>
> (Foucault 2004: 81)

This new biological racism and its theme of racial purity would not only depend on the state to protect it, but was the inevitable by-product of the birth of a new form of power exercised not only by the state but by its diverse institutions such as the family, the schools, the police, the army, healthcare and individual medicine, the prisons, the psychiatric and other institutions for the collective management of populations that were essential to the development of capitalism. Insofar as capitalism requires the reproduction and management of populations for the machinery of production, new techniques for the subjugation and control of bodies would need to be devised. These new techniques and technologies of population management and control are what Foucault refers to as biopower. However, the production and reproduction of subordinated and manageable bodies also required the deployment of mechanisms that would shape aptitudes and ideologies that would both explain and justify to the population the relations of domination, the social hierarchies and the patterns of segregation characteristic of capitalism.

In short, and in an unacknowledged nod to Gramsci, Foucault (1980: 141) argues that the exercise of biopower in its manifold forms required the production of hegemony. One of the most important functions of hegemony is to produce the normalization of social relations that in turn makes possible the exercise of biopower without having to rely exclusively on the law and the judicial system. At the same time, biological racism contradicts this tendency toward normalization and the politics of preserving life by managing it. First, biological racism allows for the creation of racial hierarchies within the biological continuity of the human race, of races deemed to be superior and others inferior. And second, it justifies killing the inferior race, or ridding society of the inferior race whose presence threatens the survival of the superior race. Unlike the old race war or race struggles against sovereignty, this new bioracism is a war, not against a political adversary, but against a biological threat. As Foucault puts it,

> In the biopower system, killing or the imperative to kill is acceptable only if it results not in a victory over political adversaries, but in the elimination of the biological threat to and the improvement of the species or race. There is a direct connection between the two. In a normalizing society, you have a power which is, at least superficially, in the first instance ... a biopower, and racism is the indispensable precondition that allows someone to be killed, that allows others to be killed.
>
> (Foucault 2004: 256)

And for Foucault, the rise of the Nazi state in the 20th century carried that logic to its extremes.

It is in the context of the rise of biopower and the politics associated with it, then, that Foucault locates the importance of sex as a political weapon and the role it would play in the development of biological racism. The management of sex here would perform a double function: that of disciplining the body to distribute forces and economize their energies for the needs of capital, on the one hand, and that of regulating populations by controlling its activities on the other hand. To that end, Foucault argues, sex would be subjected to endless mechanisms of surveillance, control, spatial orderings, medical and psychological examinations, and the micro-management of the body. Sex, in short, became "the theme of political operations, economic interventions (through incitements to or curbs on procreation), and ideological campaigns for raising standards of morality and responsibility: it was put forward as an index of a society's strength, revealing of both its political energy and its biological vigor" (Foucault 1980: 146). Thus, if in the age of sovereignty where society was threatened by famine, epidemics, and violence, the preservation of sovereignty required the formation of alliances tied to lines of descent, or to the blood line, in the age of capitalism where biopower aims to regulate the body and its reproduction, sexuality ceased to be a mark or a symbol to become both an object and a target. The politics and management of sex logically led to biological racism since the latter justified the hierarchization, segregation, and regulation of populations, the family, the educational system, the distribution of property, and the interventions to control the body, its health, and its daily activities, all in the name of ensuring the purity of blood and the survival of the superior race (Foucault 1980: 148–50).

A critique of Foucault

As elegant and seductive as Foucault's argument appears, it does not hold, theoretically or historically. On the one hand, he argues, the race struggles or the race wars of the feudal era were revolutionary because they challenged the unitary discourse of Roman sovereignty used by the feudal aristocracy as its claim to power. Moreover, the eruption of the counter-history and discourse of race war in England and France in particular since the 16th century was fundamentally an insurrectionary discourse wherein the idea of revolution permeated the politics and history of the West for more than 200 years. It was this very discourse, Foucault points out, that led Marx to acknowledge in a letter written in 1882 to Engels that "You know very well where we found our idea of class struggle: we found it in the work of the French historians who talked about the race struggle" (cited in Foucault 2004: 79). In short, for Foucault, the history of the revolutionary project and revolutionary practice in Europe is inseparable from the emergence of the "counterhistory of races and the role played in the West by the clashes between races" (Foucault 2004: 79).

On the other hand, Foucault maintains, when racism proper emerged in the 19th century and became biological racism, it replaced the race discourses of old with a new state-devised ideology of racial hierarchies whose objective was to protect the superiority of one race against the threats posed by the inferior races. However, he never explained how this new singular 19th and 20th century ideology of biological racism found its roots in the old discourse of race struggles, especially since according to him it had already metamorphosed into a discourse of class struggle and revolution. Put differently, the old race struggle was decisively against hierarchy and for equality, whereas the new racism restores hierarchy and inequality among races. Moreover, he argued, biological racism arose with the development of biopower and especially the attempt to regulate the sexual activities of women to preserve the purity of the superior over the inferior races. The old race struggle by contrast was precisely against the "purity of blood" argument used by the nobility to justify its sovereignty. Yet Foucault never argued that the struggles among the nobility and the subordinate groups gave rise to a discourse of superiority or inferiority based on unequal valuations of difference as would happen later.

In my view, then, Foucault could not establish the links between the old, revolutionary discourse of race and the new biological racism. First, this is because the social relations that gave rise to the former and those that produced the latter were rooted in very different social systems at different points in time albeit in the same geographical locations. And second, and as a result, the groups who struggled against sovereignty had not been ethnicized or racialized, and no ideology of racism had been deployed to distinguish between them as would be the case subsequent to the European colonial expansion from the 16th century on that gave rise to modern capitalism. In other words, the ideology of race used during feudalism and the one used in conjunction with the rise of capitalism had very different contents and meanings, and the latter cannot be read into the former as Foucault has done. To use an analogy between markets and capitalism, and as Marx, Weber, and Polanyi among others have shown, one cannot deduce contemporary capitalism from the existence of commodity production and markets in pre-modern societies, as

Adam Smith has done, for example, with his assumption of man's inherent "propensity to barter, truck and exchange one thing for another" (Smith 1998: 21). Yet Smith understood that the system he was analyzing could not have developed as it did without freeing land, labor, and money from their old constraints and commodifying them. Similarly, I argue, race came to have an entirely different meaning in the emergent capitalist system than it did previously, and to suggest that the latter form of racism was simply a continuation of the former concept of "race wars" is to overlook the specific historical contexts and the social relations and conditions that gave rise to the one and the other, respectively. Such an approach, I argue, is ahistorical because it assigns to the ideology of race a life of its own, independently of the context and social relations that produced it.

Thus, it is meaningless to speak of race without a concomitant ideology of racial superiority and inferiority. And the feudal relations on which the ideology of sovereignty rested could not have given rise to ideologies of racial superiority and inferiority because the social positions of the different classes under feudalism—lords, nobles, serfs, peasants—were determined by virtue of the monopoly the landlord classes had over the principal means of production, that is, land, and their ability to maintain the serfs or peasants attached to the land. Since the labor force was fixed to the land, no elaborate hierarchy in the division of labor would or could emerge among different categories of serfs or peasants to create the conditions for the deployment of ideologies to explain these different modes of incorporation and subjection. Put differently, to the extent that there was a division of labor among serfs they remained attached to their lords' estates, and the latter were not in the habit of relocating or transplanting serfs or peasants from one domain to another to displace or compete with those in other estates. Thus there were no competitions or struggles for social or economic advantages between one group of serfs and another. As such, serfs were not struggling against each other as they were against the aristocracy's claim to entitlement to rule by virtue of their birthright or their "blood line." All subordinates were thus considered equally inferior and hence subject to rule.

That is why, as many historians of the period have shown, though the nobility claimed the right to rule by virtue of their birth and lineage, the noble theorists of the 16th century such as the Comte de Boulainvilliers in France, whom Foucault referred to often in his argument, never ascribed permanent or fixed characteristics to the noble gentlemen to differentiate them from the commoners. As Hannah Arendt said, these theorists "dealt with peoples and not races; [they] based the right of the superior people on a historical deed, and not on a physical fact" (Arendt 1944: 44). Or, as Pierre Boulle, one of the preeminent historians of the period put it, in the 16th century the concept of race "remained narrowly defined as direct lineage and had none of the genetic connotations of its modern counterpart" (Boulle 2003: 13).

Even the closest attempt to use a discourse of "purity of blood" during the heydays of the Spanish Inquisition in the late 15th and early 16th centuries did not result in the invention of lines of racial demarcations to produce a racist ideology. Try as they might to claim that the true Castilian nobles were those who had fought against the Moors in the 8th century and had not been tainted by the blood of the infidels, the Inquisitors could never get the accused to provide such proofs. Many members of the nobility came under suspicion as they had intermarried with Moors and Jews, and the Church itself had admitted Moorish and Jewish converts into its ranks. That did not prevent the Inquisitors in Seville from considering those among the *marranos* who had fled because they could not prove their "purity" as apostates and persecuting them as such. And on that basis the Inquisition nurtured the idea that, in addition to being apostates, the *marranos*, as Jews, had consumed the blood of Christian children after murdering them (Hannaford 1996: 122–25).

Both Ivan Hannaford and David Davis have used the history of the Inquisition's persecution and expulsion of Jews and Moors from Spain to argue that what Davis calls an "incipient racism" had emerged in the 15th century around the interpretation of the biblical "Curse of Ham" that Iberian Muslims transmitted to Christians who were "becoming obsessed with the alleged danger that Jews and New Christians posed to their own purity of blood"; and that such racism "became magnified" when the Portuguese imported more West African slaves in Portugal and Spain. "Still," Davis goes on to say, despite "Spain's expulsion of Jews and then Moriscos (converted Moors), Iberians became accustomed to coexistence of a range of skin colors from black to white" (Davis 2006: 79). Hannaford suggests that the idea of purity of blood which was used to determine who was of good lineage among people "who could not be set apart by their physical appearance in later times became the mark of Cain and then absorbed by logic and association of ideas into the mark of race" (Hannaford 1996: 126).

However, this transition to the "mark of race" did not occur until after the European colonization of the Americas, the establishment of the system of chattel slavery, and the transportation of slaves from Africa to supply the labor force for the plantations. On this point Oliver Cox is categorical. Even when the Italian, Spanish, and Portuguese merchants needed to expand trade with the East by making their way down the coast of Africa and navigating around it to reach India because the Mohammedans blocked their in-land trade routes through the Near East, they did not develop racial antipathy towards the Africans they encountered, killed, and enslaved. This was because the Church was still obsessed with the "spiritual values of conversion" and the Portuguese and Spaniards had not yet shed their "crusading spirit [that] constantly held in check their attainment of a clear appreciation of the values of competitive labor exploitation." This "matter of cultural conversion," Cox goes on to say, "is crucial for our understanding of the development of racial antagonism. For the full profitable exploitation of a people, the dominant group must devise ways and means of limiting that people's cultural assimilation" (Cox 1970: 328).

As Cox put it,

so long as the Portuguese and Spaniards continued to accept the religious definition of human equality [and the Church was still obsessed with the spiritual values of conversion], so long also the development of race prejudice was inhibited ... [They] never became fully freed of the crusading spirit, which constantly held in check their attainment of a clear appreciation of the values of competitive labor exploitation.

(Cox 1970: 328–29)

Western European colonial expansion in the Americas in the 16th and 17th centuries would set that latter process into motion. No other than Adam Smith expressed clearly the contradictions of this emergent world-economy:

The discovery of America, and that of a passage to the East Indies by the Cape of Good Hope, are the two greatest and most important events recorded in the history of mankind. Their consequences have already been great; but, in the short period between two and three centuries which has elapsed since these discoveries were made, it is impossible that the whole extent of their consequences have been seen. What benefits, or what misfortunes to mankind may hereafter result from those great events, no human wisdom can foresee. By uniting, in some measure, the most distant parts of the world, by enabling them to relieve one another's wants, to increase one another's enjoyments, and to encourage one another's industry, their general tendency would seem to be beneficial. To the natives, however, both of the East and West Indies, all the commercial benefits which can have resulted from those events have been sunk and lost in the dreadful misfortunes which they have occasioned.

(Smith 1998: 363–64)

That dreadful misfortune, of course, was not only the genocide of the indigenous populations, but the introduction of chattel slavery in the Americas. As Cox put it, as soon as the "bourgeois world got underway,"

[the] socioeconomic matrix of racial antagonism involved the commercialization of human labor in the West Indies, the East Indies, and in America, the intense competition ... for the capitalist exploitation of the resources of this area, the development of nationalism and the consolidation of European nations, and the decline of the influence of the Roman Catholic Church with its mystical inhibitions to the free exploitation of economic resources.

(Cox 1970: 330)

I do not intend to give a full account of the various factors that led to the development of slavery and the singling out of Africans to supply the slave labor forces in the colonies of the Americas. Since the rise of capitalism meant the creation of a market for labor and the "commodification of everything" as

Wallerstein put it (1996: 15–16), the supply of labor had to keep up with the demand for it. The genocidal reductions of the indigenous Amerindian populations following the Spanish conquests and their forced labor, first in the Caribbean and subsequently in the rest of Central and South America (with Brazil going to the Portuguese), made the supply of that labor unavailable at the same time that the plantocracy was turning increasingly to the production of cash crops such as tobacco, indigo, coffee, cotton and sugar, with the latter two especially requiring large numbers of workers.

In the French and English Caribbean colonies, and the southern colonies of North America, the planter classes turned first to importing more indentured European laborers and to lengthening their terms of servitude. That worked as long as the colonies produced mainly tobacco, indigo, or cacao, but as soon as they turned to the production of cotton and sugar which required much larger work forces, the supply of indentured servants could not keep up with the demand for labor. Consequently that labor system quickly reached its limits. Normally indentured servants worked for a set number of years after which they received land and equipment and thus became independent farmers. Short of enslaving the indentured servants, their terms of servitude would eventually expire, and they demanded their freedoms and the lands to which they were entitled. Moreover, indentured servants ran away from their plantations and melted easily into the ranks of the free white population, and set themselves up as independent farmers (Williams 1970: 109). Many of them, especially in the American colonies, were also armed, and clashed often with planters and sometimes even rebelled against them and the colonial authorities (Raphael 2002: 13–58).

The inability to maintain or increase the supply of indentured servants made it necessary to find a source of labor that was "firstly adequate and in excess of the need; secondly cheap; thirdly docile or that could be whipped into docility; finally, that could be degraded to the point which sugar cultivation required. The white servant satisfied none of these desiderata" (Williams 1970: 109). Slavery, therefore, became necessary because the labor force needed for the production of cash crops for export to the metropolitan economies could not be obtained through the so-called free play of the market. And here the role of African "predatory states" like those of Futa Jallon, Dahomey, Asante, Kasanje, and the Lunda Empire played a crucial role in raiding their neighboring territories and selling their prisoners to the European traders—Portuguese, Dutch, English, French, Danes, or Americans—and whose "rulers, government officials, military officers, and merchants acquired symbols of wealth and status in exchange for the massive export of labor" (Davis 2006: 100).

However, slavery was not only crucial for the enormous wealth it created for the slave traders and the planter classes in the colonies; it was also crucial for the industrial development of the metropolitan economies. As Marx argued, in contrast to the

> indirect slavery of the proletariat [in Europe], the direct slavery of the Blacks in Surinam, in Brazil, in the southern regions of North America ...

is as much the pivot upon which our present day industrialism turns as are machinery, credit, etc. Without slavery there could be no cotton, without cotton there would be no modern industry. It is slavery which has given value to the colonies, it is the colonies which have created world trade, and world trade is the necessary condition for large-scale machine industry. Consequently, prior to the slave trade, the colonies sent very few products to the Old World, and did not noticeably change the face of the world. Slavery, therefore, is an economic category of paramount importance ... Being an economic category, slavery has existed in all nations since the beginning of the world. All that modern nations have achieved is to disguise slavery at home and import it openly into the New World.

(Marx 1982: 101–2; 1976: 167)

Marx's contrast of the indirect slavery of the (white) proletariat to the direct slavery of blacks refers to another major significance of the rise of modern capitalism: the development of an international division of labor and the processes of uneven geographical development in different parts of the world economy. Just as the Americas had been conquered and transformed into slave economies for the production of cotton and sugar for the European metropolitan economies in the 17th and 18th centuries, the further development of large-scale industry and the revolution in the means of transportation and communication gave capitalism an elasticity and the compulsion to expand "by leaps and bounds" to search for new markets and sources of raw materials by conquering foreign territories in the 19th century.

By ruining handicraft production of finished articles in other countries, machinery forcibly converts them into fields for the production of raw materials. Thus India was compelled to produce cotton, hemp, jute and indigo for Great Britain ... A new international division of labor springs up, one suited to the requirements of the main industrial countries, and it converts one part of the globe into a chiefly agricultural field of production for supplying the other part, which remains a pre-eminently industrial field.

(Marx 1977: 579–80)[4]

Returning now to the racial division of labor between free (white) and (black) slave laborers, it also gave rise to ideologies of race and racism to rationalize it. These ideologies began to develop simultaneously with the colonial conquests. However, it was roughly during the late 17th and the 18th centuries that the modern, or biological, ideological formulations of race based on phenotype (skin color, facial features, hair texture, etc.) arose. The alleged superiority and inferiority of groups ranked in a hierarchical order (with whites at the top and blacks at the bottom, with other categories in between) followed from those classifications and entered the lexicon of the modern world. And other than the descriptions of European explorers, conquerors, merchants, and traders that Cox referred to above, the task of producing an explicitly racist ideology of white superiority and black inferiority fell to the major thinkers of the Enlightenment.[5] Among them were François-Marie Arouet Voltaire, David Hume, Immanuel Kant, and Charles-Louis de Secondat Barron de Montesquieu in Europe, Thomas Jefferson in the USA, and Moreau de Saint-Méry in French Saint-Domingue. However, as Davis argues, it was

> Montesquieu, more than any other thinker, who put the subject of Negro slavery on the agenda of the European Enlightenment by weighing the institution against the general laws or principles that promoted human happiness, and encouraging the imaginative experiment of a reversal of roles in a world turned upside down.
>
> (Davis 1975: 45)

As Montesquieu himself put it in his *De l'Esprit des lois*, first published in 1748, the enslavement of Africans was justified in the American colonies because, "the peoples of Europe having exterminated those of America, they had to enslave those of Africa to clear so much land," and because "the price of sugar would have been too high if slaves did not cultivate the plant that produced it." Moreover, the slaves in question

> are black from head to toe; and their nose is so flattened that it is almost impossible to pity them. It cannot be thought that God, who is so wise, could have put a soul, especially a good soul, in a body so completely black ... It is so natural to think that color is the essence of humanity ... [that] it is impossible to suppose that these people could be men; because, if we supposed them to be men, we would start to believe that we ourselves are not Christians.
>
> (Montesquieu 1973: Vol. 1, 265; my translation)

In his *Essai sur les moeurs et l'esprit des nations*, which he wrote between 1745 and 1778 with long periods of interruption along the way (Pomeau 1963: iv–v), Voltaire claimed that the

> black race is a species of men different from ours, as the race of spaniels is from the greyhound ... the form of their eyes is not like ours. Their wooly hair in no way resembles ours, and one could say that if their intelligence is not different from ours as we understand it, it is far inferior. They are incapable of great attention; they don't contrive much, and they do not appear to be made neither for the advantages nor the abuses of our philosophy ... They believe they were born in Guinea to be sold to whites and to serve them.
>
> (Voltaire 1963: Vol. 2: 305–6; my translation)

None the less, unlike Montesquieu, Voltaire opposed the brutal exploitation of the slaves who were said to be men like us, [and were] redeemed from the blood of Christ who died for them, but then are worked as beasts of burden. They are undernourished; and if they flee, their legs are cut, and are made to turn the wheels of the sugar mills by hand after they've been fitted with wooden legs. And after that we dare to speak of the rights of people!

(Voltaire 1963: Vol. 2: 305–6; my translation)

For his part, in his essay "Of National Characters," Hume rejected that the differences among peoples and nations were due to "physical causes," that is, "the qualities of the air and climate" that supposedly affect the "temper, the tone and habit of the body ... which, though reflexion and reason may sometime overcome it, will yet prevail among the generality of mankind, and have an influence on their manners." Against this view he argued that the differences among nations were "moral," that is, caused by the differences in "the nature of the government, the revolutions of public affairs, the plenty or penury in which the people live, the situation of the nation with regard to its neighbors, and such like circumstances" (Hume 1742: Vol. 1, 214). After comparing and contrasting different nations and peoples to make his point, he concluded by excluding Africans from such considerations:

I am apt to suspect the negroes (sic) to be naturally inferior to the whites. There scarcely ever was a civilized nation of that complexion, nor even any individual, eminent either in action or speculation. No ingenious manufactures amongst them, *no arts, no sciences*. On the other, the most rude and barbarous of the whites, such as the ancient Germans, the present Tartars, have still something eminent about them, in their valour, form of government, or some other particular. Such a uniform and constant difference could not happen, in so many countries and ages, if nature had not made an initial distinction between these breeds of men. Not to mention our colonies, there are Negro slaves dispersed all over Europe, of whom none ever discovered any symptoms of ingenuity; though low people, without education, will start up amongst us, and distinguish themselves in every profession. In Jamaica, indeed, they talk of one negroe (sic) as a man of parts and learning; but it is likely he is admired for slender accomplishments, like a parrot who speaks a few words plainly.

(Hume 1742: note [M], 222, emphasis in original)

Kant seconded Hume's argument in his "Observations on the Feelings of the Beautiful and the Sublime." After comparing Arabs, Persians, Japanese, Indians, and Chinese to Europeans in terms of their moral, aesthetic, religious, and intellectual predispositions, he argued that:

The Negroes of Africa have by nature no feeling, which rises above the trifling. Mr. Hume challenges everybody, to produce a single example where a Negro has shown talents, and maintains, that among a hundred thousand blacks who are transported from their native home, though many of them are emancipated, not a single one of them has ever been found that has performed anything great, either in the arts and sciences, or shown any other commendable property, though among the whites there are constantly some, who raise themselves up from among the populace and acquire consideration in the world by distinguished talents. So essential is the difference between these two races of men, and it appears to be equally great with regard to the mental capacities, as with regard to the color.

(Kant 1799: 73)

In my view, given his stature and influence as a "Founding Father" of the USA, no one did more to lay out a justification for a politics of racial oppression and marginalization of black Americans than Thomas Jefferson. In his *Notes on the State of Virginia* published in 1787, Jefferson offered the reasons why blacks and whites could not live together on American soil, and if and when they were emancipated it would be better if they were deported. As he put it:

Deep rooted prejudices entertained by the whites; ten thousand recollections, by the blacks, of injuries they have sustained; new provocations; the real distinctions which nature has made; and many other circumstances, will divide us into parties and produce convulsions which will probably never end but in the extermination of the one or the other race. To these objections, which are political, may be added others, which are physical and moral. The first difference which strikes us is that of colour. Whether the black of the negro (sic) resides in the reticular membrane between the skin and scarf-skin, or in the scarf-skin itself; whether it proceeds from the colour of the blood, the colour of the bile, or from that of some other secretion, the difference is fixed in nature, and is as real as if its seat and cause were better known to us ... The improvement of the blacks in body and mind, in the first instance of their mixture with the whites, has been observed by everyone, and proves that their inferiority is not the effect merely of their condition of life ... I advance it therefore as a suspicion only, that the blacks, whether originally a distinct race, or made distinct by time and circumstances, are inferior to the whites in the endowments both of body and mind.

(Jefferson 1984: 264, 267, 270)

As Barbara Fields has written, the reason this racial ideology arose as it did was to "[explain] to people whose terrain was a republic founded on radical doctrines of liberty and natural rights ... why some people could rightly be denied what others took for granted: namely, liberty, supposedly a self-evident gift of nature's God" (Fields 1990: 114).

Similarly in the Caribbean colonies, especially those of England and France where the slave-based sugar plantation economies were established, there also arose in the 18th century "a systematic racist ideology that identified the slave, in turn, with nonhuman and antinatural attributes" (Lewis 1983: 98). However, in contrast to the USA, a different discourse on race developed as a result of the significant demographic, social, and political characteristics of that region. Whites were also dominant economically, politically, and socially, but they were a numerical minority confronted by a much larger population of black slaves and *affranchis* or free people of color as they were called, the majority of whom were classified as mulattoes. In Saint-Domingue, for example, which was the largest, most productive and wealthiest of the French Caribbean colonies in the 18th century, whites there were outnumbered by a ratio of 13 to 1: 40,000 whites, 28,000 *affranchis*, and 452,000 slaves, the vast majority of whom were black (Moreau de Saint-Méry [1797] 1958: Vol. 1: 28). The significance of this demographic fact is not only that of the lower ratio of whites to blacks, but the emergence of a recognized, and self-recognized, category of people who were not classified as white but were free, and, equally as important, enjoyed the right of private property in land and in slaves, even though they were denied other social and political rights reserved for whites.[6]

Consequently, a more nuanced racial ideology was produced in the Caribbean to account for a stratification system that corresponded with color classifications and degrees of freedom and rights: full social, political, and economic rights for whites; freedom and limited rights for the *affranchis*; and no rights for slaves. It was in this context that Moreau de Saint-Méry, the Martiniquan-born white Creole jurist turned historian/ethnographer wrote, with subsidies from both the royal and Saint-Domingue administrations, his three-volume *Description de la partie française de l'Isle de Saint-Domingue* originally published in 1797 (Maurel and Taillemite 1958: xv–xvi). He proceeded therein to list 128 possible color gradations combined into 13 classifications, which he admitted were arbitrary, that resulted from admixtures between those who are "white at one end and black on the other," mulattoes with other mulattoes, mulattoes with blacks, and blacks with what remained of the indigenous population (Moreau de Saint-Méry 1958: Vol. 1, 86–101). He then went on to say this: "Of all the combinations of the White with the black (sic), the Mulatto combines the most physical advantages; of all these racial mixtures it is he who extracts the strongest constitution, the most analogous to the climate of Saint-Domingue. To the sobriety and the strength of the black (sic), he combines grace in the manners and the intelligence of the White" (Moreau de Saint-Méry 1958: Vol. 1, 90).

As I will show in later chapters, mulattoes as a class would use a similar argument to fight for full equality with whites during the colonial period and, after Haiti became independent in 1804, to compete for power with the newly emergent black bourgeoisie. For the white colonialists, however, if what Antoine de Cournand (1968) critically called the *aristocratie de la peau* (aristocracy of the skin) had to be maintained, they had to erect a defensive barrier against any "crossing of the line" by mulattoes (Dupuy 1989: 28). Moreau de Saint-Méry added weight to that claim by asserting that

> One can be assured that in all the families designated by a single traditional line, these indiscreet markers of the African characteristic show up from time to time and are always noticed. Moreover, whatever whiteness the mixed race may have, it does not always have the shade of the pure white and that is what serves the eyes of those familiarized with the comparison.
>
> (Moreau de Saint-Méry 1958: Vol. 1: 100)

A *mémoire du roi* (king's memorandum) issued in September 1776 went straight to the point:

> [The] people of color are either free or slaves; they are either *affranchis* or descendants of *affranchis*; whatever distance they may have from their origin, they always keep the stain of slavery, and are declared incapable of all public functions; even gentlemen with the slightest trace of Negro blood cannot enjoy the prerogatives of nobility. This law is harsh but wise and necessary: in a country where there are fifteen slaves to one white, one could not put too much distance between the two species; one could not impress upon blacks too much respect for those to whom they are subjected. This distinction, rigorously observed even after freedom, is the key to the subordination of the slave, and follows from the opinion that his color is doomed to servitude, and that nothing can make him the equal of his master.
>
> (cited in Debien 1950: 222; Gisler 1965: 99–100; Dupuy 1989: 29)

The representative examples of the views cited above leave little doubt that by the end of the 18th century a biologically based racist ideology had been elaborated to justify and perpetuate the racial division of labor that colonial slavery had created. All later attempts by social Darwinians to give scientific clothing to these beliefs following the second wave of European imperialism in the 19th and 20th centuries added nothing new to what the European and American Enlightenment thinkers had already said. As George Fredrickson put it succinctly, "the scientific thought of the Enlightenment was a precondition for the growth of a modern racism based on physical typology" (cited in Davis 2006: 75). Philip Nicholson also argued that the development of a more strictly biological racism by the French, the Germans, the English, and the Americans stemmed from the intensifying national and imperial rivalries in the Pacific, the Arabian Peninsula, Persia, Asia, and Africa from the mid-19th century on. By extending Darwin's theory of the inevitable conquest, domination, and destruction in the evolutionary world to the relationships of human society, Social Darwinians "put aside humanitarian impulses as unscientific barriers to real human progress. In a jungle-like struggle of classes, nations, and races, it was both natural and proper ... for the winners not only to dominate their inferior rivals but to destroy them for the long-term good of the human species" (Nicholson 1999: 117–20). Or, as Hanna Arendt put it so well:

> The fact that racism is the main ideological weapon of imperialistic politics is so obvious that it seems as though many students prefer to avoid the beaten path of truism ... For the truth is that race-thinking entered the scene of active politics the moment the European peoples had prepared, and to a certain extent realized, the new body politic of the nation. From the very beginning, racism deliberately cut across all national boundaries, whether defined by geographic, linguistic, traditional, or any other standards, and denied national-political existence as such. Race-thinking, rather than class thinking, was the ever-present shadow accompanying the development of the comity of European nations.
>
> (Arendt 1973: 160–161)

In short, race-thinking and racism did not emerge in 19th century Europe with the formation of the biopower state, or as a reformulation of the old discourse on race wars to reestablish the sovereignty of the state, as Foucault contends, but rather was produced to explain and justify the gobbling up of the world by Western Europeans from the 16th century onward. The inevitable violence unleashed would subdue and incorporate the populations of the conquered territories in the global division of labor without which capitalism would not have been possible. Because he ignored the historic roots of racism in the processes of forceful incorporation of non-European peoples as one of the foundational pillars of that global division, Foucault treated Europe as if its modern history was decoupled from its imperialist practices. He therefore failed to see the connection between those practices and their internal articulations as ideologies in the imperial countries themselves.

This was as true in the 17th and 18th centuries as I have indicated for the Enlightenment thinkers, as it was in the 19th and 20th. Nicholson argues, for example, that Hitler got many of his ideas about inferior races while in prison in 1923 from the book *The Principles of Human Heredity and Race Hygiene* by the German geneticist Eugen Fischer. Fischer, who taught at the University of Freiberg, developed his views in the German colony of Southwest Africa (today's Namibia) where the German forces pursued a policy of extermination of the Herero people between 1904 and 1907 for daring to resist their colonization. Hitler later appointed Fischer rector of the University of Berlin where he taught SS doctors (Nicholson 1999: 118). As Jean-Paul Sartre put it more broadly in his "Preface" to Frantz Fanon's *The Wretched of the Earth,*

> By rejecting metropolitan universalism, our soldiers overseas apply the numerus clausus to the human species: since none can rob, enslave, or kill

his fellow man without committing a crime, they lay down the principle that the colonized subject is not a fellow man. Our military forces have received orders to change this abstract certainty into a reality … Colonial violence not only aims at keeping these enslaved men at a respectful distance; it also seeks to dehumanize them.

(Sartre 2004: xlix–l)

It is that reality that also led Aimé Césaire to conclude in *Discourse on Colonialism* that what Europe

cannot forgive Hitler for is not crime in itself, *the crime against man*, it is not the *humiliation of man as such*, it is the crime against the white man, the humiliation of the white man, and the fact that he applied to Europe colonialist procedures which until then had been reserved exclusively for the Arabs of Algeria, the coolies of India, and the blacks of Africa.

(Césaire 1972: 14)

Late in his argument, Foucault realized that race and racism had something to do with capitalism and the need to explain and justify both the unequal incorporation of different human populations in its division of labor and the invidious treatment of those assigned to the so-called inferior groups by those in the so-called superior groups. However, by the time he came to that conclusion it was too late for him to revise his argument that saw race and racism as sui generis and linear developments in Western Europe. He also misunderstood the dual role of racist violence in the history of capitalism. While that violence can lead and has led to genocide, its main objective was not to eliminate the "inferior races" in order to preserve the purity of the "superior race" as he put it, but rather to incorporate populations unequally in the division of labor of the capitalist world-economy, and to normalize, that is fetishize, their racial identities such that both those who benefited and those who were despoiled came to accept "race" as natural and unchangeable, and hence as determining the relations between "the races." Thus, once so fetishized, "race," or "color," would henceforth become part of the arsenal for the struggles for power and privilege, as well as for the recognition and equality of the unprivileged without necessarily questioning the social relations of production and divisions of labor that gave rise to these ideologies and reproduce the grievances they seek to redress.

Notes

1 All references to Foucault are from the English texts.
2 Although Marx often argued that wage-labor was essential for the production of surplus-value, he understood that other types of workers could and did produce it as well. For example, he compared slave labor in the American South and the West

Indies with wage laborers in the northern American states and Europe, and argued that "in proportion as the export of cotton became vital to those [southern] states, the over-working of the Negro, and sometimes the consumption of his life in seven years of labour, became a factor in a calculated and calculating system. It was no longer a question of obtaining from him a certain quantity of useful products, but rather of the production of surplus-value itself. The same is true of the *corvée*, in the Danubian Principalities for instance" (Marx 1977: 345).

3 That is, the production of surplus-value or profit.

4 Marx argued that the international division of labor capitalism created between the developed industrial economies and the colonized territories that were transformed into raw material producers for the former anticipated by more than a century the arguments of contemporary theorists like Andre Gunder Frank and Immanuel Wallerstein on the exploitation and uneven development of what Frank calls the metropole/satellite and Wallerstein calls the core/peripheral countries. It was Frank (1969) who originally advanced the argument that once incorporated in the capitalist world economy subsequent to the colonial conquests of the 16th century, the metropolitan countries exploited the resources of the colonized or satellite regions and caused their underdevelopment while promoting that of the metropole. Building on Frank's argument, Wallerstein later argued that since the 16th century the capitalist world-system was characterized by a single international division of labor between core, semi-peripheral, and peripheral zones comprising different modes of labor control—such as wage labor in the core areas and slave or other coerced labor relations in the peripheries—and that in addition to the exploitation of labor by capital, the core or advanced industrial countries exploited the resources and appropriated the wealth produced by the peripheral or underdeveloped economies (Wallerstein 1979).

5 There were some notable exceptions. Jean-Jacques Rousseau, for example, categorically rejected the notions of racial superiority/inferiority by offering a very modern and cosmopolitan view of the diversity of the human populations of the world in his *Discours sur l'origine et les fondements de l'inégalité parmi les hommes* (1782). He argued that, in addition to the differences of health, age, bodily strength, and the quality of mind, which he considered natural, the other kinds of inequality that existed among mankind and which he called moral or political, were those due to differences in the "privileges that some men enjoy to the prejudices of others, such as being wealthier, more honored, more powerful than they, and even of getting obeyed by them" (Rousseau 1782: 62). The causes of these moral or political inequalities, he went on to argue, originated with: (1) the invention of the right of property and the laws created to safeguard those rights; (2) the institution of Magistracy (government); and (3) the shift from legitimate to arbitrary power,

> such that the state of the rich and the poor was authorized by the first period, that of the powerful and the weak by the second, and by the third that of the master and the slave, which is the last degree of inequality, and the end which finally all the others reach, until new revolutions dissolve the Government completely, or bring it closer to the legitimate institution.
>
> (Rousseau 1782: 193)

He then went on to say this:

> Among the men we know, either for ourselves, or from historians, or from travelers, some are black, some white, others red; some wear long hair, others have nothing but curly wool; some are almost covered with hair, others don't even have a beard; there have been and there may still be nations of men of

gigantic size: and leaving aside the fable about pygmies, which may well be no more than an exaggeration, we know that the Laplanders and especially the Greenlanders are well below the average height of man ... [If] it had been possible to make good observations in ancient times where different peoples followed different ways of life than they do today, then many more striking varieties in the shapes and habits of the body would also have been noted ... All these facts ... can surprise only those who are accustomed to look only at the objects around them, and who ignore the powerful effects of the differences in climates, the air, foods, ways of life, habits in general, and especially the surprising force of the same causes, when they act continuously on successive generations. Today, when commerce, travels and conquests bring diverse peoples closer together, and their ways of life become constantly more alike as a result of frequent communication, one can see that national differences diminish ...

(Rousseau 1782: 232–33; my translation)

Rousseau's cosmopolitan views, however, were drowned out by the cacophony of the pro-slavery, racist discourse of his contemporaries.

6 I will discuss the significance of the rise of the *affranchis* or free people of color class economically, politically, and socially at greater length in the next chapters.

2 Toussaint Louverture, the Haitian Revolution, and Negritude

A critical assessment of Aimé Césaire's interpretation

Now in its 53rd year since its publication in 1960, Aimé Césaire's *Toussaint Louverture: La Révolution française et le problème colonial* (Toussaint Louverture: The French Revolution and the Colonial Problem), which has not yet been translated into English, retains its status as a classic statement on the role of Toussaint Louverture in the slave revolution of Saint-Domingue that was by all measures the most radical of the 18th century revolutions. For unlike the American Revolution of 1776 and the French Revolution of 1789, both of which sought to maintain the system of chattel slavery and declared black men and women unfit for liberty, equality, citizenship, and self-rule, the Saint-Domingue Revolution (also known as the Haitian Revolution) abolished slavery and declared that the ideals embodied in the philosophies of the Enlightenment belonged to all of humanity and not only to those segments of it privileged by skin color or social status as many of its philosophers proclaimed.[1] By challenging "the ontological order of the West and the global order of colonialism," as Michel-Rolf Trouillot put it (1995: 89), the Saint-Domingue Revolution turned the supremacist ideologies of the West and of many of the Enlightenment philosophers upside down.

Before I come to my assessment of Césaire's argument in *Toussaint Louverture*, it may be useful to situate that book in the context of his previous writings, especially his 1939 *Cahier d'un retour au pays natal* (*Notebook of a Return to the Native Land*), and *Discours sur le colonialisme* (*Discourse on Colonialism*) published in 1955. For it was in Notebook that Césaire first introduced the concept of *Négritude* into the lexicon of the 20th century black literary, cultural, and political movements. Its objective, he argued, was to challenge the dehumanization, devaluation, and oppression of black Africans and their descendants in the Caribbean and the USA, and to nurture their self-esteem, their consciousness, and their self-confidence and belief in their ability to shape their own destiny (Césaire 1972: 65–79). In keeping with that thrust, Césaire claimed in Notebook that Haiti was "where Negritude rose for the first time" with the Revolution (Césaire 2013: 19).

In *Discourse* Césaire expanded his critique of the racism, barbarism, and degeneracy of European bourgeois civilization that was also at the heart of *Notebook*. He opened *Discourse* with this indictment of Europe:

A civilization that proves incapable of solving the problem it creates is a decadent civilization. A civilization that chooses to close its eyes to its most crucial problem is a stricken civilization. A civilization that uses its principles for trickery and deceit is a dying civilization. The fact is that the so-called European civilization—"Western" civilization—as it has been shaped by two centuries of bourgeois rule, is incapable of solving the two major problems to which its existence has given rise: the problem of the proletariat and the colonial problem ... Europe is indefensible.

(Césaire 1972: 9)

In an interview he had with the Haitian poet and political activist René Depestre at the Cultural Congress of Havana in 1967, Depestre asked Césaire how he applied the concept of Negritude to the history of Haiti in Notebook. Césaire replied that "Haiti represented for me the heroic Antilles, the African Antilles ... [The] first Negro epic of the New World was written by Haitians, people like Toussaint Louverture, Henri Christophe [and] Jean-Jacques Dessalines" (Césaire 1972: 74). Depestre did not challenge Césaire's assertion, but the problem with his answer is that these three revolutionary leaders did not have the same attitude toward France, the colonial question, and the future of Saint-Domingue. As I will show below, though he was steadfast against slavery, Louverture pursued a pro-French policy that sought to preserve Saint-Domingue as a French colony and make the former slaves citizens of France. In effect, it could be said, he pursued a politics of assimilation into French culture and society, a policy which Césaire said Negritude opposed and led to what he called *boravisme*, or the failure to decolonize one's consciousness (Césaire 1972: 73). Unlike Louverture, Christophe was not steadfast against independence if the French gave any thought of reconquering Saint-Domingue and reinstating slavery. Dessalines, however, wanted nothing to do with the French and was determined to expel them from Saint-Domingue and declare its independence. And to make his point, as soon as Saint-Domingue became Haiti on January 1, 1804, he ordered the arrest, military trial and execution of French citizens who had been guilty or suspected of participating in massacres of blacks during the last year of the French occupation, a process that led to a summary execution of French citizens by anyone who had grievances against them. Part of the reason Dessalines gave to justify this act was the need for Haitians to decolonize their consciousness by freeing themselves from those who had "hitherto held our minds in a state of most humiliating torpor, [and had] every hope of enslaving us again" (cited in Dupuy 1989: 75). Unlike Louverture, therefore, Dessalines seems to come closest to embodying Césaire's definition of Negritude as a "resistance to the politics of assimilation ... a process of disalienation ... and detoxification" (Césaire 1972: 68, 72).

There is another line of questioning that Depestre did not pursue but that will form the main thrust of my argument. This has to do with what these three revolutionary leaders came to represent in terms of the emergence of a new black propertied ruling class whose interests diverged from and were opposed to those of the former slave masses, and the implications of this fact for Césaire's argument. I will argue that, contrary to his interpretation of the interests and political objectives of the *grands blancs* and the mulattoes in class terms, Césaire eschewed such an approach when analyzing the actions of Louverture and the other black revolutionary leaders. While critical of some of Louverture's policies when he took control of the colony in 1800, Césaire depicted him as sharing and defending the interests of the emancipated slaves. Contrary to Césaire I will show that Louverture and the other revolutionary leaders had in fact transformed themselves into a new ruling class opposed to the interests of the former slaves, while at the same time vying with the mulatto leaders for control of the emergent state that would become Haiti on January 1, 1804.

The class and racial structures of Saint-Domingue before the revolution

Established in 1697 after the Treaty of Riswick officially transferred the western third of the island of Hispaniola to the French, Saint-Domingue would become the most productive and wealthiest of the French sugar-producing colonies in the New World in the 18th century. It not only out-produced all the other French and English Caribbean colonies in sugar but in other export crops such as cotton, coffee, indigo, and cacao. Its sugar exports alone were valued at 115 million francs in 1789, and the total value of its revenues for that year was estimated at 150 million francs, the sum that France would later impose on Haiti as the price for recognizing its independence.[2] In addition to its exports, Saint-Domingue, along with the other French Caribbean colonies, also contributed directly to the economic development of France, especially the port-cities tied to the slave and colonial trades such as Bordeaux, Nantes, La Rochelle, Marseille, Rouen, Dieppe, Lille, and Dunkerque. Among the industries that grew from the colonial trade were those involved in sugar refining, shipbuilding, and textiles, as well as food exports. Despite the trade monopoly that France sought to exercise over its colonies, Saint-Domingue was actively involved in trading with the USA (or the southern and northern American colonies before independence), England, Holland, and Spain, both in terms of exports and imports. There is no question, then, that Saint-Domingue was fully integrated into and contributed significantly to the commercial and manufacturing-industrial development of the core economies of the capitalist world-system in the 18th century, France in particular (Dupuy 1989: Chs 1, 2, passim).

Although Saint-Domingue produced enormous profits for, and contributed to the accumulation of capital in France (and Western Europe and the USA), it does not follow that its own economy was developing or creating the infrastructure for its own sustainable commercial and industrial development. France imposed restrictions on the development of manufactures in Saint-Domingue in order to keep it as a supplier of raw materials (cotton, indigo), sugar and coffee to France, and as a market for French consumer and manufactured goods, including the equipment (e.g., the mills) used in sugar production. However, these restrictions could have been easily overcome if the dominant classes in Saint-Domingue had had an interest in doing so. And the reason they did not had to do with slavery.

First, free wage-laborers, Marx argued, depend on the renewed sale of their labor-power to the capitalists in order to earn their living. Thus, they must satisfy the demands of their employers both in terms of the quantity and quality of their labor so as not to be driven out by their competitors in the labor market. Moreover, in general workers can also increase their wages, and hence their standard of living, by developing their skills and their abilities. In short, insofar as there are variations in the wages paid to workers

> depending on whether a particular type of work requires a more highly developed labour-power at greater cost or not ... this gives scope for individual variation while, at the same time, it also provides the worker with an incentive to develop his own labour-power ... and raise [himself] to higher spheres by exhibiting a particular talent or energy.
>
> (Marx 1977: 1031–32)

The situation is the exact opposite for the slave. Unlike the wage-laborer, the slave works only under the direct supervision of the slave-master or overseer, "under the spur of external fear but not for *his existence* which is *guaranteed* even though it does not belong to him ... *The continuity in the relations* of slave and slave-owner is based on the fact that the slave is kept in his situation by *direct compulsion*" (Marx 1977: 1031, emphasis in the original). Since slaves did not sell their labor in exchange for wages but were bought whole by their master, they were not free as wage-laborers to refuse employment or offer their services to other employers for higher wages or better conditions of employment. As such, they had to be confined to the plantations. Lastly, since slaves were not paid for their labor they were not consumers who purchased their means of existence in a market as were wage-laborers but depended on the master to provide for their subsistence (food, clothing, and shelter).[3]

And second, the drive to accumulate more capital by making labor more productive inevitably leads to the development of machinery (or better technology), which reduces the need for workers and displaces them. Again as Marx explains the process, as the division of labor characteristic of capitalism develops the skill of the worker, machinery renders that worker superfluous. Consequently the "self-valorization of capital by means of the machine is related directly to the number of workers whose conditions of existence have been destroyed by it" (Marx 1977: 557).

In the capitalist slave system of the Americas such substitution of slaves by machines would have been against the interests of the slave-owners who were not just buying the labor-power of slaves, that is, their capacity to labor in return for wages, but buying the slaves themselves. As Elizabeth Fox-Genovese remarked, the plantation "reflected the principles of capitalism that informed the market," but in its internal relations it "reflected the principles of slave labor that dominated the production of the staple crop and the reproduction of the labor force" (Fox-Genovese 1983: 238). Slavery, then, severely constrained the mobility of labor and as such limited the extent to which machinery could be used as a substitute for workers while improving the productivity of those employed. Slaves were the most important part of the capital equipment of the plantations, and combined in their persons both labor-power (or variable capital) and constant capital. Their purchase represented a fixed investment by their master, and the latter recouped their investment by having the slaves produce commodities for sale in a market; and since the slaves were bought for life, they could produce surplus value for the master far beyond their original purchase price (Hall 1962: 305; Post 1978: 23). The slave-owners, then, and the merchant bourgeoisie tied to the slave trade, would have gone against their self-interest and undermined the entire system of slavery if they had rendered their slaves redundant with technological innovation.

Put differently, idle slaves would not produce surplus value for their owners who had already invested their capital to purchase them. Idle slaves, therefore, were of no use and of no value to their owners. That is the reason why none of the slave economies in the Americas industrialized. As Eugene Genovese observed for the USA, "[p]lantation slavery so limited the purchasing power of the South that it could not sustain much industry. That industry which could be raised usually lacked a home market of sufficient scope to permit large-scale operation" (Genovese 1967: 173).

Given the limits on technological innovation imposed by the slave relations of production, then, planters could improve productivity only by employing more slaves:

> The cultivation of the Southern export articles, cotton, tobacco, sugar, etc., carried on by slaves, is only remunerative as long as it is conducted with large gangs of slaves, on a mass scale and on wide expanses of naturally fertile soil, that requires only simple labor. Intensive cultivation, which depends less on fertility of the soil than on investment of capital, intelligence and energy of labor, is contrary to the nature of slavery.
>
> (Marx and Engels 1971: 67)

In Saint-Domingue, as elsewhere in the Caribbean, production also remained labor-intensive throughout the 18th century. Planters increased output by working their slaves as much as possible to the point of exhaustion or death. Their brutal exploitation, coupled with inadequate diet and health-care, resulted in a high rate of death among slaves, leading most plantations to renew their slave population every ten years on average (Debien 1962; Léon 1963).[4] As a former governor of Martinique put it,

I have always been astonished to see that, since the founding of the colonies, the slaves have never reproduced themselves sufficiently to [completely] eliminate the need for slaves from Africa, but at least to create a population base whose continuous reproduction would not always be at the mercy of the trade ... [Here] is to what I attribute this lack of reproduction. Most of the planters malnourish their slaves and work them beyond their strength, all to increase their revenues. They also force pregnant slaves to work under the same conditions until the last moment, and often they are mistreated.

(cited in Dupuy 1989: 39)

The slave uprising in August 1791 would destroy this system, the interests it served, both in the colony and in France, and eventually lead to the independence of Haiti and the creation of an entirely different social order. To better understand those interests and why the revolution took on such a violent character, it may be useful to analyze the class and racial structure of the colony as it stood then. At the top of the class and racial/color hierarchy were the white French planters who owned the majority of the 793 large sugar plantations and most of the 452,000 slaves in the colony. For the most part the large planters settled in the colony permanently to form the dominant class of Creoles, but a wealthy minority returned to France and left their properties to be managed by overseers or procurators. In France, these absentee planters became the allies of the maritime or merchant bourgeoisie in control of the slave and colonial trading system. Together, the resident Creole planters, the absentee owners, the representatives of the merchant bourgeoisie, and the colonial administrators formed the ruling class of *grands blancs* or big whites.

Immediately below the class of *grands blancs* was a middle class that comprised owners of smaller cotton, cacao, indigo, and coffee plantations, and fewer slaves than the large sugar planters. The significant characteristic of this class is that it included white Creoles and members of the *affranchis* (i.e. freed slaves or those born free). Even though the mulattoes served as the reference group for the *affranchis*, many freed blacks also belonged to that class.[5] The *affranchis* came into their own as a class during the so-called coffee revolution of the 1750s and 1760s, when, as a by-product of the racial discrimination they suffered at the hands of whites, the mulattoes retreated into the interior and hilly areas of the colony where they were able to acquire or take possession of unclaimed lands to cultivate coffee and other crops. Their stronghold was primarily in the western and southern provinces of Saint-Domingue. They not only owned property but slaves as well.[6] By 1791, in fact, they owned up to one-third of the productive properties, and one-fourth of the slaves of the colony, thereby making them a significant bloc of property owners (Moreau de Saint-Méry 1958: Vol. 2, 1110, 1138, 1154–55; Vol. 3, 1400; Debien 1950: 213–16; Trouillot 1982: 337).[7] In addition to the property and slave owners, the middle class included professionals such as physicians, lawyers, retail merchants, colonial military officers and administrators, plantation overseers, shopkeepers, and self-employed craftsmen and artisans. Again, within this group were to be found both whites and *affranchis*. There was also a white and *affranchis* working class of skilled and unskilled workers, sailors, store clerks, apprentices, and dockworkers, among others. Taken as a whole, the whites who belonged to the middle and working classes formed the *petits blancs*, or small whites, so-called because they distinguished themselves from the *grands blancs* whom they opposed politically, and the class of *affranchis* whom they despised because of the immediate competition they faced from that group for access to employment, property, and other positions.

Below the dominant, middle, and working classes that constituted the free population of Saint-Domingue and counted some 40,000 whites and 28,000 *affranchis*, were the 452,000 slaves, most of whom had recently arrived from Africa before the revolution started in 1791 (Moreau de Saint-Méry 1958: Vol. 1, 28, 111). The slaves worked primarily as laborers on the plantations, but also as domestic servants, coachmen, and in myriad other jobs that whites and *affranchis* would not perform. It is they who produced the enormous wealth that earned Saint-Domingue the designation as the "pearl of the Antilles" and the envy of all other colonial powers in the 18th century, England in particular.

The class system of Saint-Domingue, then, did not exclude free mulattoes and blacks from the ranks of property and slave owners. By contrast, the racial system that slavery engendered worked to exclude free mulattoes and blacks socially, politically, and even economically from certain occupations, such as medicine, law, or any public function, especially after 1750 when whites pushed to deprive the *affranchis* of the previous powers and privileges they had gained. As I argued in the preceding chapter, in all other New World slave societies of the 18th century, the institutionalization of a racial hierarchy engendered by slavery produced its corresponding fetishized ideologies of race and the fierce defense of "the color line" to maintain the privileges of the skin. As such, that "line" made it possible for whites of any class to assert their social supremacy over mulattoes or blacks of any class to constitute what came to be known as the *aristocratie de la peau* (aristocracy of the skin) or simply white supremacy (Cournand 1968). Whites, however, did not have a monopoly on the exercise of skin privilege in the colony. Mulattoes practiced their own racism against blacks by excluding blacks from their social networks and intermarrying among themselves or with whites if possible. The *affranchis* also defended slavery, and free blacks were not allowed to buy mulatto slaves. Mulattoes who were slaves were not only treated differently than black slaves, but also considered themselves superior to blacks (Labelle 1978: 51). These practices were at the root of the reproduction of the class relations and divisions that came to be expressed ideologically as relations between whites, mulattoes, and blacks complete with arguments about the "natural" superiority of one group over the other derived from their biology, that is, their phenotype, as I have shown in the previous chapter.

The system of racial stratification, therefore, straddled the class system, in such a way that alongside the vertical divisions of class there emerged an impermeable horizontal racial division among whites, mulattoes, and blacks. Race and racism, therefore, became parts of the system of social and class closure to enable whites to monopolize the positions of power and privilege in the colony. However, while the racial order united whites against mulattoes and blacks, it did not change the class divisions between whites. In fact, by fostering a sense of solidarity between whites, the racial system reinforced the dominance of the *grands blancs* over the *petits blancs* and prevented the latter from challenging the former by forming an alliance with the mulattoes with whom they shared much in common. At the same time the mulattoes who opposed the racism of the whites and fought to achieve equality with them, also despised the blacks and defended the slave system. They therefore could not turn to the blacks to unite with them to oppose the slave and racial system until they realized later that freeing the slaves was in fact the only way they could win their own freedom from racial exclusion and oppression. As Aimé Césaire put it so poignantly, "the black stain of the mulatto, indelible as it must be, must mark his place. Forever" (Césaire 1960: 14).

Thus, the race question cannot be understood independently from the class relations in a specific society. Individuals with the same skin color may be classified differently depending on their structural location or class position in different societies. This explains why the construction of a system of racial/color hierarchy and the elaboration of ideologies of racial/color differences to justify the unequal positions of members of such racial/color groups differ from society to society, or even within the same society to reflect the shifts in the structural location of and power relations between different groups. Put differently, class divisions cut through racially designated social groups, and race/color relations never exist independently of class relations but in fact derive from them as I have shown. Practices of racial distinctions and racism, therefore, always articulate with other class practices and their economic, political, and ideological manifestations in a specific society in the context of that society's position in the hierarchical division of labor of the capitalist world-economy. However, saying that race/color ideologies derived from class relations does not mean they do not take on a "life or their own" once created. Otherwise the fetishism of race/color argument I developed in the previous chapter would be meaningless since it posits that race/color takes on an objective existence and determination independent of the social relations that produced it. To recall the point Barbara Fields made earlier (in Chapter 1), race continues to live because the individuals who identify themselves as "belonging" to a race continue to verify and recreate it in their daily lives and relations with each other.

In the case of Saint-Domingue, then, the class relations and divisions between the property owners, the middle classes, and the slaves came to express themselves as relations between whites, mulattoes, and slaves, with their corresponding fetishized identification of freedom and privilege with whiteness, unfreedom and servitude with blackness, and something in between for the mulattoes. Or, to quote Césaire again, the colonial slave system was

> more than a hierarchy; it was an ontology: on top, the white—the *human being* in the full sense of the term—and below, the black, with no juridical personality, a furniture; a thing, that is, *nothingness*; but between this all and this nothingness, there was a forbidding in-between: the mulatto, free man of color.
>
> (Césaire 1960: 11)

The balance of class forces between masters and slaves, and between whites, mulattoes, and slaves determined the significance of the race question, and not the other way around. It is precisely because the class divisions expressed themselves in terms of racial/color ideologies and generated such intense hatred and conflicts among them that they engulfed Saint-Domingue in one of the bloodiest civil wars the Caribbean has ever known, and to which I now turn.

The revolution and transformation of Saint-Domingue

Toussaint Louverture was not among the original leaders of the slave revolution when it started, but he soon emerged as its leader when the growing revolutionary army defected to the Spanish army in neighboring San Domingo, which along with the English was fighting the French in Saint-Domingue. Feeling threatened and wanting to bring the rebellious slave forces back on their side, the French government decreed the emancipation of the slaves in all the French colonies in 1794. Louverture and his now seasoned army of former slaves switched over to the French and helped them expel the Spanish and English forces from Saint-Domingue. By mid-1800, Louverture emerged as the dominant force in Saint-Domingue after expelling the colonial administrators and defeating the mulatto army led by General André Rigaud who had launched a war against him in 1799. He then proceeded to reorganize the colony to reflect the new order, including writing a new constitution in 1801 that abolished slavery and racial discrimination in all aspects of public life and administration, declared all those born in the colony to be free, equal, and French citizens, guaranteed the right to private property, declared Catholicism the official religion and outlawed Vodou, and proclaimed Louverture Governor General for life with the right to name his successor (Schoelcher 1889: 294–95; Nemours 1925: Vol. 1, 103–5; Cabon 1929: Vol. 4, 165–68; Ardouin 1958: Vol. 4, 34; Pluchon 1979: 255–57; Dupuy 1989: 64).

As one would have expected, the French government then under Napoleon Bonaparte was not about to accept this fait accompli and ordered a military expedition in October 1801 led by his brother-in-law General Emannuel Leclerc to recapture Saint-Domingue. He declared part of this objective to be "[the] crusade of civilized people of the West against the black barbarism that was on the rise in America" (cited in Dubois 2004: 256). However, as history would have it, after Haiti had won its independence and the English had defeated Bonaparte and exiled him to St Helena in 1815, he admitted that the expedition to retake Saint-Domingue was a mistake and that it would have been better if he had ruled over the colony through Louverture. As C. L. R. James put it so clearly, "[Bonaparte] had been convinced at last by the only argument that imperialists understand" (James 1963: 373).

However, this was 1802, not 1815, and after months of raging battles between Bonaparte's and Louverture's armies, Louverture surrendered to Leclerc once he realized that the previous surrender of Henri Christophe, one of his top generals, made it impossible for him to continue to fight. Louverture did so only after signing an agreement with Leclerc that all his officers would preserve their rank and their functions, and be incorporated in the French army. In June 1802, under orders from Leclerc, General Brunet arranged to meet with Louverture and proceeded to arrest and deport him to France.

This, in brief, is the historical context that frames Césaire's argument in *Toussaint Louverture*. He divides the book into three sections that deal successively with the three major social and political forces confronting each other in Saint-Domingue, namely the whites, the mulattoes, and the blacks. The first section, which he calls *La Fronde des Grands Blancs* (The Revolt of the Big Whites), meaning principally the French bourgeoisie tied to the slave and colonial trades and the class of large sugar planters, deals with the opposition of those classes to the demands of the free people of color for equal political rights with whites. The position of the whites in the colony also resonated with that of the revolutionary government in France where they realized that tackling the questions of slavery and full equality for the mulattoes would jeopardize the prosperity of the French merchants, the slave traders, the planters, and the French economy itself. Thus, they avoided the issue altogether. Césaire argues that Marat was the only revolutionary in the Legislative Assembly or the National Convention who articulated a consistent anti-colonial and anti-slavery position, including the right of the colonies to revolt against the mother-country and declare their independence, and the right of the mulattoes and blacks to revolt and even massacre the white colonialists to gain their liberty and their rights (Césaire 1960: 156–58).[8]

Essentially, the representatives of the colonial bourgeoisie argued that granting the free people of color political equality with whites was the thin edge of the abolition of slavery, and everyone knew that abolishing slavery would mean the ruin of the colonies and the immense wealth they generated for France, especially Saint-Domingue. Césaire's main point in that section was that for the French bourgeoisie the question of political equality for the free people of color was intimately tied to its fundamental class interest in preserving slavery as the source of its wealth. Thus, one could not equivocate on the race question. Give an inch on that question and the entire system of exploitation it justifies crumbles. As Le Noir de Rovray, a spokesman for white colonial interests, put it, "Mulattoes today, slaves tomorrow!" (cited in Dupuy 1989: 44).

The second section, titled *La Révolte Mulatre* (The Mulatto Revolt), deals with the demands by that social group for full political equality with whites but not, at first, for the abolition of slavery and equality for all. The issue here was that as a class, or, more precisely, the dominant faction of the *affranchis* who, as I mentioned above, came into their own as a property- and slave-owning class in the mid-18th century, tied their demand for political equality with whites to the proposition that they would be a buffer against a revolt by the slaves. That is, propertied mulattoes as a class shared the same interests as the bourgeoisie in preserving the slave system. However, they warned the whites that unless they granted them full political, and not just social equality, the whites would lose them as allies against the slaves and put the entire system in jeopardy. Indeed, the mulattoes argued that to deny them equal rights with the whites would destroy whatever opportunity existed for an alliance between the "free classes" on the question of slavery and prevent a full-scale uprising by the slaves. Raymond Julien, a wealthy mulatto property and slave owner and spokesman for mulatto interests in Paris, argued that after all property interests should take precedence over the color of one's skin (Raymond 1793; Césaire 1960: 88–91).

In May 1791, the French National Assembly yielded and decreed in favor of mulatto rights, but limited them to those born of free mothers and fathers, a small minority among the *affranchis*. Even that limited concession was intolerable to the whites of Saint-Domingue who revolted against the French government and unleashed a wave of terror against mulattoes. Open warfare broke out between them, and in 1794 the French government tried again to grant full civil and political rights to all mulattoes. However, the whites in the colony would have none of it and renewed their offer to England to take possession of Saint-Domingue. England, which along with Spain was at war with France, sent an expeditionary force to Saint-Domingue in 1793 and occupied the West Province and most of the southern part of the colony until Louverture's army drove them out in 1798.

Granting equality to the *affranchis* mulattoes was all well and good for them, but it did nothing for the slaves who were now determining events in the colony. With the slave revolution spreading, Césaire pointed out, "the mulatto question was no longer essential ... [The] essential question [now] was that which no deliberative assembly had yet confronted: the enormous, terrifying black problem" (Césaire 1960: 135). This then leads Césaire to the third and final section titled *La Révolution Nègre* (The Black Revolution). Here he focuses on Louverture's relationship with France and whether or not he should have declared Saint-Domingue's independence once he took control of the colony in 1800. As I will argue, by focusing on that question Césaire downplayed other important contradictions that characterized this historical juncture, namely those among different factions of the emerging indigenous bourgeoisie, on the one hand, and between that bourgeoisie and the former slave masses on the other.

For Césaire, as it was for James, the progressive aspect of Louverture's project was that he sought to preserve the best that France had to offer while rejecting the worst. He saw Louverture as a visionary who was ahead of his time and its possibilities. For what he wanted was to make the former slaves of Saint-Domingue French citizens, keep Saint-Domingue as a self-governed colony, and preserve the plantation system and the trade and financial ties with France. As Césaire put it,

> [Toussaint's was] a brilliant intuition. The idea of a French Common-wealth was there from the beginning. Toussaint had only one fault: he was ahead of his time, by a good century and a half. His offer was to Europe; it was to France, an "offer of destiny": an opportunity which after a time cannot be renewed and that no nation can reject with impunity. And it was for France an exceptional opportunity to liquidate the colonial misadventure under good conditions, without any loss and with greater prestige. We know how he was answered.
>
> (Césaire 1960: 241)[9]

As John Walsh suggests, perhaps thinking of his own role in Martinique, Césaire was portraying Louverture as being willing to sacrifice himself for the future of Haiti (2011: 112). We can also see that theme of sacrifice in how Césaire depicted Louverture's decision to surrender to Leclerc. Louverture could have continued to fight, he argues, even if he was in a much weaker position after Christophe's surrender, but he decided not to for political and not military reasons. He believed that with the indigenous army and its officers kept in their positions, the real motives of Leclerc would become clearer, and with the rainy season and the yellow fever returning, the war would resume and be decisive this time, even if he himself would no longer lead it. Moreover, Césaire goes on to say, Louverture never trusted Leclerc. When, acting on orders from Leclerc, General Brunet asked Louverture to meet with him to discuss the repositioning of troops in the area surrounding Louverture's estate and residence, he no doubt realized this was a trap. At that point, Césaire suggests, Louverture had two choices: resume the war or sacrifice himself so that others, meaning the mulatto and black forces, could unite to carry on the struggle to the end when the time was right. He chose the latter because he believed that given the rift with the mulattoes since he defeated them, he would stand in the way of that unity. For Césaire, then, Toussaint saw himself as an obstacle to unity and thus concluded that he "had to disappear to unite the Haitian forces" (Césaire 1960: 267).

Césaire's argument is unconvincing. In his recent biography of Toussaint Louverture, Madison Bell, citing the same letters Louverture wrote from his prison cell at Fort-de-Joux, points out that those letters

> do suggest that some such idea may have entered his mind, but however fervent his Catholicism, it seems doubtful that he would have wanted to push the imitation of Christ quite so far. And while he was certainly able to put the welfare of his people ahead of his own, it was rare for him to

lose sight of his personal interests so completely. It's more likely that, under the extreme pressure of his situation, he gambled and lost.

(Bell 2007: 265)

Bell's point is similar to that of C. L. R. James and Thomas Madiou, both of whom argued that Louverture made the decision to meet with Brunet, not because he trusted him or Leclerc, but because he believed that Leclerc would not dare or have the power to arrest him while Christophe, Dessalines, and the other officers of the revolutionary army still had command of their troops. Indeed, Louverture took 300 of his own troops with him to meet Brunet, but when the latter refused to let Louverture's troops pass the French lines, Louverture took only two of his officers with him to go to Brunet's headquarters to protest this affront to his authority. He was immediately arrested when he got there (Madiou 1989: Vol. II, 325–26; James 1963: 333–35). In other words, as Bell said, he gambled and lost.

Louverture also lost his second bet that Dessalines and the other general officers of the revolutionary army would come to his rescue if Brunet dared to arrest him. They did not. The question then is why? Césaire never asked that question, yet it is fundamental in explaining Louverture's downfall. By the time of his arrest, Christophe and Dessalines, among other top general officers of the revolutionary army, had come to the conclusion that Louverture was an obstacle to the struggle for independence and had to be pushed aside. When Leclerc decided to arrest Louverture and spoke to those officers about his plan, they gave him their approval. According to Madiou, Dessalines told Leclerc that "Toussaint's banishment from the colony would please me, [and my continued] devotion to my former leader is contrary to my interests" (Madiou 1989: Vol. II, 321). Or, as Bell put it, Leclerc probably "would not have dared arrest Toussaint without some assurance from the black generals that the move would not provoke a revolt on their part" (2007: 263). What's more, Louverture seems to have suspected this. In a letter he wrote to his warrant-officer he accused Dessalines and Christophe of having abandoned him and embraced the French side (Madiou 1989: Vol. II, 323). In short, Louverture did not sacrifice himself for the cause; he was betrayed by some of his top generals so they could pursue their own interests.

What then were those conflicting interests that led Dessalines and Christophe to break with Louverture that Césaire does not address? I am referring here to the emergence of conflicting class interests and objectives among the leaders of the new regime Louverture created in 1800, and between them and the former slave masses. As I mentioned above, the Constitution of 1801 codified and sanctioned the new order Louverture created and also ratified his dictatorship by making him governor for life and granting him absolute power and the right to name his successor.

As both Césaire and James show, since Louverture decided that Saint-Domingue could not go it alone and should remain a colony, it was essential that he revitalize the economy. That meant first and foremost resuming production on the sugar plantations that had made Saint-Domingue the wealthiest of all the French colonies in the New World. But both white and raw sugar production declined by 99 percent and 80 percent, respectively, between 1789 and 1801 (Dupuy 1989: 54). If Louverture was to succeed in revitalizing the economy, he needed to do at least two things. First, he needed to encourage the colonial planters who had fled the colony during the war to return to manage their properties. Most did not and the government then took over their properties and either leased or sold them to the high ranking officers of the revolutionary army who were now managing them. Through such means Louverture and most other high-ranking military officers, including Dessalines, acquired several plantations and transformed themselves into a new black propertied class alongside the old class of white and mulatto property owners. Military officers and administrators of the new political order did not only appropriate properties from former French planters; they also pilfered the public treasury (Sannon 1933: Vol. 3, 103; Pluchon 1979: 248–49, 287–92; Ardouin 1958: Vol. 4, 68–69).[10]

Second, since this new landowning class sought to preserve the plantation system, it had to compel the former slaves to remain on the plantations as wage-laborers. For their part the laborers aspired to become landowning farmers and steadfastly refused to remain on the plantations. They fled to the hills to settle on unclaimed public lands. This created such a labor shortage that Louverture contemplated contracting with Spanish and English slave traders to bring new slaves to work on the plantations but freeing them once they got there and paying them for their labor (Lacroix 1820: Vol. 2, 58; Ardouin 1958: Vol. 4, 77). That plan never materialized.

To maintain order Louverture imposed harsh discipline on the laborers and confined them to their plantations. At the same time, he adopted a conciliatory attitude toward the French planters who remained in the colony. Louverture knew that he could not trust the French planters because they were without principles and were only interested in their properties and their wealth. However, he needed them because they had the knowledge, the experience, the market connections, and the capital the colony needed to prosper. Louverture also appointed many whites to administrative positions in his government. In general, the whites came to realize that Louverture could be trusted to protect their interests and many returned to the colony to regain control of their properties.

As James points out, however, Louverture was no naive politician. As the unchallenged master of the colony in 1801, he was well aware that the whites had no choice but to accept his regime; that the planters hated the laborers; and that they and the maritime bourgeoisie in France were anxious to return to the old regime. None the less, James maintains, Louverture

> set his face sternly against racial discrimination. He guarded his powers and the rights of the labourers by an army overwhelmingly black. But within that wall he encouraged all to come back, mulattoes and whites.

The policy was both wise and workable, and if his relations with France had been regularized he would have done all he hoped to do.

(James 1963: 261)

Given this to be the case then, Louverture's error was not that he took the masses for granted, as James suggests, but rather that he believed he could convince the French colonial planters, and even Bonaparte, to accept the new social order he had created because he preserved Saint-Domingue's colonial status and defended the properties of the whites who remained. In other words, except for the question of emancipation and of formal equality for all, Louverture, as the leader of an emerging black property-owning class, came to share the same interests as the white and mulatto property owners (Dupuy 1989: 62; 1995).

Césaire understood that a process of class transformation was unfolding under Louverture. He realized that Louverture stubbornly opposed the break-up of the plantations, and that to maintain order and the production system he imposed harsh discipline on the laborers. Césaire, as did James before him, recognized that this system amounted to a "new despotism," but one that was none the less different from the old regime because the laborers were now free and paid for their labor. In effect, Césaire argues, Louverture had substituted a form of "state capitalism" for the barbaric slave system (Césaire 1960: 232), but this came at a cost. "If Toussaint's ideas were good," Césaire writes,

> his method was much less so. The most delicate problem for a revolutionary is that of his relationship with the masses, it calls for suppleness, creativity, a sharp sense of the human. And it is here where Louverture erred ... The social situation was preoccupying, and the economic situation dire. He thought he could resolve everything by militarizing everything ... If the link with the masses is the connective tissue of the Revolution, his was becoming ossified. He no longer persuaded; he issued decrees.
>
> (Césaire 1960: 228)

The best evidence of Louverture's failure to mobilize the masses by convincing them of the rightness of his aims, Césaire points out, was that he had to have recourse to repression. Everywhere the masses were rebelling against his system. When, in October 1801, General Moïse, Louverture's adopted nephew who was believed to hate the French planters and favor an agrarian reform, took the side of the laborers who had rebelled against the government, Louverture swiftly suppressed the rebellion, arrested Moïse and had him executed. For Césaire, this was the surest sign of a crack in the system (Césaire 1960: 233–34).

As James argues,

> every observer, and Toussaint himself, thought that the labourers were following him because of his past services and his unquestioned superiority. The insurrection proved that they were following him because he

represented that complete emancipation from their former degradation which was their chief goal. As soon as they saw that he was no longer going to this end, they were ready to throw him over.

(James 1963: 276)

Thus, when Louverture had Moïse executed the laborers thought of him as favoring the whites over them, and they never forgave him for this crime. For his part, Moïse defended his actions by arguing that the land should belong to those who till it, that he "was not the executioner of his own color [and that] the blacks had not conquered their liberty to labor again under the rod and the whip on the properties of the whites" (Madiou 1989: Vol. II, 144). Again, as James puts it so well,

> In allowing himself to be looked upon as taking the side of the whites against the blacks, Toussaint committed the unpardonable crime in the eyes of a community where the whites stood for so much evil. That they should get back their property was bad enough. That they should be privileged was intolerable. And to shoot Moïse, the black, for the sake of the whites was more than an error, it was a crime.
>
> (James 1963: 284)

Thus, the issue here was more than just a crack in the system as Césaire put it. The confrontation with Moïse symbolized the new class conflicts that Louverture's regime gave rise to; it is one that opposed the interests of the new black propertied ruling class in control of the state to those of the former slave laborers who fought against their proletarianization to become independent landowning farmers. Put differently, the black revolutionary leaders turned into a new property-owning class and in so doing created a proletarian problem. The former slaves, on the other hand, in practice if not in theory,[11] were trying to solve it. By saying that "Toussaint's ideas were good," Césaire took the side of the new bourgeoisie against those of the workers because he believed their interests were the same. They were not.

Neither did Césaire pursue the unfolding contradictory interests between Louverture and other key leaders of the revolutionary army like Christophe and Dessalines over the colonial problem. As I mentioned above, and as James argues he should have, even when it became clear that the objective of Bonaparte's expedition was to restore slavery, Louverture hesitated and refused to call the people to arm, declare the independence of Saint-Domingue, and give the whites a choice to either remain and accept the new black order or leave (James 1963: 284).

Unlike Louverture, however, Dessalines knew what to do and say to the masses: "If France wishes to try any nonsense here, everybody must rise together, men and women," Dessalines said to loud popular acclamation, words that James says "were worth a thousand of Toussaint's equivocal proclamations reassuring the whites. Dessalines had not the slightest desire to reassure whites"

(James 1963: 287). Moreover, Dessalines had his plan for national independence ready long before the French expedition, and he was simply waiting for the right moment to act. That moment came when Leclerc told him of his plan to arrest and deport Louverture, and Dessalines and other generals gave him the green light (333–34). With Louverture out of the way, Dessalines was now in a position to reorganize the revolutionary army, unite with the mulatto forces, and prepare to drive the French from Saint-Domingue for good.[12]

Let me now offer some concluding remarks about my reading of Césaire's *Toussaint Louverture* in the context of his views on Negritude and colonialism expressed in *Notebook* and *Discourse*. First, if "Negritude first rose in Haiti," it was because Dessalines, Christophe, and other high-ranking revolutionary officers broke with Louverture, formed a new army with the mulatto leaders, and resumed the war of independence. Césaire was aware of this rift and responded to it thus: "It is fashionable today to diminish Toussaint, to elevate Dessalines ... One can end the debate with one word: at the beginning is Toussaint Louverture and without Toussaint, there would not have been a Dessalines, this continuity" (1960: 282). The first assessment is true. The second is not. Had Louverture's project succeeded, Saint-Domingue would have remained a colony and become what Martinique, Guadeloupe, and French Guiana became in 1946: overseas departments of France. Thus, it is not accurate to claim as he did that Louverture made a "colony into a state; better yet, a nation" (ibid.).

Second, whether one called the new social order Louverture and the revolutionary leaders created a form of "state capitalism" as Césaire suggested, or simply a substitution of a capitalist economy based on free wage-labor for one previously based on slave labor, it is clear that these leaders became a new ruling class that opposed the interests of the laboring classes and sought to keep and exploit them on the plantation system they tried to revitalize. On that point there was no difference between Louverture and Dessalines or the other leaders of the revolution, save for some like Moïse who, to his peril, sided with the laborers. However, if Negritude stood for the black revolt against slavery and white domination and for self-determination, where does it stand when the revolutionary leaders (Louverture, Dessalines, Christophe) sought to substitute the exploitation of the black masses by a white bourgeoisie for the exploitation of the black masses by a black (and mulatto) bourgeoisie? In *Toussaint Louverture* Césaire answered that question: he sided with the bourgeoisie.

Returning to the interview he had with René Depestre, Césaire said that for the black man to establish his identity he needed to "have a concrete consciousness of what we are – that is, of the first fact of our lives: that we are black and have a history" (Depestre 1972: 76). Moreover, in his *Lettre à Maurice Thorez* (Letter to Maurice Thorez) of October 24, 1956, announcing his break with the French Communist Party, Césaire wrote that:

> [we black men] have consciously grasped in its full breadth the notion of our peculiar uniqueness, the notion of who we are ... The peculiarity of

our problems, which aren't to be reduced subordinate forms of any other problem.[13] The peculiarity of our history, laced with terrible misfortunes which belong to no other history.

(Césaire 1957: 6)

In light of the history of the Saint-Domingue Revolution I summarized above and of the subsequent history of dictatorial rule, repression and exploitation of the black men and women of the laboring classes in post-colonial Haiti by a new black and mulatto ruling class, to whose irreducible peculiar consciousness, peculiar uniqueness, peculiar problems, peculiar history, and peculiar misfortune is Césaire referring?[14] Perhaps it might be appropriate to give the last word to René Depestre who, since his interview with Césaire in 1967, had broken with Negritude and wrote the following:

From its anti-racist origins, the concept of Negritude came to acquire ambiguous and paradoxical meanings: formulated to awaken and nurture the self-esteem, the trust in their own powers, of social beings that slavery had reduced to beasts of burden, Negritude dissolves them into a somatic metaphysics. Far from arming their consciousness against the violence of underdevelopment, Negritude dissolves its blacks ... into an essentialism that is perfectly harmless to the system that dispossesses the men and women of their identity ... regardless of the positions they occupy in the system of production, property ownership, and the distribution of material and spiritual goods.

(Depestre 1980: 82–83)

Notes

1 See Chapter 1.
2 See Chapter 3.
3 The masters in Saint-Domingue allowed slaves to produce their own food on plots allotted to them on the margins of the plantations to cut down on food imports. Over time the colony relied increasingly on that food supply. Slaves also engaged in the production of other goods, such as cooking wares and clothes which they sold on local markets. These practices gave rise to what Sidney Mintz referred to as a "proto-peasantry" that represented an alternative social organization developed and controlled by the slaves (Mintz 1974: 152; Trouillot 1985: 6).
4 Marx also made the same point. See the citation in Chapter 1, Note 2.
5 Among them was Toussaint Louverture. Freed in 1776, he became the owner of a slave and the tennant-farmer and manager of a coffee plantation of 13 slaves before the slave uprising of 1791 (Debien, Fouchard and Menier 1977: 74).
6 There is always a tendency when talking about mulattoes to treat them as a homogeneous group. Mulattoes, or the free people of color, differed in terms of skin color (from lighter to darker skin complexions) as in their social status. Though many among them were property and slave owners, others were employed in all sectors of the economy ranging from artisans to plantation overseers, professional soldiers in the colonial militia to semi-skilled and unskilled workers. A

small number of mulattoes (2–5 percent at most) were slaves (Rogers 2003: 89). In other words, they neither shared similar class positions, similar relations with the whites, nor similar interests on the burning questions of the day. Though most wanted equality with whites, not all of them supported equality for blacks, the abolition of slavery, or independence from France. Thus, when I speak about "mulatto" interests here, I am referring primarily to the interests of the property and slave owners and their leaders, even though divisions existed among them as well.

7 Though he does not deny that the free people of color became a class in their own right, John Garrigus contends that the claim about their owning one-third of the properties and one-fourth of the slaves is probably exaggerated. He also argues that coffee was not the major factor in their ascendancy (2006: esp. Chs 2 and 6; 2009: 49–64). From my point of view, whatever the percentage of property or slaves they owned, there is no question that they emerged as a class to be contended with, and that their ownership of coffee plantations was significant in their rise, albeit not the only factor (see Rogers 2003: 88–94). And neither does the actual number of properties and slaves they owned change the argument I am making here about their politics and aspirations as a class.

8 Carolyn Fick also made the same point when she argued that, with the exception of Marat, none of the Jacobins club members (Robespierre, Camille Demoulins), or any of the radical left-wing revolutionaries in France "wanted to touch the burning question of the slave trade … [or] the abolition of slavery" until 1794 when the slave uprising gave them no choice (Fick 1997: 53).

9 For anyone who does not know it, this was a direct reference to 1946 when France made Guadeloupe, Martinique, and French Guiana into overseas departments.

10 At the same time, Ardouin points out: "Louverture took measures to prevent labourers from being able to buy property by issuing decrees that prohibited the sale of property smaller than 50 carreaux (1 car = 3 acres); and those who wished to buy such land had to prove they were not previously attached to a plantation" (Ardouin 1958: Vol. 4, 68–69).

11 In his defense of the laborers who wanted to become independent farmers Moïse at least raised the principle that the land should belong to those who till it.

12 As I argued in *Haiti in the World Economy*, before the revolutionary leaders could fight the final war of independence, they had to defeat the independent guerilla bands who refused to submit to them (1989: 72–74; see also Fick 1990: 230–34). In *The Making of Haiti* Fick shows how at every stage of the revolution it was the independently organized bands of slaves and former slaves who initiated the struggles that paved the way for the successes of the revolution, including the final war of independence. She also depicts the conflicting interests between Louverture and the masses but not those between Louverture and other leaders of the revolutionary army like Dessalines and Christophe. For his part in *Toussaint Louverture* (2007) Bell discusses the rifts between Louverture and his top general officers but overlooks the conflicting class interests between them and the former slave masses.

13 Here Césaire was referring to the tendency among some Marxist theorists to reduce the "race question" to the "class question," and, therefore, to resolve the former by first resolving the latter.

14 One could add the rulers, government functionaries, military officers, and merchants of the African states of Futa Jallon, Dahomey, Asante, Kasanje, and the Lunda Empire who raided neighboring territories to capture prisoners and sell them into slavery to European slave traders and "acquired symbols of wealth and status in exchange for the massive export of labor" to the Americas (Davis 2006: 100).

3   From revolutionary slaves to powerless citizens

Haiti was born as an independent nation-state in 1804 after a unique and successful revolutionary war that not only ended French colonial rule, as the American Revolution against England had done for the USA in 1776 but also, unlike the latter, abolished racial slavery and declared all citizens, men and women, to be equal. On the one hand, I will argue that this extraordinary achievement by the revolutionary slaves proved to be a Pyrrhic victory for the laboring classes who soon became subordinated to, and exploited by a new but divided dominant class, and, on the other hand, that it also led to the stalemate of the new Haitian ruling class and Haiti's continued underdevelopment and subordination to foreign capital. There were two primary reasons for these outcomes.

First, the dominant class became divided between those factions whose power was derived from the ownership of property and the commercial sectors and those who controlled the state. Given the specific configuration of the dominant class that emerged during and after the revolution, the state itself became a primary site of conflict between factions of that class. Thus, rather than acting to promote the growth of commodity relations, i.e., develop the productive forces of the economy to expand the scope of production and of private capital accumulation, the holders of state power would do the exact opposite. They would stifle such expansion by competing directly with the private sector to accumulate wealth. Therefore, rather than serving as an instrument for the development of the economy as a whole, the state became a primary site for the promotion of the interests and enrichment of those who controlled it. As such, corruption became systematized as a modus operandi of the prebendary or predatory state in Haiti (Dupuy 1997; Fatton 2002).[1]

It is in this sense, then, that I speak of the Haitian bourgeoisie comprising two factions: one which accumulates wealth through its private ownership of means of production, and the other through its control of the state and its various apparatuses; or, if one prefers, an economic and a state bourgeoisie. As Michel-Rolph Trouillot observed, despite the competition and conflict between the holders of state power and the economically dominant class, the two have always entered into a bargaining relationship, or a pact of domination, with one another. If the economically dominant class always had to pay its "dues to the state to maintain [its] dominance," the holders of state power also had to reach compromises with the economically dominant class, "even while [they] limit[ed] the reach of representative institutions, including those that represent the dominant classes" (Trouillot 1990: 28). However, an important distinction needs to be made between these two factions of the dominant class. Although the state bourgeoisie could and did operate relatively autonomously and at times even contrary to the interests of the private-sector bourgeoisie, it none the less remained dependent on the latter whose links to the markets of the dominant capitalist countries were crucial for Haiti's exports and imports as its primary source of foreign currency.

Moreover, the economic bourgeoisie reproduced itself by bequeathing its wealth to its descendants and by its continued participation in the world market. By contrast, the state bourgeoisie could not as a matter of right transfer power to its offspring, hence the tendency of those who came to control the state apparatuses to prolong their power as long as possible through dictatorial means. Haitian rulers have even tried to make power hereditary, as François Duvalier did in 1971 when he transferred power to his son Jean-Claude before he died.[2] And this practice could endure as long as dictatorship and the *coup d'état* were the principal means of accessing power. This was the case throughout the 19th and most of the 20th centuries until a mass movement in the mid-1980s toppled the 29-year Duvalier dictatorships (father and son) and ushered in a transition to democracy.

The institutionalization of democratic governance and transfer of power is not to be equated with the empowerment of "the people" and their ability to determine effectively the public (economic and political) agenda. That is because in a capitalist society the fiscal health or well-being of the state usually depends on the growth and well-being of the economy, and the latter in turn depends on the extent to which those who own or control the principal means of production (i.e., capitalists) invest their wealth (i.e., their capital) to generate economic growth and can sell their products to consumers for profit. As many have argued, this fact grants the (private) owners of the means of production and of capital (whether domestic or foreign) much greater sway over state policies than it does to the non-owners, that is, the people. Thus, a capitalist democracy must disempower the people if it is to serve the interests of (private) capital, thereby establishing an inverse ratio between capitalism and democracy.[3]

The second factor that led to the Pyrrhic victory of the laboring classes and the stalemate of the bourgeoisie was the inability of the latter to transform the former slaves into proletarians because of their success in gaining access to land, either as outright owners, with or without legal land titles, or share-croppers. At the same time, the former slaves who succeeded in transforming themselves into subsistence farmers could not block their subordination to and exploitation by the dominant classes. The latter were able to appropriate wealth by imposing taxes and other mechanisms of extortion, raising the rents on the lands they leased to sharecroppers, and controlling the prices they paid to farmers for the crops they produced and resold on the market. For its part, unable to proletarianize the peasant classes, the new bourgeoisie could not revitalize the sugar plantations that had been the basis of Saint-Domingue's wealth in the 18th century, or lay the conditions for the development of national industries to create an integrated national economy. This essentially restricted the dominant classes to accumulating their wealth mainly from the circulation (commerce, finance, trade, taxes, corruption) rather than from the production of commodities (capital and consumer goods) for the domestic and export markets. This fact, as we will see, also made it possible for the return of foreign capital to dominate the national economy, in the form of commercial-financial capital in the 19th century and industrial-manufacturing capital in the 20th and 21st.

Pyrrhic victory of the peasantry

When Haiti emerged as an independent nation in January 1804 its class structure was characterized by a dominant class that comprised two factions that were formed during the colonial period and the revolutionary war. The first was that of the *affranchis* ("free people of color") property-owning class of the ancien régime, most of whom were mulattoes. The second was that of the *nouveaux libres* (newly freed) comprised mostly of black military officers of the revolutionary army who appropriated properties from the former French planters and the new lands that fell under the domain of the revolutionary government. The conflicts between the dominant classes and the former slave masses to decide the land question, on the one hand, and those between the factions of the dominant class to control the state, on the other, would characterize the first major social and economic transformation of Haiti in the 19th century. These conflicts would result in what I call the stalemate of the bourgeoisie and the Pyrrhic victory of the peasantry, factors that contributed significantly to the underdevelopment of the Haitian economy and its continued subservience to foreign capital.

The conflicts between the black and mulatto elites can be understood better by an examination of the class configuration of Haiti in the 19th century and the articulation of the Haitian economy with the global capitalist economy. The former slave masses successfully resisted the attempt by Toussaint Louverture to compel them to return to work on the sugar plantations as wage laborers. They also resisted such attempts by the governments of Jean-Jacques Dessalines (1804–06), Henri Christophe (1806–20) and Jean-Pierre Boyer (1818–43) (Dupuy 1989: 51–66).

No sooner had Haiti declared its independence on January 1, 1804 than the struggle between the black and mulatto factions of the new ruling class erupted into a full-blown civil war in 1806 after Dessalines, Haiti's first head of state who named himself Emperor, was assassinated. That conflict led to the partition of the country into the State of Haiti in the north under the black General-turned-King Henri Christophe who renamed the territory the

Kingdom of Haiti in 1811, and the Republic of Haiti in the west and south controlled by the mulatto General-turned-President Alexandre Pétion. Though neither Christophe nor Pétion pursued "color politics" per se—each appointed mulattoes and blacks, respectively, to top positions in their administrations—each regime none the less favored the factions of the dominant class allied with them in their land redistribution policies. As with Louverture and Dessalines, Christophe tried to maintain and revive the plantation system by putting military officers in charge of running them and compelling the laborers to work on them under harsh discipline. In return the laborers received a fourth of the value of the crops as wages and were granted access to small plots for their own cultivation. Christophe also used forced or *corvée* labor for public works projects and on the plantations under military control. These repressive methods sparked rebellions against the regime. Plantation laborers fled to the mountains, or to the south where they faced less harsh conditions and more personal freedom under Pétion. Christophe tried to counter this erosion of support for his regime by redistributing land to military officers and soldiers according to their rank (larger properties to the former, smaller to the latter). However, these measures did not end the discontent that erupted into rebellions that ultimately led to Christophe's downfall and suicide in 1820.

Facing strong resistance from below, including a rebellion led by Goman— a former maroon slave—that succeeded in occupying large areas of the southwest until it was defeated in 1819, Pétion pursued a more liberal land redistribution policy that favored the wealthy but also benefitted small landowners. Whether through the sale or granting concessions of public lands to high-ranking military officers, civil service administrators, or influential politicians, the wealthy elites under Pétion acquired or received large estates of 100 hectares or more (1 ha = 2.5 acres), lower-ranking officers and mid-level civil servants received between 40 ha and 25 ha, and lower civil servants and rural laborers received concessions of 5 ha. Pétion also tried to adopt a more lenient policy for laborers working on the plantations, but that was not enough to prevent their break-up, as the laborers opted to cultivate their own lands or took to the hills to squat on unclaimed lands to become their de facto possessors (Bellegarde 1938; Leyburn 1941; Moral 1961; Manigat 1962; Cole 1967; Pierre-Charles 1967; Nicholls 1979; Péan 2000).

The mulatto Jean-Pierre Boyer assumed the presidency of the Republic after Pétion's death in 1818 and reunified the country after Christophe's death in 1820. His would be the last administration to attempt to restore the plantation system by reversing or at least blocking the continued redistribution or parceling of land and transforming the former slave masses into a permanent proletariat. That attempt came in the form of the *Code Rural* of 1826 that declared that laborers were obligated to work the land and bound to the soil; that all Haitians except those who owned their land legally, government functionaries, military officers, professionals, artisans, and shopkeepers, were to be attached to a plantation permanently; and, as with the three previous governments, the laborers would be paid between one-fourth and one-half of the gross revenues of the estates. That decree and efforts to implement it met stiff opposition from the laboring population as well as from rank-and-file soldiers who were also compelled to work on the plantations. The government's repressive measures only fueled more opposition that culminated in an insurrection (known as the Praslin revolution, which started on the plantation that bore that name in Les Cayes) and the overthrow of Boyer in 1843 (Dupuy 1989: 92–97).

By the mid-19th century, three categories of landed peasant farmers had emerged: those who owned land (i.e., had legal titles); those who possessed unclaimed or public lands but did not own them (i.e., had de facto but not de jure ownership); and those who leased land through the métayage or share-cropping system from large landowners. Those who owned/possessed land were also those who had larger, though still relatively small farms of approximately 4 ha to 7 ha. Sharecroppers, on the other hand, leased their land from the landed bourgeoisie (properties larger than 40 ha or 100 acres), who subdivided their estates into smaller units. And below the categories of landowning/possessing peasants or sharecroppers were those without land (i.e., a proletariat), who were compelled to hire themselves out as day laborers to those with land.

The changes in the pattern of land ownership and the rise of a landed peasantry had significant effects on the relations between the dominant and subordinate classes, on the one hand, and between the dominant classes and foreign powers such as France in particular, on the other hand. First, because the majority of the rural population were farmers with access to land, they controlled the means and processes of production, and hence the rate of their exploitation. This was the case even where the landed bourgeoisie tried to extract more surplus from the sharecroppers.[4] Expressed theoretically, the majority of the working population continued to be part of what Marx refers to as the "objective conditions of labour," that is, they entered the market place as producers and sellers of commodities rather than as sellers of their labor, or labor-power to capitalists. As Marx wrote,

> where capital has not yet taken over agriculture, a large proportion of agricultural produce is still used directly as means of subsistence and not as commodities. In that event a large proportion of the working population will not have been transformed into wage-labourers and a large proportion of the conditions of labour will not yet have become capital.
>
> (Marx 1977: 950–51)

Second, unable to defeat the majority of the peasantry, expropriate, and proletarianize them, the bourgeoisie was stymied in its efforts in the mid-19th century to develop a national infrastructure in both the rural and urban areas, expand public, technical and professional education, diversify agriculture, promote the growth of small, medium, and large industries, and create a coastal maritime service. In short, the bourgeoisie could not create an inte-grated national economy that could make possible an expanded process of capital accumulation and development. Consequently the dominant classes were limited to accumulating wealth primarily through the circulation rather than the production process. They became a commercial and a rentier bour-geoisie that engaged in commercial and trade relations with other countries to which they could export Haitian agricultural products (principally coffee), and from which they could import durable and consumer goods they resold on the domestic market.

Haiti, then, had retained all the characteristics of a peripheral economy in the capitalist world-system. It had a divided and weak state that became the site of intense conflicts between factions of the dominant class.[5] Those who controlled the state appropriated the revenues generated from taxes[6] (domestic, import, and export) and other means of extortion, including *corvée* labor. There was a low level of proletarianization. The majority of the population engaged in subsistence production as well as production for the local market. Farmers also engaged in the production of agricultural crops (principally coffee) and raw materials (cotton, cacao, lumber) for export. However, urban merchants con-trolled the export of the crops as well as the importation of the manufactured and consumer goods they resold on the domestic market.

The combination of these factors explains the political weakness of the dominant class and the relative ease with which foreign capital, especially commercial and banking, was able to reassert its dominance soon after Haiti gained its independence because of the constant need for the successive gov-ernments to borrow money from foreign governments and banks to make up for their budgetary shortfalls and keep the government functioning.

The turning point in Haiti's re-subordination to foreign, especially banking or finance capital in the 19th century, came with the indemnity Haiti agreed to pay to France in return for its recognition of Haiti's independence. Estab-lishing and extending normal, that is, legal trade, commercial, and financial relations with France and the other major powers of Western Europe and the USA, required first and foremost their recognition of Haiti's independence. But they all steadfastly refused to do so. For the USA in particular, recog-nizing Haiti's independence would have legitimized the slave revolution that achieved it, thus undermining its own slave regime and ideology of white supremacy. The USA also pushed to prevent the other independent states of Latin America from recognizing Haiti's independence at the Panama Congress of 1826. Trouillot remarked: "Diplomatic rejection was only one symptom of an underlying denial [of the revolution]. The very deeds of the revolution were incompatible with the major tenets of Western ideologies" (Trouillot 1995: 89, 95). In my view, however, the major powers were more bent on making Haiti pay dearly for its defiance rather than denying the revolution.[7]

France's hands were thus strengthened. According to François Blancpain's recent account, in October 1814 France sent two emissaries to Haiti to attempt to negotiate the return of "Saint-Domingue"[8] to French control. Pétion categorically rejected Dauxion Lavaysse's proposition, but then raised the idea of Haiti paying an indemnity to France in exchange for its recognition of Haiti. For his part, Christophe immediately arrested Medina, the second envoy, and had him shot.[9] Christophe subsequently published the secret instructions that Medina had brought with him from Malouet—with the intention of showing Pétion's weakness if not treason—the French Minister of Colonies, which made clear France's intentions to reconquer "Saint-Domingue" militarily if necessary, and to reinstate slavery and the racial order of the old regime (Blancpain 2001: 43–48).

The French government of Louis XVIII disavowed Malouet's instructions and tried again to renew negotiations with Pétion and Christophe in 1816. Although it had abandoned the idea of a military expedition, it still contemplated establishing a protectorate over Haiti. Pétion, affirming Haiti's determination to safeguard its independence, broke off negotiations with France in November 1816. For his part, and under advice from the Englishman Thomas Clarkson who assured him that France was in no position to use military force against Haiti, Christophe refused to meet with the French envoy (Blancpain 2001: 48–49).

France tried again in 1821, but this time it realized that no Haitian head of state would agree to surrender to French sovereignty over Haiti. Boyer had twice broken negotiations with France as long as it continued to entertain that idea. In a letter he wrote on May 16, 1821 to Esmangart, a former colonialist who had been charged with opening negotiations with Haiti, Boyer mentioned that England had recognized the independence of the USA and asked:

> the efforts France made on its part to ensure Washington's triumph, did they not bring fame to the reign of Louis XVI? Impressed by these examples, Haitians are asking themselves often why that latter power hesitates to repudiate such vain rights to reap more honorable benefits ... Could the difference in skin color be the reason for this hesitation?
>
> (cited in Madiou 1988: 198–99)

Commenting on that letter, Madiou argued that skin color was not the issue but rather France's "regret at relinquishing a bountiful colony over which it wanted at the very least to establish a protectorate in the interest of its preponderance in the Antilles and the Gulf of Mexico which centrally overlook the two Americas" (Madiou 1988: 199).

Madiou missed the point, however. Until the slave revolt forced it to act otherwise, France considered the slaves and the *affranchis* (free people of color) as inferior beings who did not deserve equal rights with whites, and Bonaparte's objective in sending Leclerc to retake possession of the colony was to reinstate the slave regime and its racial order, as was the intention of Louis XVIII exposed in Malouet's instructions mentioned above. And, as I pointed out, the very existence of a "black republic" in the midst of a colonial order where racial slavery was still the norm was ontologically intolerable to the

West. Boyer, therefore, was justified in raising the "color question" which could not be separated from French imperialist policies as Madiou suggested.

Finally, in 1825, and now under the rule of Charles X, France sent a new emissary with an ordinance to Haiti that proposed for the first time the full and complete recognition of Haiti's independence in return for an indemnity of 150 million francs, a reduction by 50 percent on duties for French imports and paying half the duties on Haitian exports to France. Disregarding the advice of his own representatives, Boyer decided to accept the French conditions. Other than the veiled threat of 14 French war ships in the vicinity of Haiti at the time of the negotiations, Boyer had inherited a near empty treasury. When Christophe died in 1820 it was believed that he had left a treasury worth around 17.5 million gourdes in gold and silver, but most of it had been pillaged and only about 1.5 million remained. Boyer also understood that without French recognition the other major powers would not recognize Haiti either (Turnier 1985: 25; Blancpain 2001: 43–62). Still, there is no question that Haiti's

> full and complete independence was not recognized but granted on condition of commercial and financial compensations, that is, blackmail. It was not placed at the head of the ordinance, which, subsequently, could have settled on commercial and financial concessions sanctioning an agreement reached between two sovereign nations. Quite the contrary, it appears to have been bought, just as in the old days a slave could buy his freedom.
>
> (Blancpain 2001: 56)

The sum of 150 million francs was calculated on the estimated value of the revenues generated by the colonial properties in 1789. That amount was compared to the value of Haitian exports in 1823, which amounted to 30 million francs and were estimated to yield a 50 percent profit. On that basis France decided that the colonial properties Haiti seized were worth 10 years of benefits or 150 million francs. Again, as Blancpain concluded, "a political demonstration is never better than when it proves what had been decided a priori" (Blancpain 2001: 57).

The indemnity was equivalent to ten years of fiscal receipts for the Haitian government, which depended heavily on customs duties for its revenues. In 1838 Boyer succeeded in reducing the indemnity to 60 million francs; lowering the interest rate from 6 to 3 percent on the remaining balance of the 30 million francs borrowed from French banks to make the initial payment on the indemnity; and eliminating the half-duties Haiti had to pay on exports to France (which Haiti had suspended on its own in 1827). At the conclusion of that second agreement, France recognized Haiti's independence, as did the other major powers of Western Europe and England, but not the USA, which did not do so until 1862. Due to interruptions in the annual payments of the debt after Boyer's overthrow in 1843, and political turmoil between 1867 and

1869, the debt was fully paid off in 1883 instead of the original contractual date of 1867 (Blancpain 2001: 56–74).[10] In all, Haiti paid France 90 million francs for what has been called the "double debt"—the original indemnity of 150 million francs reduced to 60 million francs, plus the 30 million borrowed to make the first installment with interests (Blancpain 2001: 79; Blancpain and Dorigny 2004: 103–4).

Péan argues that the national debt "neutralized early on the willingness of [those in power] to economize by subtracting from [them] the foundation of an accumulation that could have led to some type of development" (Péan 2000: 245). By contrast Turnier maintains that while the indemnity caused the country great harm, the role of the debt in impeding national development has been exaggerated. By the time Sylvain Salnave came to power in 1867 the "weight of the indemnity had already diminished considerably" and in 1876 the balance of the indemnity with interests was 7.76 million francs (or US \$1.5 million) (Turnier 1985: 27). As Benoit Joachim notes, despite the criticisms of Boyer and the factions of the dominant class who campaigned against him for having agreed to this "shameful tribute," all the subsequent heads of state

> agreed to repay the indemnity, even at the cost of great difficulties ... not because they believed it was fair to indemnify the former colonialists, [but] to curry the favors of the French governments, and to live in peace with the France they all venerated. Because the interests [of the rulers of Haiti] did not coincide with those of the large majority of the nation, the ruling classes of Haiti often gave in to the pressures exercised by the metropolitan rulers, even without any significant strengthening of relations between the two countries.
>
> (Joachim 1971: 364)

Indeed, according to Turnier (1985: 27), when President Lysius Salomon made the last payment on the indemnity he proudly exclaimed that "I paid France the last term of the double debt of 1825".

As with Turnier, I argue that the debt was not the primary cause of Haiti's underdevelopment. Rather, I believe that the primary factors that blocked a sustained process of economic development were the divisions and internecine conflicts between the two factions of the dominant class for control of the state that started long before the debt was incurred. They involved the use of public funds as a source of enrichment for those who controlled the state rather than to promote national economic development and the failure of the bourgeoisie to expropriate/proletarianize the landowning/possessing peasantry to create the pre-conditions for the development of industries (either labor- or capital-intensive) and the expanded accumulation of capital.

However, if the national debt was not the principal obstacle to economic development, there is no doubt that it caused great harm as Turnier has remarked, and made Haiti vulnerable to exploitation by foreign bankers and financiers backed by the power of their governments, especially France in the

19th century. As Péan (2000: 243) points out, the "double debt" became instead an eternal debt. Foreign debt, in effect, became the Achilles heel of the heads of state who, until the US occupation of Haiti (1915–34), borrowed large sums from foreign and domestic banks, ostensibly to pay off the remainder of the indemnity and to finance infrastructural and development projects, most of which never materialized, and also to keep themselves in power. But the nefariousness of the conditions imposed on the governments by the creditors also led to their undoing. The most notorious of these was the so-called Domingue debt of 1875 incurred by President Michel Domingue who came to power in 1874 and was overthrown in 1876 directly as a result of the scandal the debt caused. That debt, renegotiated to obtain somewhat more favorable terms by President Salomon in 1885, was followed by two other substantial debts by subsequent governments in 1896 and 1910. In all, these debts amounted to over 113 million francs (or US \$22.6 million), the last of which was repaid fully in 1961 (Turnier 1985: 27–42; Blancpain 2001: 79–88). The money to repay these debts came from taxes on coffee exports which were the principal source of Haiti's foreign currency: for every three dollars earned on coffee exports in 1875, \$0.33 went to service the foreign debt; \$1.20 in 1896; and \$1.00 in 1910 (Turnier 1985: 35).

Foreign lenders and their governments would use Haiti's debts to wrench concessions for their capitalists who sought to establish a foothold in Haiti. It was through such means that foreign commercial interests would re-enter Haiti in the 19th century (German, French, English, American, Syrian), begin to supplant Haitian businesses, and pave the way for the investment of foreign capital in other sectors, from mainly commercial (import/export), financial, and banking in the 19th century to banking, agricultural, extractive, and industrial-manufacturing under the US occupation and afterwards. There is also no doubt that the external debts incurred by Haitian governments primarily benefitted the high banking and financial sectors of France (or other creditor countries) and, to a lesser extent Haitian banks (for the internal debt), and that the biggest losers were the Haitian economy and the Haitian commercial and financial bourgeoisie who saw themselves being displaced by foreign banks and merchants (Dupuy 1989: 126; Péan 2000: 256–66). Péan observes that the Haitian state thus became "a vulgar agent for the condottieri of international trade and finance" (Péan 2000: 245). And for Turnier,

> to stop the descent into hell, good will, competence, and patriotism were not enough, and foreign aid was essential, whereas imperialism aimed to carve up its prey. External finance succeeded in transferring to the economy the colonialism that was politically defeated on the battlefields of Saint-Domingue, and thus perpetuate the past.
>
> (Turnier 1985: 40)

For their part, and for all their ability to prevent their expropriation and lessen their exploitation to some extent, the peasant farmers remained powerless economically and politically. They could never fully block the different mechanisms of exploitation or extraction to which they were subjected, such as the derisive prices they received from the coffee speculators (middlemen between the peasants and urban merchants) for their crops, the direct and indirect taxes appropriated by the state, and the *corvée* labor rural state officials forced them to perform on public works projects, on pain of fines or imprisonment for those who refused. Peasants resisted these measures and even revolted against particularly abusive or corrupt governments during the 19th century. But these movements remained disorganized and decentralized, and never coalesced into national movements that articulated the aspirations of the "peasantry" as a whole. That is, to borrow a phrase from Marx, the peasantry could never become a unified class "for itself" because the primary interest of the farmers was to safeguard their property rights or their right to have access to land as the sine qua non of their independence. But this was a veiled independence, for, while the farmers waged a successful struggle to become a landed peasantry (whether as titled owners, de facto owners, or sharecroppers) they remained generally poor, subsistence producers subordinated to and exploited by a dominant class through both direct and indirect means. For its part, the bourgeoisie (state and private), unable to proletarianize the peasants and engaged in endless internecine conflicts to control the state, was stalemated in its ability to lay the foundations for industrial development and remained essentially a parasitic class whose wealth derived from commercial and financial transactions, land rents, extortion, exporting coffee and other goods such as lumber, and reselling imported manufactured and consumer goods on the national market.

Democratization, proletarianization, and powerlessness

The 20th century began with the 19-year US occupation (1915–34),[11] which led to the second major transformation of the economic, social, and political landscape of Haiti. That process of transformation was characterized by: (1) the substitution of US dominance for European, primarily French, in the 19th century; (2) the proletarianization of Haitian peasants combined with the export of Haitian workers to other parts of the Caribbean and North America; and (3) a transition to a weak or minimalist democracy and the disempowerment of the people to effect substantive change.

As I have argued elsewhere, the US invasion and occupation of Haiti must be understood in the context of the projection of US power in Central America and the Caribbean since the 1870s to displace its European rivals, establish its hegemony, and facilitate the penetration of US capital throughout the region. Far from being peaceful, this process was often preceded by military interventions in and occupations of many countries in the region between 1853 and 1916, including Nicaragua, Honduras, Guatemala, Mexico, Cuba, and the Dominican Republic. Threatening to seize the Virgin Islands if the Danish government refused to sell them to the USA, Denmark did so in 1916. In short, since peaceful trade alone would not guarantee the dominance of US capital in the region, military power became its necessary handmaiden (Dupuy 1989: 129–30).

Once the USA crushed the guerrilla war against the occupation in 1920, it replaced the old Haitian army with a new army and police force that became the dominant political force in Haiti until former President Jean-Bertrand Aristide disbanded the army in 1995.[12] The USA also drafted and imposed a new constitution that for the first time since Haiti became independent allowed foreigners to buy and own property (without the need to marry Haitians as required by previous constitutions). It also created a centralized public administration, expanded technical education, and developed a modern infrastructure of roads and other transportation and communication networks to facilitate foreign, primarily US, investments. Though US businesses had been established in Haiti before 1915, many new ones followed on the heels of the occupation, including those involved in electricity, port and railroad construction, mining, banking, and large-scale plantation production such as pineapple, sisal, and sugar. The occupation definitively uprooted France as the dominant power in Haiti, economically and politically. Haitian banking and finance were placed under the control of US banks, and the Haitian currency, the gourde (HTG) was henceforth pegged to the US dollar rather than the French franc. And the USA became the single most important market for Haitian exports and imports.

Foreign capital investments in Haiti necessitated the proletarianization of farmers. From the outset that process had a dual aspect: creating a supply of labor for businesses operating in Haiti, and exporting between 300,000 and 400,000 laborers to work in plantations in other parts of the Caribbean, and Central America between 1915 and 1930 (Dupuy 1989: 137) . First, to supply the labor force for the businesses that came to Haiti, occupation and Haitian authorities evicted tens of thousands of peasant farmers from the lands they had occupied or leased from the government and ceded them to the companies. That process had begun prior to the occupation when, for example, in 1910 the government of Antoine Simon granted land and other concessions to James McDonald to build a railroad and grow bananas for export.[13] Between 1917 and 1955 tens of thousands of hectares of land were transferred to foreign companies. The authorities adopted other measures to expropriate farmers, such as imposing a tax on alcohol that forced hundreds of small distilleries out of business, or not renewing leases or increasing their costs to farmers on rented state lands. Agricultural companies, such as those producing sisal, bananas, and pineapple, foreclosed the provision grounds of the farmers on their large estates, or as did the newly formed Haitian American Sugar Company, contracted with the small peasants to sell them their crop at low prices, eventually ending up hiring them as wage-laborers. Thus, just as US military power served to implant US capital throughout the region, the occupation authorities used their power to proletarianize Haitian peasants and accomplish in short order what the Haitian bourgeoisie could not do for over 100 years. Force, in other words, was the midwife of proletarianization and capital accumulation.

Once unleashed, this process continued unabated after the occupation. In the 1930s, 1940s and 1950s, foreign companies came to Haiti to cultivate bananas and rubber, and to mine copper and bauxite for export. And since the 1970s, the USA, through the United States Agency for International Development (USAID), the World Bank, and the Inter-American Development Bank, championed the export assembly industries as Haiti's main development strategy. Though initially these industries produced electronic component parts and baseballs, as well as apparel, the latter has become the only basis for the operation of that industry today. And, as it did then, the industry relies on the constant supply of an unskilled and the lowest paid labor force in the Caribbean region, made possible by the decline of agricultural production, a large reserve army of unemployed labor, a large and unregulated informal sector, or what Wallerstein (1996: 23–29) calls semi-proletarian households where members engage in some wage-labor work, and the dogged resistance of the USAID, the World Bank, and foreign investors and their subcontracting Haitian partners to raising wages in that sector in combination with the suppression of labor unions and labor rights.

As mentioned, the proletarianization of Haitian peasants was not limited to supplying a labor force for the businesses operating in Haiti only. During the occupation Haitian workers were also recruited to work on US-owned sugar and other agricultural plantations in Cuba, the Dominican Republic, and Central America. Though Haitians stopped migrating to Cuba after the Cuban Revolution, migration to the neighboring Dominican Republic, the Caribbean, and North America increased dramatically: in 2010 about 546,000 Haitians lived in the USA, 280,000 in the Dominican Republic, and 74,000 in Canada (IOM) .

The occupation also transformed the class structure and balance of power in Haiti in ways other than the proletarianization of the peasantry, even though the latter still constitutes the majority of the population. The most significant in my view was the rise of a small but significant urban middle class of professionals and white-collar workers spawned by both the expansions of job opportunities in the private sector and the growth of a civil bureaucracy and state institutions (e.g., in education, public works, sanitation and health), in addition to the new Haitian army and police. The political significance of the rise of the middle class was the growth within its ranks of an intelligentsia and various currents and political tendencies that expressed the new class forces and interests that would form broad coalitions with factions of the dominant class as well as working-class organizations and trade unions.

Two broad political and ideological tendencies crystallized during the 1930s and 1940s that would have great significance for subsequent political developments. On the left were communist, socialist, social democratic, and populist parties which, along with some progressive trade unions, prioritized the "class question," democracy, and social justice. And on the right were those parties, organizations and trade unions that were staunchly anti-socialist/communist, nationalist and populist, and prioritized the "color question" and the conflicts between the mulatto and black bourgeoisie. The US occupation authorities exacerbated that conflict by installing or supporting mulatto presidents and placing mulattoes, already dominant economically, in the top administrative and civil service positions, as well as in the top echelons of the new Haitian army.

Though mulattoes and blacks belonged to the middle class and the subordinate stratum of the bourgeoisie, blacks predominated in both and were intensely conscious of the correlation between skin color and upward social mobility. Thus, when mulattoes regained control of the government and monopolized key positions in the various state apparatuses, including the military, they directly challenged the black middle class's traditional means of social ascension, thereby elevating the "color question" to the center stage ideologically and politically. The struggle between those two factions reached a decisive turning point in 1946 when the black-nationalist forces succeeded in electing Dumarsais Estimé as President.[14] Though Estimé's presidency was short-lived, it allowed the black middle class, in alliance with the provincial and urban black bourgeoisie, to regain its dominance in the government and public administration. However, it was in 1957 that the black-nationalist forces reached their apogee with the election of François Duvalier to the presidency,[15] which he transformed into a 29-year dictatorship by transferring power to his son Jean-Claude in 1971 before his death. The son ruled until he was overthrown and exiled in 1986.

For the purpose of my argument here, I want to focus on three essential aspects of the Duvalier regime that were consequential for future political and economic developments. First, the principal objective of the regime under François Duvalier was not to alter the class structure of Haiti and hence the economic dominance of the predominantly mulatto bourgeoisie,[16] but to recapture political power for the black bourgeoisie and middle class. It achieved this by purging most, but not all, mulattoes from the top positions in the government, public administration, and the military.[17] And, never fully trusting the military even after having chosen officers to run it, the regime created a parallel military force to the Haitian army called the Volunteers for National Security (popularly known as the *Tontons Macoutes*) that Duvalier controlled directly, and which was used as the regime's security and terror apparatus. Once in place, the state unleashed a reign of terror unprecedented in Haiti's history. Going beyond the repressiveness of previous dictatorships, the regime spared no one from its violence. Men, women, children, families from all classes, and even entire towns were subject to the regime's ruthless and unpredictable terror. No major state and civil society institutions were left untouched or allowed to function independently. The legislature, judiciary, and civil administration were all brought under the direct control of Duvalier, and the regime suppressed all hitherto independent political, trade union, media and other civil society organizations by arresting, killing, or exiling their leaders who were considered a threat to the regime. Even the Catholic Church came under the regime's control when Duvalier expelled all foreign clergy and replaced them with Haitians.

The cost of capturing and consolidating power for the black-nationalist bourgeoisie and middle class, therefore, was quite high. In addition to the tens of thousands of citizens killed by the regime, the economy and the standard of living of the majority of the population deteriorated; and the regime had alienated the mulatto bourgeoisie as well as the USA and other Western European powers, which suspended direct military and financial aid, but made no effort to topple the regime. To attract new foreign investments and financial and military aid, the regime made overtures to the mulatto bourgeoisie and offered advantages to foreign investors—such as tax exemptions, an abundance of cheap labor, and a climate of labor peace due the suppression of all independent labor organizations and the banning of strikes. These measures led US President Richard Nixon to resume full financial and military aid in 1969.

However, it was not until after Jean-Claude Duvalier assumed power in 1971 that foreign businesses began to invest in Haiti. This third aspect of the regime was characterized by what I have called a triple alliance among the Duvalier regime, that is, the black bourgeoisie and middle class, the mulatto bourgeoisie, and foreign capital, with the first two components as junior partners (Dupuy 1989: 168–69). Essentially the Haitian government turned over the formulation of economic policy to the USA and the international financial institutions—the World Bank, the International Monetary Fund, and the Inter-American Development Bank. Capitalizing on Haiti's poverty, a climate of labor peace achieved through brutal repression, and an abundant and unskilled labor force, these institutions proceeded to transform Haiti into a supplier of the cheapest labor in the western hemisphere for the export assembly manufacturing industries established by foreign investors and domestic entrepreneurs as subcontractors.

Though they would not be implemented fully until after the overthrow of the regime in 1986 and the transition to democracy in the 1990s, a set of "structural adjustment" policies—reductions on tariff and trade restrictions, tax incentives to investors, privatization of public enterprises, reduction of public spending and public-sector employees—would destroy Haiti's near food sufficiency and turn it into the largest importer of US-produced foods, especially rice, in the Caribbean. But rather than generating sustainable economic development, these policies exacerbated poverty and income and wealth inequalities, and spurred more migration. An estimated 19–20 percent of the Haitian population (i.e., 2 million) now live abroad, the majority of whom are in the Dominican Republic, the USA, and Canada. Migration is not only a safety valve or an alternative to unemployment and poverty; it has become an increasingly important lifeline to the economy itself. The remittances of Haitian emigrants are estimated at around 20 percent of Haiti's gross domestic product, which is more than Haiti earns from its exports.

Even though it was not as brutally repressive as the father's, the son's regime could not reform itself sufficiently to accommodate the popular demands for democratic reforms and civil and human rights that emerged in the early 1980s. As that movement grew and became more radical, Jean-Claude Duvalier was finally forced to leave Haiti in 1986 and sent into exile in France. The fall of Duvalier unleashed a power struggle among the neo-Duvalierists and the military for the next four years to regain control of the state. But the relentless struggle of the democratic movement prevented any of the successive military governments from imposing a dictatorship and led instead to the elections that resulted in the landslide electoral victory of the then radical liberation theology priest Jean-Bertrand Aristide in December 1990.

The democratic movement fought to rid the country of dictatorship, democratize the government, eliminate corruption in public office, reform the military and police, and create a more just and equitable society. The popular movement comprised many different political, religious, civic, human rights, neighborhood, women's, student, professional, labor, peasant, and media organizations that gave voice to the people and formulated their collective aspirations. Although no single political organization, individual, or group of individuals controlled the popular movement, its aggregate demands amounted to nothing short of a call for what I termed a maximalist egalitarian democracy in Haiti (Dupuy 2007: 19–20, 60–61).

Vowing to carry out the popular mandate for change, Aristide earned the enmity of the neo-Duvalierists, the military, the Haitian bourgeoisie, and the USA. Once in power, however, the Aristide government pursued a two-fold and contradictory strategy. On the one hand, the government encouraged the people to remain mobilized and to press their demands, and incorporated many of them in the program of government it presented to parliament in February 1991, including greater access to education, healthcare, land reform, and a higher minimum wage. On the other hand, while it called on the bourgeoisie to cooperate with the government to bring about change, it also threatened to unleash the power of the people against them if they refused. The bourgeoisie responded by backing a military coup against Aristide in September 1991 that sent him into exile until US President Bill Clinton returned him to power in October 1994 on the back of 20,000 US troops.[18]

By the time Aristide returned to finish the 18 months left in his first five-year term he had abandoned his radical views and broken with the interests of the majority of Haitians he championed in 1990. As a quid pro quo for returning him to power, Aristide accepted the neoliberal program drafted by the international financial institutions in 1994, but managed to avoid implementing the reforms fully by the time he left office and transferred power to the newly elected government of René Préval in February 1996. When Aristide won re-election for a second and final five-year term in November 2000,[19] the balance of class forces had shifted even more in favor of the bourgeoisie and the organized political opposition. The popular movement that brought him to power in 1990 had been decimated after three years of brutal repression under the junta (1991–94) and Aristide never attempted to revive it. Moreover, the left-of-center or social democratic parties that had coalesced around him in 1990–91 had broken with him and now opposed his new Lavalas Family Party created in 1996. Thus, in the absence of a strong popular movement to back him, Aristide pursued an accommodation with the bourgeoisie and foreign capital, but they rebuffed him and supported the opposition instead.

Be that as it may, Aristide pursued the recommended neoliberal policies of privatizing public enterprises and reducing tariffs to their lowest levels, and negotiated deals with the World Bank and the Inter-American Development Bank to create a free-trade zone in northern Haiti that required the expropriation of farmers and the appropriation of more than 1,000 acres of farm land in the region. However, none of these measures won him the support of the international community, especially the USA under the Bush Sr Administration, the Haitian bourgeoisie, or his political opponents. Fully backed by the USA, France, and Canada, the Haitian bourgeoisie and the opposition coalition blocked any and all negotiated solutions that would allow Aristide to remain in power until the end of his second mandate in 2006, and succeeded in removing him once more from power in February 2004—and again exiling him—with the help of an armed uprising by former members of the Haitian army that Aristide had dissolved in 1995.

An interim government installed by the international community[20] succeeded Aristide, and its main task was to pacify the country—i.e., neutralize the remnants of Aristide's more militant, and sometimes armed, supporters known as *Chimères*. René Préval was then re-elected for a second and final term in 2006 and ceded power to the elected government of Michel Martelly in 2011. But neither of these two governments challenged the policies outlined above that were dictated by the international community. If anything, the dominant political and economic classes of Haiti have become even more subservient to and dependent on the international community since the devastating earthquake that hit Haiti in January 2010 and from which it is still far from recovering.

Immediately after the earthquake, the Préval government surrendered the decision-making process to an Interim Haiti Recovery Commission (IHRC) co-chaired by former US President Bill Clinton and then Haitian Prime Minister Jean-Max Bellerive. Though the commission comprised equal numbers of representatives from Haiti and the international community, the latter made all the key decisions from which most of the Haitians were excluded.[21] Predictably the Commission and the international community pursued the same policies discussed above that exacerbated Haiti's poverty, inequalities, and dependence on foreign aid and foreign capital. The objective of those policies had never been to generate sustainable and equitable development in Haiti, but to serve the interests of foreign investors to take advantage of the lowest-cost labor for garment production in the hemisphere, as well as US agricultural exports for which Haiti has become the largest importer in the Caribbean region, rice in particular. The mandate of the IHRC expired in October 2011, but the government of President Martelly, which came to power in May of that year, had already made clear its intention to pursue the agenda developed by the international community.

However, if the Haitian bourgeoisie (economic and political) has surrendered its independence and accepted its subservience to foreign capital, it has in turn gained the support of the latter in suppressing the popular demands for a more just and more equal society. Nowhere can this be seen more clearly than in the struggles of Haitian workers to improve their standard of living by pushing for a higher minimum wage in both Haitian- and foreign-owned apparel industries operating as subcontractors for Haines, Bali, Champion, L'eggs, Gildan, Fruit of the Loom, and Levi's for firms such as Kmart, Wal-Mart, GAP, J.C. Penny, Jos A. Bank, and Levi's, among others. These factories produce knits and woven-based garments (from T-shirts to uniforms, medical scrubs, undergarments, nightwear, sportswear, to pants and men's suits), making Haiti the fifth largest supplier of such garments to the USA after Honduras, Mexico, El Salvador and the People's Republic of China. Some 68 percent of the approximately 25,000 workers employed in the assembly industries are women, and only one of the 23 factories operating in Haiti is unionized. As a result, wages in Haiti have remained the lowest in the region, a fact which, accounting for the overall lower-than-average rate of productivity of Haitian workers and the costs of production per unit (wages, utilities, transportation, rent, and other overhead costs), yield the apparel industry an average profit rate of 22 percent (Nathan Associates Inc. 2009: 31, 33, 39, 42).

To keep these industries profitable and attractive to foreign investors, the World Bank, USAID, and the Association of Haitian Industries representing those Haitian entrepreneurs involved in subcontracting production fought continuously to keep them low. Whenever a government tried to raise the minimum wage of workers in these industries, the Haiti business-international financial institutions partnership fought against it. None the less, thanks to the struggles of the workers and students who persisted despite retaliation by the factory owners, the Haitian parliament increased the minimum wage across the board to 200 HTG (or US $3.75) a day in 2009. However, under pressure from Washington and the subcontractors in Haiti, President Préval vetoed the bill, forcing a compromise with parliament that raised the wage to 125 HTG ($3.13) a day. Though subsequent wage increases the law required did not take place, the minimum daily wage was raised in October 2012 to 300 HTG ($7.20) across the board, although the government did not enforce the law, allowing the apparel industries to continue to pay their workers 200 HTG ($4.20) (Doucet 2013). In 2011, however, and accounting for inflation, the average wage was one-third less than the value of the wages that were paid under the Duvalier dictatorship in 1982 when the assembly industries were at the height of their operation. Such a wage covers less than half of the most basic needs of the workers and their families for housing, food, clothing, schooling, and transportation. According to the American Federation of Labor-Congress of Industrial Organizations (AFL-CIO) Solidarity Center, a worker would need to be paid at least $29/day to meet those needs for a family of four (Ayiti Kale Je 2011a; Bell and Ekert 2013).

Even the report of Nathan Associates written for the World Bank notes:

> the costs of transportation to and from work and food purchased away from home eat up a substantial share of that minimum wage. At 10 Gourdes

(HTG) per ride in the informal "tap-tap" transports, and with three or four rides required each way to and from work, it is easy to see that the minimum wage barely covers work-related expenses. Nevertheless, even though total apparel industry employment in Haiti is small by international standards, even though the minimum wage of 125 HTG per day [in 2009] is relatively low, and even though production incentives are only paid when workers achieve their production targets, factory work with its steady paycheck represents a significant employment opportunity for Haitians.

(Nathan Associates Inc. 2009: 37; also cited in Bell and Ekert 2013)

Given the high rate of unemployment[22] and the fact that employment in the apparel industry is the second highest source of full-time work in the formal sector after the public sector, six to seven people apply for every job opening in the assembly industries. Such competition is a boon to the employers who are "pleased by the low levels of absenteeism (2 percent) and turnover (4–6 percent per year)" (Nathan Associates 2009: 37). As the Haitian owner of one of the largest apparel industries acknowledged, "When you have a country where 80 [sic] percent of the people don't work, anything is good!" The manager of another plant justified the low wages thus: "If you don't work, you don't have anything. [With the wages they get] at least [they] can survive … It's better than nothing" (Ayiti Kale Je 2011b).

Expressed theoretically, the point these two employers are making is this: Haiti's large reserve army of labor allows employers to have maximum advantage in exploiting their workers by paying them rock-bottom poverty wages and denying them the most elementary labor rights because they have no other means of providing for their needs and are therefore compelled to sell their labor-power well below their value. As Marx explained the role the reserve army of labor plays in the accumulation of capital,

> the greater this reserve army in proportion to the active labour-army, the greater is the mass of a consolidated surplus population, whose misery is in inverse ratio to the amount of torture it has to undergo in the form of labour. The more extensive, finally, the pauperized sections of the working class and the industrial reserve army, the greater is official pauperism. *This is the absolute general law of capitalist accumulation.*
>
> (Marx 1977: 798; emphasis in original)

For those who are not employed in agriculture, in the apparel industry, in the public sector, or in other commercial, service, transportation, or industrial enterprises, the alternative to unemployment and starvation is either employment in domestic labor or the informal sector where wages are even lower, or, failing that, emigration.[23]

Popular and grassroots organizations and labor unions and peasant organizations in Haiti have called for the rejection of the neoliberal policies and prioritizing the rebuilding and expansion of Haiti's infrastructure, communication, transportation, public schools, public health, and public housing; promoting Haiti's food security and sovereignty by launching an agrarian reform and subsidizing production for the local market as well as for export; subsidizing the development of industries that use domestic inputs to produce consumer and durable goods; and protecting the rights of workers to form trade unions and to strike, and providing a living wage to all workers, including those in the export assembly industries. However, in order to achieve these goals, these organizations, and the working people in general, would need to mobilize themselves on a scale not seen since the days (years) of relentless struggles to overthrow the Duvalier dictatorship to bring to power a government that raises the specter of an alternative, as the government of 1991 had done for a short time, and before it that of 1800 had done for the slaves who overthrew colonialism and slavery.

Notes

1 Leslie Péan, for example, has undertaken the most extensive study to date of what he calls the political economy of corruption in Haiti (2000, 2005, 2006, 2007).
2 There is a long precedent for such efforts in Haitian history. When Toussaint Louverture took control of Saint-Domingue he created a new constitution that gave him the right to choose his successor. Jean-Jacques Dessalines's constitution did the same when he came to power in 1806.
3 See Chapter 6 for a fuller discussion of this point.
4 Sharecroppers did not own the land they worked and lived on, but they owned the tools and animals, and hence controlled when and how they worked.
5 Between 1804 and 1915 (the year the US occupation of Haiti started), there were 29 insurrections to overthrow or install a government led by a leader from one of the two factions of the ruling class.
6 Normally taxes appropriated by the state cannot be considered exploitation in the strict sense of the word insofar as these revenues are used to provide social and welfare services or to build infrastructures—that is public goods—for the population as a whole, especially the poor, the working classes, and the most vulnerable sectors of the population. This has never been the case in Haiti.
7 While refusing to recognize Haiti, the United States and Britain exploited the divisions between the two factions of the emergent ruling class to reinforce Haiti's economic dependence on them and weaken France's dominance. See Vertus Saint-Louis (2003) for a succinct analysis of how the rivalries among those three big powers played themselves out during and immediately after the Haitian Revolution.
8 France refused to use the name Haiti since that would signal a tacit recognition of its independence.
9 Contrary to Blancpain, Jean-Baptiste Wallez asserted that he was not executed but died several weeks later after he was made to attend a Requiem mass and imprisoned (1826: 16).
10 Turnier noted that it was 1886 (1985: 27).
11 For some excellent analyses of the US occupation of Haiti and its consequences, see: Bellegarde (1929), Schmidt (1971), Gaillard (1973–85), Labelle (1978), Millet (1978), Nicholls (1979), Renda (2001), and Smith (2009).
12 Elected in 1990, Aristide was toppled by the Haitian army and exiled in 1991. In October 1994 the USA led a United Nations multinational force to remove the military junta from power and return Aristide to finish the 18 months left in his first term as president.

13 The peasants who were forcefully expropriated sparked the Caco rebellion in 1911 that led to Simon's downfall. The rebellion was not fully defeated until 1920 by the US Marines.

14 Until 1957, Haitian presidents were elected indirectly by the legislature, which itself was elected by popular vote, though only men could vote. However, as I mentioned previously, such elections were meaningless since most heads of state ruled as dictators who ignored or suspended the legislature, and the coup d'état was the primary means of creating and undoing governments during the 19th and most of the 20th centuries.

15 Contrary to most accounts, the first universal election in which both adult men and women participated was in 1957, not 1990 when Jean-Bertrand Aristide was elected president. Despite a heavy military presence during the election, and the latter's support for Duvalier, he won 71 percent of the popular vote. See Ferguson (1987: 37).

16 When I speak of the mulatto bourgeoisie I also include among its ranks members of the Levantine immigrants who came to Haiti at the beginning of the 20th century and many of whom and their descendants married into native-born Haitian families. They are part of the two percent of the population who today control about 26 percent of the country's wealth and nearly 50 percent of the national income.

17 Though they were few in number, several high-ranking mulatto officers and members of the bourgeoisie were among the strongest defenders of the Duvalier regime in its early years. Duvalier also had support from members of the Levantine business groups who were despised and socially excluded by the mulatto haute bourgeoisie.

18 See Dupuy (1997), Ballard (1998) and Shacochis (1999).

19 To prevent the possibility of consecutive and unlimited presidential terms, the Haitian Constitution of 1987 allowed an elected president to be re-elected to a second and final five-year term separated by an interval of a five-year term by a different president.

20 By international community I mean the dominant powers, principally the USA, France, and Canada, and the international organizations, principally the International Monetary Fund, the Inter-American Development Bank, the World Bank, and the United Nations, involved in designing and implementing policies for Haiti. The international organizations, however, do not operate autonomously, but do so in accordance with the interests of the major powers, principally the USA in the case of Haiti.

21 For a fuller analysis of the role of the IHRC in the post-earthquake policy-making decisions and their consequences, see Chapter 6.

22 The CIA Factbook for Haiti puts it at 41 percent (2013).

23 Migration may have some possible, and as of yet unrecognized, positive effects for the working class as a whole. There is good evidence that the remittances Haitian migrants send to Haiti help reduce poverty, provide for about 25 percent of Haitian families, and even allow them to have bank and saving accounts (Fajnzylber and López 2008: 4, 8). This fact, then, may well reduce the need for individuals to work for low wages, reduce the labor force, and hence put upward pressure on wages. This, in fact, was a conclusion reached by a World Bank study: "The impact of remittances on labor supply is in principle ambiguous. For individuals in households with migrants, the net additional income derived from remittances could have the 'income effect' of increasing the demand for leisure and reservation wages, with a consequent reduction in labor force participation. However, out-migration also has the direct effect of reducing the size of the labor force, and the ensuing upward pressure on local wages could in turn create a 'substitution effect' away from leisure, with a consequent increase in labor supply for those living in areas with high migration rates." See World Bank (2006).

4   The transition to democracy and the demise of color politics in Haiti

One of the major casualties of the struggle against dictatorship and for a democratic alternative in Haiti since the 1980s has been the interpretation of Haiti's history as a struggle for power between the mulatto and black factions of the dominant class rather than a conflict between this factionalized dominant class and the subordinate classes they exploited. The former argument has been most compellingly defended by David Nicholls, whose 1979 seminal work *From Dessalines to Duvalier: Race, Colour and National Independence in Haiti* remains influential and is essential reading for all serious students of Haitian history. Much of Haiti's post-independence history, Nicholls argued, "must be seen as a struggle between a mulatto, city-based, commercial elite, and a black rural and military elite" (Nicholls 1979: 8). These two elites, moreover, do not constitute two distinct classes but are part of a single but factionalized class. In other words, Haitian history has been mostly an intra-class rather than an inter-class conflict. However, Nicholls suggests, during the US occupation of Haiti between 1915 and 1934, which favored the mulatto faction, an urban working class and a small but important black middle class emerged and henceforth began to play a significant role in Haitian politics. The middle class especially would play a crucial role in the ascendency first of Dumarsais Estimé in 1946 and later of François Duvalier in 1957, both leaders of a resurgent *noiriste* or black-nationalist movement that sought to displace the mulattoes from power. Thus, Nicholls argues, the power struggles in the period since the US occupation must be understood in terms of the changing class structure of the country. But, he concludes, it is wrong to account for political developments in that period primarily or solely in terms of class and to ignore the central role of color divisions (Nicholls 1979: 9–10).

A critique of Nicholls

I agree with Nicholls that color divisions played a role in Haitian politics before and during the Saint-Domingue/Haitian Revolution, and since Haiti gained its independence in 1804. However, we differ in our understanding of the connection between color and class. Contrary to Nicholls, I argue that ideologies of color were not simply symptomatic of a struggle for power between two factions of the dominant class, but most importantly a struggle for a share in the exploitation of the subordinated classes in terms of which faction controlled the state and its apparatuses, on the one hand, and the private sector and its links to the world market and foreign capital, on the other hand.

Put differently, the ideologies of color in post-colonial, independent Haiti were not produced to justify the subordination and exploitation of a racial/color group different from the new Haitian ruling class, the middle class, or other segments of the working class, as was the case in the colonial era.[1] Rather, they were produced to justify the struggle for state power between two contending factions of the ruling class precisely because one faction—the mulattoes—tended to be more dominant economically and the black faction sought to counter that power by controlling the state and its various apparatuses.

For me, the "color question" is derivative from the "class question" and cannot be understood independently of the system of class relations that emerged in post-independent Haiti. However, as I explained in Chapters 1 and 2, "derived" from is not to mean that once formed these ideologies did not become a force in their own right, that is, appear to be "objective facts" with their own determinations. But it does mean that these ideologies "have a life" of their own only to the extent that they are reproduced by social actors in their daily lives or politically to pursue political or economic objectives. Thus, ideologies of racial or color distinctions, always articulate with other class practices and their economic, political, and social manifestations in a specific society at specific points in time.

Moreover, to see "colorism" (short for ideologies of color) as operating independently of the shared interests of the factions of the dominant class in the exploitation of the subordinated classes makes it impossible to explain the shift that occurred in the political discourse in the wake of the movement for a democratic alternative to dictatorship since the 1980s, the rise of Jean-Bertrand Aristide to power in 1990 and again in 2000, as well as the subsequent presidential electoral contests of 2006 and 2011. That shift, I argue, displaced "colorism" as the ideological claim to power and replaced it with the question of legitimacy, that is, government by consent of the governed and whose interests the state defends regardless of the "color" of who governs. That question may have always been present, but the exclusion of the majority of the population from participating directly in the political process through the exercise of universal franchise and the transfer of power by means of *coups d'état* throughout most of the 19th and 20th centuries made it possible to justify the de facto claims to power on the basis of identity politics rather than the right to govern by legitimate consent.

I also disagree with Nicholls's interpretation of the meanings of race and color. For him, "race" refers to the subjective beliefs that a set of people holds about itself and is generally regarded by others as being connected genetically to some extra-familial common descent. By contrast, he sees "color" as referring to objective phenotypical or somatic characteristics such as skin color, type of hair, or facial features, and argues that in New World societies like those of the Caribbean, all those who had "non-white blood" were considered by colonial whites and came to accept themselves as sharing a common "African race," even if they made distinctions among themselves as mulattoes or blacks depending on their phenotypical or color characteristics (Nicholls 1979: 1–2).

The difference Nicholls makes between "race" and "color," however, does not hold. First, both definitions are based on the ideological premise that people who share a "common" biological heritage belong to the same "race." But this assumes that someone who is said to belong to a "race", say in the 19th or the 21st centuries, is connected to a member of that same "race" in the 15th or 17th centuries through an invariant common line of descent. Going that far back in history, however, would surely mean that everyone who lived in the 19th or the 21st centuries would be descended from many people by more than one route, as modern DNA (deoxyribonucleic acid) testing is revealing, thereby making it impossible to hold that those who belong to a particular "race" today shared a common biological or genetic heritage with the presumed members of that same "race" several centuries removed (Appiah 1986: 25–27). As I have argued in Chapter 1, "race," which came to be defined on the basis of skin color, is a purely ideological construct developed in the 17th and 18th centuries to justify the enslavement of Africans in the European colonies of the Americas and the differential incorporations of non-Europeans in the global division of labor of the capitalist world-system resulting from the European colonial empires in the 19th and 20th centuries. There is nothing in the facts of visible physical differences that in themselves explain racism or "colorism." Thus, the fact that mulattoes and blacks came to be defined by the European colonialists as belonging to the black "race," and that they, in turn, came to accept that classification, is the result, not of biology but ideology. To quote Barbara Fields again, racial or color classifications are not elements "of human biology ... nor [are they ideas] that can be plausibly imagined to live an eternal life of [their] own. Race [and color are] not [ideas] but [ideologies]. [They] came into existence at a discernible historical moment for rationally understandable historical reasons and [are] subject to change for similar reasons" (Fields 1990: 101).

Though it may not always have been easy, white Europeans who colonized the New World were fairly clear about where they drew the line. Again, to recall Moreau de Saint-Méry's point made earlier (in Chapter 2), "indiscreet markers of the African characteristic ... are always noticed ... [W]hatever whiteness the mixed race may have, it does not always have the shade of the pure white and that is what serves the eyes of those familiarized with the comparison" (Moreau de Saint-Méry 1958: Vol. 1, 100). And notwithstanding the distinctions whites made between the free people of color, or mulattoes, and blacks, they considered them both part of the "inferior race," and therefore undeserving of the rights and privileges reserved for whites. That those who were defined and defined themselves as mulattoes or blacks in turn came to distinguish among themselves along the continuum of color characteristics is simply a variation on the same theme. Whether or not whites saw them as belonging to the same "race," they themselves behaved as if they were different. But the fluidity of these categorizations and the difficulty of drawing a clear cut-off line between mulatto and black or mulatto and white make them just as arbitrary and socially and politically contingent as the distinctions between whites and blacks.

As I showed in Chapters 2 and 3 and other writings,[2] the dominant class that emerged during the revolutionary war and after independence in Haiti was neither homogeneous in terms of the socio-economic origins or the complexions of its members, nor unified politically. That factionalized class consisted, on the one hand, of the class of predominantly mulatto property owners who descended from the *affranchis,* or free people of color as they were called during the colonial era, and, on the other hand, the new land-owning black bourgeoisie formed during the regimes of Toussaint Louverture (1801–03), Jean-Jacques Dessalines (1804–06), and Henri Christophe (1806–20). A major consequence of the class structure of post-colonial Haiti was that the state became a source of wealth accumulation and social advancement for those who controlled it. Failing to maintain the sugar-based plantation economy created by the French slave-owning class and to expropriate the former slave masses from the lands they appropriated during and after the revolution and transform them into a proletariat (i.e., wage-laborers), the bourgeoisie turned to the importation and exportation of commodities, the extraction of rents from tenant farmers, the small rural and urban proletariat, and to its control of the state as its bases of accumulation. As such, it derived its wealth primarily from the circulation rather than the production process. Since the state also depended primarily on the circulation process—through direct or indirect taxation, or extortion/corruption—for its revenues, the state bourgeoisie entered into conflict with the private-sector bourgeoisie to appropriate part of the surplus wealth produced by the working and farming classes. Under such conditions, then, it became difficult to establish government by legitimate consent, thereby making dictatorship the most common form of government and the *coup d'état* the most common mechanism for the transfer of power in the 19th and most of the 20th centuries.

The class divisions described above, therefore, expressed themselves in terms of ideologies of color. As they developed during the 19th century, "colorism" consisted of a reformulation of the racist ideology created during the colonial period by the French, and became an expression of the conflicts between the mulatto and black factions of the bourgeoisie and middle class to justify their claims to power and impose their dominance. The black elite used "colorism" as a means of social advancement by countering the mulattoes' contempt for and devalorization of blacks. For their part, mulattoes used it to preserve their dominant social and economic positions (Péan 2000: 112–13).

The mulatto ideology rejected the notion of racial inequality proposed by European racism, but adopted none the less the European somatic norm image, with one important modification. Contrary to the European racist ideology which eschewed all notions of "racial intermixing" to depict its ideal type of "whiteness," the mulatto ideology claimed that all advanced civilizations, most notably European, were the products of racial intermixing, and that Africa remained "backward because she has always been outside the great currents of immigration" (Laroche, cited in Martinez 1973: 29; and also in Labelle 1978: 57). From this it followed that the mulattoes, as the product of miscegenation between Europeans and Africans, considered themselves "closer" to the Europeans and therefore "more civilized" and "more advanced" than the blacks who were "nearer" the Africans. Thus, mulattoes believed they should rule Haiti because they were the "most competent." Edmond Paul, a leading defender of the mulatto ideology, put it thus:

> The incapacity of the greatest number is exploited in our country ... by those who sought to place at the head of the state the least competent among the people, and this to elevate their own prestige, and so that their merit would not be challenged, and their ambition would not be rivaled.
>
> (Paul 1976: 37)

By contrast, the *noiriste* or black-nationalist ideology claimed that the selfishness of the mulattoes since independence caused the ills of the country and that only blacks could articulate the interests of the black majority against those of the minority mulatto elite. Therefore blacks, and not mulattoes, should be in power because they alone could be the "authentic" spokesmen for the black masses and represent their genuine interests. As Louis-Joseph Janvier, one of the leading intellectuals of the 19th century and an articulate proponent of the black nationalist ideology put it, "a government of the majority by the majority and by those who respect the majority is the only one possible in Haiti" (Janvier 1885: 248).

The two factions or blocs of the dominant class, then, redefined the racist ideology of the slave and colonial era to legitimize their claim to political power. As Nicholls recognized, it was not always easy to distinguish between mulattoes and blacks since the definition of who was "mulatto" and "black" tended to coincide with the class position of the individuals being defined, a fact well captured in the popular yet racist dictum in Haiti and elsewhere in the Caribbean and Brazil that "money whitens." None the less, as a social category, skin color and color classifications, fluid as they were, tended to correlate more or less with social class position in such a way that those of lighter skin complexion tended to be found more among the dominant and wealthier than among the poorer and powerless sectors of the population (Trouillot 1990: 110–13). Though not always observed scrupulously, elite mulattoes certainly used skin color strategically to exclude blacks with non-identifiable mulatto or upper-class lineages from their social circles and as "proper marriage" partners, and the black elite avoided marrying with "unknowns," or those who "don't belong" to that elite (Paquin 1983: 213–21). Thus, as Leslie Péan put it, "matrimonial alliances don't escape the color question to ensure the reproduction of the social stratification" (Péan 2007: 108).

Be that as it may, neither faction could exclude the other from having access to the means of production, whether landed, commercial, or industrial property, or political power. The wealth or power of individuals from both factions of the dominant class made it possible for them to acquire similar standards of living, to educate their children in the same schools, to bequeath their wealth to their offspring, to reproduce their particular racisms through social or familial alliances, and hence to reproduce the system of class domination and its characteristic cleavages. As such, there is a significant difference between the role that the ideologies of race and color played during the colonial slave era and the role that "colorism" came to play in post-colonial Haiti. In the former case,[3] the ideologies of race and color were integral to the social division of labor between whites, mulattoes (or free people of color), and blacks to maintain them in their corresponding socio-economic and political positions: whites as the dominant slave-owning class, and whites of all ranks—those in the middle or working classes—having political rights and privileges denied to the mulattoes or free people of color of any rank—even property or slave owners; and the black slaves who had no rights or property but were themselves the property of others.

By contrast, the class structure of post-colonial Haiti was not characterized by a division between mulattoes as the exclusively dominant class subordinating blacks in the middle and laboring classes. Instead, the class structure comprised a dominant class of mulattoes and blacks, a majority black middle class, and an overwhelmingly black laboring class. However, and this is the crucial point, unlike in the colonial-slave era, there were powerful economic but no institutionalized—social, cultural, or political—barriers that excluded blacks or mulattoes from belonging to any class, especially the property-owning and political classes, even if, as mentioned above, those of lighter skin complexion tended to be found more among the dominant and wealthier economic class than among the poorer and powerless classes. Put yet another way, the racial/color hierarchy was essential to the survival of the slave regime of Saint-Domingue and crumbled when the slaves rose against it. In post-colonial, post-slavery Haiti, ideologies of color expressed a struggle between the two factions of the dominant class for a share in the political and economic means of wealth appropriation, but they are not essential to the reproduction of that class system. As I will show below, the class system can survive unscathed without "colorism."

Carolle Charles, for example, argues that to see "race" or "color" in Haiti primarily as either an ideology of domination or a manifestation of class strife between dominant and subordinate groups is to make it a residual category. Instead, "race" or "color" is best understood as a product of collective practice embedded in both social relations and individual identity. For Charles, then, "in the former case [race/color] participates in the creation and ascription of place, in the latter it is a matter of identity formation manifested in taste, networks of friends and clients, strategies of reproduction through marriage, and self-identification, as well as in other ways" (Charles 1992: 108).

However, the two facets of the "color question" in Haiti, that is, its role in class domination and conflicts between factions of the dominant class for a share in the spoils of the economic system, and its role in individual identity and social practices, are not mutually exclusive. As I noted before, the "color question" cannot be understood independently of the system and history of class and political relations in Haiti. Race and color ideologies were the product of the class structuring and social division of labor of the colonial-slave era to justify them, not the other way round. Similarly, the reinterpretation and perpetuation of the "ideologies of color" in Haiti stemmed from the reconfiguration of its class system of domination/exploitation, and not the other way round. Charles herself understands this to be the case when she argues that the "perception of race/color is conditioned by class and culture," and that "blackness in Haiti is a conceptualization of class interest in the language of race. It is a racial symbol whose meaning hides class conflicts, in particular between those dominant groups" (Charles 1992: 107–8). "*Mulâtrisme*," or the self-perception, identity formation, and individual practices of members of the mulatto population, served a similar function as *noirisme* did for members of the black factions of the dominant and middle classes. Each formulation provided their proponents with a set of cultural references with which to negotiate their personal and social relations with other groups and classes, and to justify their dominant and privileged positions in the society. There is no question, then, that cultural/ideological perceptions or references play an important role in the reproduction of the factions of the bourgeoisie. However, it does not follow, as Leslie Manigat (and Nicholls) argue that the "cleavages of color" aligned the "mulatto bloc comprising bourgeois and petit bourgeois mulattoes vis-à-vis the black bloc comprising the middle classes and the black masses, despite class differences within each bloc," and that these conflicts were decisive over the conflicts between classes (Manigat 1975: 16–21).

As suggested above, the dominant classes included both mulattoes and blacks, and though each faction used the ideologies of color for its respective purposes, they were identical in all other respects vis-à-vis the subordinate classes. Moreover, no president or dictator, mulatto or black, could rule without including members of the "opposite color" in his government and without cross-class and "cross-color" alliances to form a "pact of domination" whose character is determined by the "interrelations between the various parts of the state apparatus, on the one hand, and the most powerful classes or class fractions, on the other" (Rueschemeyer and Evans 1985: 47). Insofar as an ideology is not reducible to the class or racial group whose structural location provided the contents for its formulation, one could find mulattoes espousing a black-nationalist ideology as much as blacks could defend the mulatto counterpart (just as a member of the bourgeoisie could espouse a proletarian ideology and vice versa). It is worth quoting Jean Price-Mars's reply to René Piquion who advanced a proposition similar to that of Manigat and Nicholls:

[The] fortunate and the powerful who constituted the ruling class and which included blacks as well as mulattoes, and on the other hand, the immense majority of jobbing laborers, the workers, the non-specialized, the unemployed of all colors, and especially the mass of rural laborers, the mass of peasants ... constituted the *social question* [since] 1804 ... [This question] has been misrepresented, has been systematically masked by cloaking it with false claims ever since, for a long time, blacks and mulattoes killed one another to conquer power without the success of one or the other faction having changed in any way the living standard of the unfortunate more or less black, or more or less light skin.

(Price-Mars 1967: 20–21)

Neither faction ever became socially, economically, politically, or ideologically hegemonic because neither could crystallize the ideology of color into structures of institutional exclusion or discrimination. In other words, precisely because racism or colorism never became institutionalized in postcolonial Haiti, and because the barriers between mulattoes and blacks could not be enforced and were therefore permeable socially and politically, the ideology of color remained transparent as an ideology of power rather than becoming fetishized as the ideologies of race did in those countries, such as the USA, where they served to allocate people of different "races" or "ethnicities" differently in the social division of labor. Consequently the ideology of color could be challenged more easily and more successfully as I will show below.

Duvalierism and black nationalism

Since the reunification of Haiti in 1818, a balance of power or "pact of domination" had been formed between the mulatto and black factions of the dominant class, with the former retaining its advantages in the economy and the latter tending to predominate in controlling the state and in land ownership. The US occupation from 1915 to 1934, however, would change that precarious balance of power in favor of the mulattoes, a fact that set into motion important new processes that would ultimately set the stage for the rise of François Duvalier to power in 1957 as the purported champion of the black-nationalist cause.

During the 1930s and 1940s there emerged two currents within the broad *Indigéniste* movement of that period. Linked internationally to the Négritude movement, the *Indigénistes* in Haiti criticized and rejected the racist claims of Western culture and the re-articulation of those beliefs in Haiti by the bourgeoisie (both mulatto and black) which valued European and especially French culture and language as a mark of its social superiority. By contrast, the *Indigénistes* promoted a "genuine" Haitian culture that recognized and validated its African roots and contents. An explicitly racist offshoot of the *Indigéniste* movement, known as the *Griots* (of which François Duvalier was a founding member), also emerged and went further by claiming that there existed a specifically African psychology and culture that was biologically determined and present in the collective personality of the predominantly black Haitian population. Accordingly, and in a formulation similar to that of Louis-Joseph Janvier referred to earlier, the solution to Haiti's ills, which the *Griots* attributed to the mulatto elite's European cultural values and support for the American occupation, consisted of transferring political power to the "authentic" representatives of the black majority and reorganizing the institutions of the society to express the African cultural values of the masses. Thus, the differences between mulattoes and blacks were said to stem principally from their cultural differences determined by their biological (i.e., color) characteristics rather than from their divergent class or economic positions. Moreover, contrary to those in Haiti who advocated a democratic form of government, the *Griots* nationalists maintained that Haiti needed a black leader who embodied the aspirations of the black masses and would defend them.

This more explicitly anti-mulatto articulation of the *Griots* nationalists served as the rallying cry for those sectors of the black middle class and bourgeoisie who opposed the economic and especially political resurgence of the mulatto bourgeoisie during and after the US occupation. That movement succeeded in bringing Dumarsais Éstimé to power in 1946 with the aim of shifting power back to the black elite and middle class. The so-called Estimist Revolution of 1946 was short-lived, however, as mulattoes seemed to gain the upper hand once again with the rise to power of Colonel Paul Magloire in 1950. Though not a member of the mulatto faction, Magloire none the less was allied with and served its interests. As a member of the *Griots* group and supporter of the "1946 Revolution," Duvalier set himself the task of conquering power on behalf of the black bourgeoisie and middle class in 1957.

It is in this historical context that one can understand better the objectives of the Duvalier regime between 1957 and 1971 and its use of black nationalism in achieving them. Once he was elected president with the help of the Haitian military in 1957, Duvalier proceeded to consolidate his control over the state apparatuses. Duvalier did not seek to alter the class structure of Haiti and thus the social and economic dominance of the mulatto bourgeoisie. Neither did Duvalier aim to reduce the economy's subordination to and dependence on foreign capital. Duvalier's and the black nationalists' objectives were to capture political power for the black bourgeoisie and middle class as a counterweight to the mulatto bourgeoisie's economic dominance. This would be achieved by forging an alliance with other class factions under the leadership of the black bourgeoisie and middle class. The other classes that formed the power base of the Duvalier regime included members of the expatriate and white Levantine business groups resented and socially excluded by the mulatto bourgeoisie, sectors of the medium-size farmers, and elements from the urbanized lumpen-proletariat. Duvalier had very little support among the urban working classes.

For all its anti-mulatto ideology, however, Duvalier did not exclude mulattoes who shared his views and objectives from his administration. Though they were few in number, several well-known high-ranking mulatto officers and members of the mulatto bourgeoisie were among the staunchest defenders of the Duvalier regime in its early years. This shows once more that ideologies of color cannot be reduced to the color of one's skin or to the class faction that produced it, but rather to one's self-identification, interests, and objectives. As Cary Hector points out, however, one needs to distinguish between the ideology of conquest of power and the ideology of power, that is, between black-nationalism as a contesting and revanchist ideology and black-nationalism as the ideology of the black bourgeoisie and middle class in control of the state. The former justified the claim to political power by Duvalier as the incarnation of the "historic mission" of the black elite to gain power in the name of the black majority against the exclusivism and elitism of the mulatto minority. Once in power, Duvalier moved to monopolize the political space by suppressing all competing political opposition (Hector 1972: 52).

Duvalier did not limit his attack to ideological and political opponents, however. To achieve the black nationalists' objective of a social and political balance with the mulatto bourgeoisie, the latter had to be removed from positions of power or authority in the apparatuses and agencies of the state, including and especially the military. To be effective against the mulattoes, the government's purge and repressive measures had to be ubiquitous and include all opposition or potential opposition, and it could know no bounds. Therefore Duvalier's first order of business was to consolidate his power within the state and over the society, and he spent the first seven years of his rule implementing that policy. The regime created a vast clientelistic network by staffing all the apparatuses of the state, including and especially the military, with those loyal to Duvalier.

From 1957 to 1964, Duvalier unleashed a reign of terror hitherto unknown on all opponents, real, potential, or imagined, and on the population in general. No one was spared the tyrannical and unpredictable violence of the state: men, women, children, families from all classes, and even entire towns, such as in Jéremie, where members of 27 mulatto families were exterminated (Péan 2007: 121–26). By striking against all, anywhere, and at any time, the new violence became as symbolic as it was preventive. Moreover, Duvalier sought to extend his control over all major state and civil society institutions, from the military to the legislature, the media, the Catholic Church, the public schools, and the trade unions. Still distrusting the military for its historic role in the making and unmaking of governments, however, Duvalier built an alternative armed force directly under his control, the so-called Volunteers for National Security, more popularly known as the *Tontons Macoutes*, recruited mainly from the ranks of the lumpen-proletariat in the urban centers and landless peasants, section chiefs, and Vodou priests in the rural areas. With some 10,000 members, the militia readily became much larger than the regular armed forces, including the police, which numbered slightly over 5,000. As Michel-Rolph Trouillot observed succinctly, Duvalierism

> did not seek the physical intervention of the State in the battlefield of politics; it aimed to create a void in that field to the benefit of the State. It wanted an end to that struggle for a lack of combatants in the sphere occupied by the totalitarian executive.
>
> (Trouillot 1986: 189)[4]

In my view, the significance of Duvalierism was not only the form in which it exercised power, but also that it used it to restore the balance that the black bourgeoisie and middle class had achieved with the mulatto bourgeoisie under Estimé in 1946–50 but had lost in the subsequent years. The Duvalier regime shifted the balance of political power in favor of the black bourgeoisie and middle class and achieved a greater degree of autonomy from the bourgeoisie as a whole. Those were its primary objectives. Control over the state apparatuses offered the only sure avenue for the social and economic advancement of the black middle class because of the limits of private-sector development and the barriers of entry in the major commercial and industrial sectors (i.e., private property ownership and wealth) imposed by the mulatto bourgeoisie and foreign capital. It did not intend or attempt to eliminate the economic dominance of the mulatto bourgeoisie as such, or the exploitative economic system on which that dominance rested. The regime simply sought to force the social and political accommodation of the mulatto bourgeoisie with the black bourgeoisie and middle class as the only way for the latter to share the spoils of the extant economic system.

Though Duvalier was willing to risk alienating the mulatto bourgeoisie to consolidate his power, he could not afford to do so without the backing of some of the Western European powers and especially of the USA. It was therefore essential for Duvalier to maintain good relations with the latter, but not at the expense of his regime, its objectives, and its practices. In short, Duvalier accepted his dependence on foreign capital, but under certain conditions that he was not willing to compromise. Duvalier was willing to offer all the necessary advantages to foreign capital, such as tax exemptions, an abundance of cheap labor, and a climate of labor peace due to the suppression of all independent labor organizations and the banning of strikes. In return, Duvalier expected to be given foreign economic and military assistance, especially from the USA, but without the latter interfering in how he governed the country.

Through his clever exploitation of the US fear of communism during the Cold War era and Haiti's proximity to Cuba, Duvalier managed to win its support. After the successful Cuban Revolution and the US botched Bay of Pigs invasion, Duvalier managed to get a reluctant USA to increase its aid package to Haiti when Richard Nixon took power in 1968. Duvalier may have been a barbaric tyrant, but he was also staunchly anti-communist and knew how to exploit the East–West conflict. The USA, which had failed to launch a successful invasion against Castro, had also drawn strong international criticism for invading the Dominican Republic and overthrowing its democratically elected president, and was getting more deeply involved in an unpopular war in Vietnam. Under those circumstances, it was far more desirable to acquiesce to the Duvalier regime than to alienate it further and push it to seek ties with the Eastern bloc, as Duvalier feigned. For its part, the Duvalier regime, now secured in its power, could rein in the militia. Repression was no longer a daily necessity because the regime had succeeded in silencing the internal opposition and/or forcing it into exile. Thus repressive practices could be relaxed and targeted against selected opponents.

Besides winning renewed economic and military aid from the USA, the regime sought reconciliation with the mulatto bourgeoisie, now politically tamed, and encouraged foreign capital investment, now that a climate of political stability had been created. The reconciliatory moves toward the mulatto bourgeoisie also entailed a marked decrease in the anti-mulatto rhetoric of the early years. For its part, the mulatto bourgeoisie realized that the Duvalier regime concerned itself primarily with the monopoly of state power and a share in the spoils rather than with its expropriation. Faced with the choice of joining the opposition, most of which was in exile, or acquiescing to the rapacious Duvalier dictatorship to protect its own interests, the mulatto bourgeoisie chose the latter. Besides, the regime's repressive policies toward workers benefitted the bourgeoisie directly and offered other advantages such as tax evasion and participation in the generalized corruption of the government.

Foreign capital, too, especially that sector that relied on intensive labor production, such as in garment assembly manufacturing, saw many advantages to investing in Haiti. The abundance of cheap labor, the containment of all labor discontent, the generous fiscal concessions of the government, and the proximity of Haiti to the USA, all served to attract foreign assembly manufacturers to Haiti. By the time François Duvalier died and his 19-year-old son Jean-Claude succeeded him to the presidency in 1971, a new alliance or pact of domination had been formed between the Duvalier regime, that is, the black-nationalist faction of the bourgeoisie and middle class, the mulatto bourgeoisie, and foreign capital. As Péan has shown, the "turn" toward an accommodation with the mulatto bourgeoisie started under the regime of Duvalier *père* but became concretized under that of Duvalier *fils*, symbolized by his marriage to the mulatto Michèle Bennett and the removal of several barons of the father's regime from their once powerful positions. These overtures led the mulatto bourgeoisie to forget about the murderous brutality and humiliation they suffered under the old regime and embrace the new for the promise of "several prosperous good years" (Péan 2007: 130).

The transition to democracy and the demise of color politics

The regime of Jean-Claude Duvalier ruled Haiti until it was overthrown in February 1986 following years of protests and opposition by a growing and radicalizing popular democratic movement. A power struggle ensued among the Duvalierist forces and the military to determine which faction would control the state and impose a new dictatorship. Thanks to relentless pressure from the democratic movement none of those factions could consolidate its power, and in March 1990 a civilian government was formed to organize national elections that resulted in the landslide victory of liberation theologian Father Jean-Bertrand Aristide in December 1990. The broad popular movement comprised many different political, religious, civic, human rights, neighborhood, women's, professional, labor, peasant, and media organizations that gave voice to the people and formulated their collective *cahiers de doléances* (grievances). The democratic movement fought to rid the country of dictatorship, democratize the government, eliminate corruption in public office, reform the military and police, and create a more just and more equal society. The most important characteristic of that broad movement was its decentralization and autonomy. No single political organization, individual, or group of individuals controlled it. Nevertheless, the emergence of Aristide on the political stage in the mid-1980s led him to articulate like no one else could the multiple grievances, interests, and objectives of that movement and to become its standard bearer.

My interest here is not to analyze the contradictory practices of the first Aristide presidency which lasted a mere seven months (February to September 1991), or his second term in office (2001–04)[5] that also ended prematurely, but to emphasize the fundamental break that occurred with the racially based nationalist discourse of the Duvalier dictatorship, modified as it was under the regime of Jean-Claude Duvalier, in favor of a more democratic, egalitarian, non-racial, and inclusive discourse. Put differently, the entry of the lower classes, that is, the majority of the population, onto the political stage and their demands for a restructured and more egalitarian society made it difficult if not impossible for them to be played off by ideologies of color which the experience of the Duvalier dictatorship had exposed as a shield for brute exploitation and repression. From February 1986 to September 1991 Haiti was a vast laboratory for popular participatory democracy. The popular classes were mobilized and organized; they articulated their demands and pushed to actualize them. Once he assumed power in February 1991, Aristide tried to act on the broad demands for jobs, better working conditions, a higher minimum wage, ending corruption in the public administration and public enterprises, greater access to education, a literacy campaign, healthcare, and land reform, among others. As we know, however, that brief experiment in participatory democracy came to an abrupt end in September 1991. The dominant classes and the military felt threatened not only by the intended reforms of the government, but also by the vast popular mobilization that pressed for their implementation. That combination portended a realignment of forces the dominant classes and their foreign backers could not tolerate.

Aristide tried to infuse the emergent democratic discourse with his own interpretation of the world through the prism of liberation theology. That discourse was compatible and resonated with the demands for rights, justice, and equality formulated by the mass movement for democracy within which the base communities of the Catholic Church, known as the *Ti Legilz* (Little Church) movement, played a key role (Greene 1993: esp. Chs. 5–6). For all his shortcomings and contradictions, Aristide's most significant contribution has been to remove the veil of color in the political discourse to unmask the fundamental class interests of both factions of the dominant class and their international allies. He likened Haiti to a prison, where the rule of the game was that the "prisoners" (i.e., the poor and oppressed) were presumed guilty by virtue of being poor. They must accept their plight (i.e., their "prison sentence") without protest, without discussing their social conditions with their fellow "prisoners," and without organizing to defend their rights and their interests for fear of worse cruelty or death (Aristide 1990: 34).

In Aristide's view, the Duvalierists, which can also be read as a euphemism for dictatorships in general, intended to maintain power at any cost and, to that end, they deployed permanent violence and repression against the population. The Duvalierists sought to preserve power not simply for its own sake, but to enable them to plunder the public treasury for their own benefit. The Duvalierists ran the state and the government like an organized gang, with the Duvalier family originally at its head. Yet, even with the Duvalier family gone (which Aristide likened to the "king" and "queen" in a chess game), the "bishops," "knights," and "rooks"—meaning the lower officials of the regime or those who sought to replace it—remained to take over and perpetuate the system. The military commanders linked to the system had become a mercenary force. Its lower echelons, particularly the rural police officers known as section chiefs, benefitted from the system principally by extortion and by terrorizing the population (Aristide 1990: 26; 1992: 70–71).

The holders of state power formed an alliance with the moneyed and propertied oligarchy and protected its interests. The Haitian bourgeoisie, which included the landed and commercial-industrial oligarchy and represented a tiny fraction of the population, mediated between foreign capital and the national economy. Its primary concern was to enrich itself by exploiting the people as much as possible and without regard for their welfare (Aristide 1990: 6–9; 1992: 71, 74–76). The whole system was shored up by the imperialists from the "cold country to the north" through their military and financial aid and their economic policies. In short, the government and the oligarchy were devoid of any meaningful development or social project, save that of enriching themselves and maintaining the population in their state of ignorance and misery (Aristide 1990: 7–8; 1992: 74–76). Needless to say, that critical view of the status quo earned Aristide the bitter enmity of the dominant classes, mulattoes and blacks, as well as the USA, whose objectives were simply to get rid of him. They would never trust him, even after his return to power in 1994 and his second and also abbreviated term in office from 2001 to 2004 when he sought to appease the bourgeoisie and the USA by enforcing the latter's neoliberal policies.

When President Clinton returned Aristide to office in October 1994 on the back of 20,000 US troops to finish out the remaining 18 months of his first five-year term, Aristide had also undergone a major transformation. His main objective now was to monopolize political power for himself and his Lavalas Family (FL) party to create what Robert Fatton aptly called a "presidential monarchism bent on suppressing any alternative, independent power" (Fatton 2002: 120). To accomplish that goal, two conditions had to be met. First, Aristide had to ensure his re-election and that his FL party would also win an absolute majority in Parliament. They accomplished both in the elections of 2000. Second, the 1987 Constitution had to be amended to remove the two-term limit for the presidency separated by a five-year interval. Lavalas legislators proposed to do so in September 2003, but the USA made it clear through its ambassador in Haiti that such a move would be considered "fundamentally destabilizing." There was also opposition from within the ranks of Lavalas, even from once staunch Aristide supporters like Father William Smart and founder of Lavalas who called on the population to resist the amendment. Aristide would be forced out of office in February 2004 before his FL legislators could act on the amendment.

That Aristide and FL contemplated prolonging their hold on power indefinitely was in keeping with the historical tradition of using the state as a means of social promotion and personal enrichment. In my view, these facts more than anything else Aristide did during his second term were the principal reasons the middle and dominant class opposition coalitions backed by the USA, Canada, and France wanted him out of power. They knew that as long as he was around they would not easily dislodge him and his FL party from their grip on power through the ballot box. The main point to note here, however, is that whatever else he aimed to do, Aristide could lay his claim to power only by playing the democratic and not the color game, even if that meant manipulating elections to achieve his ends. Though he occasionally alluded to their color and chastised the mulatto bourgeoisie for their selfishness and exploitation of the masses, his language remained essentially one of class and social injustice, not pigmentation as was the case before 1986. Likewise, the opposition to Aristide did not come only from the predominantly mulatto bourgeoisie, but from the black middle-class sectors that had opposed the Duvalier dictatorship and supported Aristide in 1990. The political discourse, in short, had shifted decisively away from dictatorship to democracy, and hence from justifying one's claim to power on the basis of pigmentation, to government with the consent of the governed. This shift, I maintain, represented a fundamental turning point in Haiti's history of racial/color politics.

Aristide's break with the interests of the subordinate classes also expressed a shift in the balance of class forces since his overthrow in 1991. The popular movement was severely weakened after three years of brutal repression and a crushing economic embargo[6]; and it was now fragmented into pro-and anti-Aristide factions. At the same time, the Haitian bourgeoisie, under the hegemony of Washington, regained the upper hand. In the absence of a strong popular movement to check him as before, Aristide pursued an accommodation with the bourgeoisie and foreign capital during his exile in the USA. As a quid pro quo for returning him to power, Aristide accepted the neoliberal policies drafted for Haiti by the international financial institutions in October 1994, and continued to implement them during his truncated second term even though he got nothing in return from the international community for his compliance.

Moreover, and just as important, after assuming power in 2001 his Lavalas party and government officials engaged in rampant corruption, drugs trafficking, and the diversion of funds destined for public works projects; profited from the sale of tax-exempt imported rice and from banking and investment schemes that defrauded middle-class Haitians of their savings; and last but not least, used gangs, some of whom were armed, against their opponents. Noteworthy here is not the fact that a once popular leader brought to power by the people struggling for a more egalitarian and just social order ultimately broke with those objectives to pursue his and his party's own interests. It is rather the paradigmatic shift in the political landscape and language, which is no longer centered on which color faction of the dominant class ought to rule, but whether those who rule do so legitimately with the consent of the people. Aristide ultimately lost his legitimacy because he betrayed the trust the people had put in him to champion their interest over those of the foreign investors and the Haitian elites.

The return to democratic government after Aristide's second overthrow in February 2004 and the interim rule of Prime Minister Gérard Latortue imposed by the USA, Canada, and France, rekindled the discourse of democratic legitimacy and whose interests the elected serve or ought to serve. René Préval, who had succeeded Aristide to office after he ended his first term in 1996, won a second and final five-year term in 2006. His re-election represented a defeat for the Haitian bourgeoisie and the foreign-backed coalition—the Democratic Convergence and the Group of 184—that had forced Aristide out of office in 2004. These forces had hoped that with the crack-down on Aristide's supporters by the interim Latortue government (2004–06), one of their chosen candidates would win the election and restore the balance of power between the government and the bourgeoisie through the traditional pact of domination favorable to the latter. However, to their dismay, Préval distanced himself from Aristide, ran under the banner of his own LESPWA (Hope) Platform and not the Lavalas Family banner, and drew support throughout the country. His victory came in large part from the massive voter turn-out from the poor neighborhoods and Aristide strongholds in Port-au-Prince and its surrounding areas (see Dupuy 2006: 132–41).

On March 20, 2011, Michel Martelly, leader of the Peasant Answer party, was elected president after the second round of balloting for the elections held in November 2010 by beating his rival Mirlande Manigat, leader of right-of-center Christian Democratic Rally of the Progressive National Democrats party. As was the case before with Aristide and Préval, the vote for Martelly symbolized a rejection of the candidate of the traditional political class represented this time by Mirlande Manigat. Martelly drew his support largely from the same social sectors who voted for Aristide and Préval, namely, the younger urban and rural poor who are part of the 80 percent of the population who live on less than two dollars a day and have been marginalized, excluded, and rejected by a socio-economic order that caters exclusively to the top 10 percent of the population. This small and wealthy group appropriates 47 percent of the national income, and the richest 2 percent controls 26 percent of the wealth. And it did not matter to that sector of the population who voted for Martelly that Aristide was a left-of-center populist who once preached Liberation Theology and was feared by the wealthy elites and their international allies, and that Martelly, a popular singer from the well-to-do mulatto elite, is a right-of-center populist who despised Aristide and had ties to the neo-Duvalierist military that toppled him in 1991, and whose former members, supported by the bourgeoisie-middle-class opposition, once again forced him out of office in 2004.

However, even though they voted for him, they are realistic enough not to expect him to do what neither Aristide nor Préval could: change the social order or even reform it minimally in their favor. The reasons for this are simple. As I just mentioned, Martelly comes from the business elite and received support from a faction of the business and professional classes, and he will also rely on the major powers and international financial institutions that supply Haiti's financial aid and determine its economic policies.

Moreover, Martelly is beholden to the international community, especially the USA, for making it possible for him to go to the second round to face off with Manigat after Jude Célestin, the candidate of Préval's ruling INITÉ (Unity) party who had initially been ranked ahead of Martelly, was forced to withdraw from the race. Leaving aside the reasons why US relations with Préval soured to the point that the country did not support his party's candidate, it seems clear that the motive was more political than having to do with the refusal to accept flawed elections in Haiti as it had done many times in the past.[7] However, more important than owing his survival as a candidate to the strong-arm pressure of the USA, as president Martelly will confront the structural constraints determined by Haiti's subordinate position in the international division of labor of the capitalist world-economy and over-dependence on foreign aid and investments.

As was the case with Aristide, my objective here is not to analyze the economic policies of the new government, but to focus on the question at hand, namely, the "politics of color" in the post-Duvalier era. Of significance here was a conflict that emerged in the early months between Haiti's parliament and Martelly over his first two choices for prime minister, namely, Daniel Rouzier and Bernard Gousse, before finally ratifying the nomination of Gary Conille in October 2011, and subsequently that of the current Prime Minister, Laurent Lamothe. In rejecting Rouzier earlier in June, the Chamber of

Deputies said it did so because of his failure to pay taxes and his conflict of interests as an honorary consul for Jamaica. But the report the Chamber subsequently released also revealed its other and in my view more important motive for its rejection. Referring to Rouzier as an archetypical representative of the wealthy mulatto bourgeoisie, the Chamber questioned whether he could defend the interests of the middle class and where he stood in regard to the 19th-century credo of the mulatto elite of "power to the most competent." The document went on to say that the mulatto class was also "intimately linked to the overthrow of the democratic order during the past twenty years, and remains the principal obstacle to the growth of a strong middle class by virtue of its control over all the economic and financial levers" (*Haiti en Marche* 2011a).

In August 2011, a group of 16 senators, mostly from former President Préval's INITÉ party, voted to reject the nomination of Bernard Gousse for Prime Minister. However, since the vote was to decide whether Gousse had met the technical, i.e., constitutional, qualifications to be prime minister before the final vote for his ratification, the other 13 senators, many of whom had expressed their support for Gousse, saw no need to vote since it was a foregone conclusion that he would not be ratified. The 16 senators who voted against Gousse made it clear that, unlike the vote against Rouzier by the deputies, theirs was political and not technical. They laid out their views in a letter published the day after Gousse had released his to criticize the senators' decision. In an unmistakable reference to Gousse's role as Minister of Justice under the de facto government of Prime Minister Gérard Latortue and the crack-down he led against supporters of Aristide after he was overthrown and exiled in February 2004, the group of 16 said that they voted to "save the nation from a return in force to fascism ... and to stand against a selective or a generalized and arbitrary repression." Moreover, without referring directly to the report released by the Chamber of Deputies which I cited above, the senators' letter criticized the "famous phrase of the new political discourse" which they also obviously attributed to Gousse, that "the middle class is the motive force of the Haitian economy. But the change that is promised is a change-return to Duvalierism, a return to failure" (*Haiti en Marche* 2011b).

It is obvious, then, that there are deep divisions and contradictory tendencies in parliament between those who want to preserve the state as the purview of the black middle class, those who support Martelly's alliance with the neo-Duvalierist forces, and those who want to prevent their return to power and protect what they see as the fragile gains of the turn to democracy. Although recourse to the black-nationalist ideology of Duvalierism had been in abeyance since the end of the dictatorship in 1986, its reemergence in 2011 suggests that the black-nationalist factions of the middle class felt threatened that, by choosing Rouzier, Martelly, who is also a mulatto, was seeking to return the mulatto bourgeoisie to political power and take control of the executive branch and its offices. This is so despite the fact that Martelly initially aligned himself more with the former barons of the regime of Jean-Claude Duvalier and their descendants than with the mulatto bourgeoisie as such. But by raising the issue of Rouzier's color and the mulatto class's control of all the economic and financial levers, the Chamber of Deputies was clearly saying that they consider the state and its branches of government the preserves of the black middle class.

For its part, the group of senators who came to office under Préval's INITÉ banner and maintain a slight majority in the Senate, sent a clear signal in their vote against Gousse that they consider him a representative of those who want to return to the dictatorial past, a concern heightened by Martelly's alliance with the neo-Duvalierist forces, their inclusion in his government in the persona of their sons, and his interest at the time to reinstate the army Aristide disbanded in 1995. The Senate then joined the Chamber of Deputies in voting to confirm Conille (*Latin American Caribbean and Central America Report* 2012). As an assistant to former US President Bill Clinton who served as co-chair of the Interim Haiti Recovery Commission, and a protégé of "shock therapy" economist Jeffrey Sachs, Conille, no less than Rouzier, was a strong proponent of the dominant neoliberal ideology of free markets, free trade, and foreign investment in the export assembly industry as a panacea for Haiti's underdevelopment and poverty. Conille, however, resigned after four months of conflicts with Martelly and other members of his cabinet. Paradoxically, the same members of the Chamber of Deputies who had voted to reject Rouzier because he was a member of the mulatto elite, joined with the Senate to ratify the nomination of Laurent Lamothe, also a member of the mulatto business class, to replace Conille as Prime Minister (*AlterPresse* 2012). Lamothe also shares the same views as his predecessors. Haiti's new diplomatic objective, he said when he was serving as Foreign Affairs Minister, "is a business diplomacy … A business diplomacy is a change from a diplomacy of representation or of protocol, to one where the practical preoccupation is to encourage a pouring of foreign investment" (*Haïti Libre* 2011).

In my view, then, two main conclusions can be drawn from the foregoing analysis. First, the transition to democracy, precarious and marred as it is by fraudulent practices, has irrevocably displaced "color politics" as a means of acquiring and monopolizing power, and replaced it with the discourse of legitimacy through popular mandate. As the example of the Chamber of Deputies' rejection of Rouzier's nomination for Prime Minister showed, while the ideology of color may still have currency among some factions of the black political class, it is equally contested by other factions, not by having recourse to a "counter-colorist" discourse, but by linking such a discourse with the discredited dictatorial rule of the past.

And second, the substitution of the discourse of legitimacy and democracy for the "politics of color" has in no way altered the class structure of Haiti or the composition of the dominant economic and political class. The black middle class and elite continue to control most of the top functions in the local, municipal, provincial, and national judicial, legislative, executive, and administrative offices, with the difference that for most of those offices they now have to compete for them electorally. The bourgeoisie, as such, both mulatto and black, continues to control the main levers of the economy and hence of the production and accumulation of capital, and mulattoes are still more highly concentrated among the 2 percent of the population that control 27 percent of the country's wealth. Individuals will no doubt carry their identities and prejudices, and use them strategically in their personal and social alliances. But the emergence of the people on the political stage has also signaled the death-knell of color politics as a means to power.

Notes

1 See Chapter Three.
2 Unless otherwise noted, full documentation for the claims I am making in the rest of the essay can be found in Dupuy 1989, esp. chs 3 to 6 passim; 1995; 1997, esp. Chs. 5 and 6 passim; and 2007, esp. Chs. 5 and 6 passim.
3 See Chapter Three.
4 I have argued elsewhere against Trouillot's use of the term "totalitarian" to describe both the objectives and practices of the Duvalier regime (Dupuy 1988). See also Fatton (2013) for a more recent and more extensive critique of Trouillot's "totalitarian" argument.
5 See Dupuy 1997 and 2007 for my analysis of Aristide's truncated presidential terms.
6 For one of the most theoretically sophisticated ethnographic analysis of the "terror apparatus" the military junta that toppled Aristide deployed to crush the popular democratic movement, see Erica C. James' *Democratic Insecurities: Violence, Trauma, and Intervention in Haiti* (2010).
7 See Chapter Six for a fuller analysis of the electoral debacle and the international pressure put on President Préval to remove Célestin from the second round contest.

5 The World Bank and Haiti

Abetting dictatorship,
undermining democracy

In 1996 and again in 1998, the World Bank (henceforth the Bank) issued reports that marked a turning point in its analysis of the causes of under-development and poverty in that Caribbean nation. For the first time since the Bank began to formulate development policy for Haiti in the 1970s, it argued that poverty remained pervasive and even deepened because of the long history of political instability, poor governance, corruption, and the misuse of public funds (World Bank 1998: v). The Bank's criticism went even further. Borrowing the language of the Left, the Bank indicted the entire political system and the dominant wealthy Haitian elite. As the Bank put it,

> Haiti has never had a tradition of governance aimed at providing services to the population or creating an environment conducive to sustainable growth. Instead, a small elite has supported a "predatory state" that makes only negligible investments in human resources and basic infra-structure. At the same time, pervasive repression through army, police, and paramilitary groups has created deep-seated distrust between civil society and the state.
>
> (World Bank 1996: 1; 1998: 14)

Even after the restoration of civilian rule in 1994, the Bank argued, condi-tions had not improved. There continued to be an absence of leadership, charges of corruption, abuse of power, and human rights violations, and the issues of justice, insecurity, economic hardship, and budgetary crisis remained unresolved and exacerbated the situation (World Bank 1998: 14).

When parliamentary elections in 1997 and 2000 resulted in victory for Jean-Bertrand Aristide's political party, *Fanmi Lavalas* (FL—Lavalas Family) and when Aristide himself was re-elected president in 2000 for another five-year term, the USA, Canada, the European Union (EU), the Bank, and other international financial institutions (IFIs—the International Monetary Fund, the Inter-American Development Bank) suspended the disbursement of for-eign aid to Haiti. Also in 2000, the Bank eliminated its representative position in Haiti and managed Haiti affairs from the Dominican Republic. These organizations and governments insisted that for them to re-engage in Haiti the government must carry out critical reforms. In particular, the Bank demanded measures to increase transparency and accountability in public spending. Institutional reforms must also be undertaken, with particular attention paid to the factors that prevent the full implementation of the Bank and International Monetary Fund's (IMF) structural adjustment program. This included above all the privatization of public enterprises and the provision of social services. Lastly, a vigorous civil society must be allowed to flourish so that citizens could "challenge public authorities to enhance their performance and responsiveness to the citizenry" (World Bank 2002b: 20).

The Bank's critical attitude toward the democratically elected governments and its indictment of the predatory state were radically different from its attitude toward the Duvalier dictatorship from 1971 to 1986, as well as the military governments that succeeded Jean-Claude Duvalier between 1986 and 1990. Though the Duvalier regime and the successive military governments were ideal-typical cases of repressive and corrupt predatory states, the Bank looked for reasons to continue to work with and support them. When it criticized the practices of these regimes, the Bank refrained from calling them predatory states that engaged in widespread repression; and it never called on them to be transparent and create the political conditions for the existence of a vibrant civil society that could challenge their authority and hold them accountable. Moreover, the Bank never insisted that the continued flow of foreign aid and loans to these regimes would be contingent on their implementing the requisite reforms and eliminating corruption.

What, then, explains the Bank's suspension of aid in 1991, 1995, 1997, and 2000 to democratically elected governments when it supported the dictatorships for nearly two decades between 1971 and 1990 and again in 2004 when it worked with the unelected Interim Government of Haiti (IGH) imposed by the international community after Aristide's second ouster? Even if one argued that the Bank did not "discover" the concept of "good governance" as a necessary condition for sustainable economic development until 1989 and linked it to the need for democracy a year or two later, it was fully aware of the corruption, brutality, and unaccountability of the dictatorships with which it collaborated. Moreover, it is well known that throughout the 1960s and 1970s the Bank supported murderous military dictatorships in different parts of the world, even after they had overthrown democratically elected governments it had refused to fund, such as in Brazil, Argentina, Chile, Uruguay, Indonesia, and the Philippines (Rich 1994: 99–100). The USA opposed these democratic governments, and if it was not always directly involved in the respective *coups d'état*, it moved quickly to support the military juntas that carried them out. In that period, the Bank's decision to provide or withhold loans to a government had little to do with whether or not a government practiced "good governance" as the Bank now defines it, but with whether or not the USA supported or opposed that government, be it a dictatorship or a democracy.

As I will show below, this continues to be the case. The Bank's support of the dictatorships in Haiti between 1971 and 1990, and its decision to withhold loans from the democratically elected governments in Haiti in 1991, 1995, 1997, and 2000 had more to do with US policy towards these respective governments than with whether or not they complied fully with Bank recommendations and expectations. In 1991 the issue was Aristide's radical views about capitalism and his criticisms of the Duvalier dictatorship, the Haitian bourgeoisie and US imperialism; in 1995 it had to do with Aristide not implementing the neoliberal policies he had agreed to after the USA returned him to power in 1994; in 1997 the problem was with a parliament controlled by Aristide's FL party; and in 2000 the problem became the control of both parliament and the executive branch by Aristide and his FL party. The Bank's use of "governance" to compel implementation of its (and other international financial institutions') "conditionalities," and its disregard of that issue in earlier times, then, is selective, and is to be understood in the context of the changes in the dynamics associated with the current phase of globalization and in particular with US interests.

The politicization of economic reforms occurred in the late 1980s under the aegis of what came to be known as the "Washington Consensus." The "Washington Consensus," also known as the "neoliberal" or "structural adjustment" reforms/policies, became the new mantra of the IFIs, especially after 1989–90. The "Washington Consensus," I will argue, had nothing to do with promoting meaningful and sustainable economic development in the underdeveloped or peripheral countries that adopted its policies, but basically sought to weaken the interventionist powers of the state and open their economies to the markets and capital of the advanced or core capitalist countries, especially those of the USA, Canada, and the EU (Britain, France, and Germany in particular).

In the case of Haiti, the transition to democracy in 1991 and especially after 1994 offered the Bank the opportunity to push for the fuller implementation of the structural adjustment and institutional reforms because it (and the other IFIs) could in effect exercise greater economic leverage against the government by threatening to withhold the delivery of foreign aid monies if it refused. The fact that the post-1990 governments had been elected to office (except for the three years of military rule between 1991 and 1994 and again between 2004 and 2006 under the IGH) made them more vulnerable to external pressure than the dictatorships that retained power, or intended to do so, indefinitely. Moreover, since the collapse of the Soviet Union and the Soviet bloc in 1989, the unchallenged supremacy of capitalism and the discrediting of socialist and state-centered models of development, progressive or would-be progressive governments had nowhere to turn for possible alternative trade partners and sources of support. I will further argue that while the Bank's criticism of the predatory state's anti-developmental policies is correct, the Bank's own policies—and, by extension, those of the other IFIs—were equally anti-developmental. Those policies have led to the steady deterioration of the Haitian economy since the 1970s and its transformation into an essentially labor-exporting economy increasingly dependent on remittances from Haitian migrants, foreign aid, and drugs trafficking.[1] In short, though ostensibly designed to alleviate poverty by stimulating sustainable economic growth, the policies of the Bank and the other IFIs in fact maintained Haiti's position in the international division of labor as a supplier of cheap labor to foreign capital.

Globalization and the World Bank's political conditionalities

The term globalization began to enter popular and academic discourses in the early 1970s. It refers to a process of integration of the economies of the world in the international division of labor of the capitalist world-economy and a concomitant shift of power from nation-states to multinational corporations and other organizations controlled by the core capitalist countries (Evans 1997: 65; Meiksins Wood 1998: 1–2). Globalization may be seen as an unfolding of the internal logic of the capitalist system characterized by dramatic new developments in the international financial system, the concentration of capital, knowledge, information, and technology in the developed countries, the internationalization of production, and the intensification of competition among the core capitalist economies (Meiksins Wood 1998: 2). Competition among the core states has led to a new division of the world-economy into three distinct zones or blocs over which different core states exercise greater or lesser influence: the USA over the North and Latin American bloc (with Brazil emerging as a world player), the European Economic Community where Germany and France vie for dominance over the (West and East) European bloc, and Japan over the East Asian bloc, with the People's Republic of China as a fast-rising global economic power as well. From this it follows that nation-states are integrated in the world-economy through trade, investment, and production relations in proportion to their position in the international division of labor, such that the core economies tend to trade and invest mostly among themselves; Latin America and the Caribbean trade mostly with the USA; the Asian countries trade mostly among themselves and with Japan; and sub-Saharan Africa trades mostly with the EU.

The reconfiguration of the international division of labor associated with the globalization process has not altered the hierarchical structure of the world-economy and the division of labor between the core or developed and the peripheral or underdeveloped countries. The new international division of labor is characterized by a shift from capital-intensive to technology- or information-based production and services in the core economies, and capital- and labor-intensive industries in the lower-wage countries. Thus, the position of countries in the international division of labor is still determined by the types of goods and services they produce: whether high-value goods and services based on highly skilled and informational labor (predominantly in core countries); whether high-volume goods and services with lower-cost labor (predominantly in advanced semi-peripheral countries such as Mexico, Chile, South Korea, and Taiwan, and some sectors in core countries); or whether raw materials based on natural endowments, redundant, devalued, and marginalized labor in peripheral countries (sub-Saharan Africa, parts of Asia, Latin America and the Caribbean) (Castells 1996: 145–47; Wallerstein 2003: 45–68).

Even the World Bank recognizes that the current phase of globalization has not benefited all countries equally. Some of the countries it calls the "new globalizers," 24 in all, have experienced high levels of growth by opening their economies and improving their climates for foreign capital investment to make the shift from primary commodity exports to the production of manufactured goods and services for the world market. The rest of the developing world, incorporating some 2 billion people (excluding China and India), however, has not made the transition. These countries not only remain poor, but were (in 2002) trading even less than they did 20 years ago. The Bank simply called them "losers." Globalization, then, produced "winners" and "losers," both within and between countries; and the "losers," with declining incomes and increasing poverty, are becoming increasingly redundant and marginalized in the world-economy. For many of these countries, the Bank concluded, it may be too late for them to reverse their situation even if they pursued the Bank's policies of "openness." This is because world demand for manufactures and services was limited. Moreover, agglomeration economies lead firms from the advanced countries to locate in clusters, and while there may be room for many clusters, countries that offer the advantage of low-cost labor may find it difficult to attract firms that are already located in other labor-abundant countries (World Bank 2002b: 1–7, 38–40). Despite this conclusion, the Bank and the other IFIs have not reconsidered their argument that adopting the "right policies" is the best way for the "losers" to participate in and benefit from globalization (World Bank 2002b: 36–38).

Even analysts sympathetic to Bank policies who evaluated the performance of the developing countries that followed Bank policies during the 1980s and 1990s concluded that their response

> has not been what could have been expected ... Zero per capita growth on average after major reforms is a disappointing outcome whatever the cause ... Many, even stationary, country characteristics widely thought to be favorable for growth (or at least favorable for level of income) have improved, yet developing countries on average have stagnated. This in itself is a blow to the optimism surrounding the "Washington Consensus" prior to the experience of the last two decades.
>
> (Easterly 2001: 138)

Moreover, as William Easterly, Michael Kremer, Lant Pritchett, and Lawrence Summers found, there is no correlation between country characteristics and growth rates over time. "With a few famous exceptions, the same countries do not do well period after period; countries are 'success stories' one period and disappointments the next" (Easterly *et al.* 1993: 460). Joseph Stiglitz reached a similar conclusion:

Despite repeated promises of poverty reduction made over the last decade of the twentieth century, the actual number of people living in poverty has actually increased by almost 100 million. This occurred at the same time that total world income actually increased by an average of 2.5 percent annually.

(Stiglitz 2002: 5)

It is at this juncture that one can best understand the convergence between the dynamics of globalization and the ideological propositions clustered under the "Washington Consensus." Formulated in the 1980s[2] by the US Treasury Department, the World Bank, and the IMF, the "Washington Consensus" reflected the ideology and political objectives of the state actors and policy makers of the Ronald Reagan Administration. It corresponded with the collapse of the Soviet system and the discrediting of central planning and state-centered development models of the 1950s to the 1970s in the Third World (Naim 2000: 509). As Easterly put it, the "new consensus" emphasized "market-friendly economic policies by developing country governments. The development consensus shifted away from state planning towards markets, away from import substitution towards outward orientation, away from state controls of prices and interest rates towards 'getting the prices right'" (Easterly 2001: 135). The advocates of the "Consensus" exploited the huge debts accumulated by peripheral Third World countries—largely at the urgings of the Bank itself—to demand that they restructure their economies, open them more to the operation of the market, and facilitate the takeover of their assets by foreign capital.

Basically, the "Consensus" view held that to achieve macrostability, the debtor countries of Latin America, Asia, and Africa needed to "liberalize" their economies, that is, lower or eliminate tariff barriers, deregulate their markets, and end subsidies to and privatize their public-sector enterprises. Many of these ideas were incorporated in Bank analyses and recommendations before the 1980s, but since the end of the Cold War the Bank and the IMF began to insist even more on making loans conditional on carrying out the mandated reforms. This insistence was based on the belief that the borrowing countries could undergo economic expansion and growth only if they removed all restrictions on imports and exports, allowed foreign currency transactions, and opened their economies to outside investments (Soederberg 2001: 454). As Moises Naim points out, however, what the IFIs and the governments that were called upon to implement the core requirements of the "Consensus" understood by that term changed throughout the 1990s.

Reforming governments everywhere saw how the policy goals that just a few years, or even months, earlier had been specified as the final frontier of the reform process became just a mere precondition for success. New, more complex, and more difficult goals were constantly added to the list of requirements for an acceptable performance.

(Naim 2000: 508)

However, even when the advocates of the "Consensus" admitted that it had become a "damaged brand," as John Williamson himself did in 2002, and former British Prime Minister Gordon Brown declared it dead in 2009, the IFIs continued to adhere to its prescriptions and looked instead to lay the blame for its failures on the countries that had implemented the reforms. As Dani Rodrik summarizes the new thinking, referred to as "second generation reforms," the "developing countries had to work harder. It wasn't enough to slash import tariffs and eliminate barriers to trade; open trade policies had to be underpinned by extensive reforms in public administration, by labor market 'flexibility,' and by international trade agreements." Institutions also had to be reformed by "giving central banks independence, and of course better politics. Property rights required extensive reforms in governance and legal regimes" (Rodrik 2011: 171–72). In other words, and as Naim has argued previously, the original policy was still considered sound, but the laundry list of what developing countries had to do now to "get it right" was just extended, not reconsidered (Rodrik 2011: 172). As I will show below, the case of Haiti fits that pattern very well.

The Bank and the dictatorships in Haiti, 1971–90

By all measures, Haiti would have to be considered one of those "loser" states that did not live up to the expectations of the "Washington Consensus" even though the Bank classified it among the "more globalized" countries, that is, states that have followed Bank policies, "opened up" to foreign capital and the world market, and have had increased trade to gross domestic product (GDP) ratios from the 1970s to the 1990s (World Bank 2002a: 51, fn. 3). Given that the Bank (along with the other IFIs) seems incapable of rethinking how their policies reinforce a country's underdevelopment and inequalities, it could only focus on Haiti's poor institutions and poor governance as being primarily responsible for its failure to grow. That is, as mentioned above, Haiti had to do more than just being open to foreign capital and the world market: "Without fundamental reforms to the political and institutional obstacles to progress, no other reforms, however important in their own right, will work" (World Bank 2002b: 3–4). In addition to the political conflicts that characterized the transition to democracy,[3] the Bank identified the following factors as the primary causes of the country's poor economic performance: the lack of public-sector capacity for aid absorption; the disappearance of many of the institutions that existed under the Duvalier regime; the brain drain that has depleted the ranks of professionals and technicians; the failure to decentralize and offer financial support to public institutions and to secure political support from the center; and the absence of public financial accountability and oversight of public spending by Parliament that has encouraged corruption, and the misuse and misallocation of government expenditures as well as of external funding for public-sector projects (World Bank 2002a: 3–4).

However, the Bank did not always explain Haiti's poor economic performance in these terms. Indeed, the Bank believed that the Duvalier and post-Duvalier military dictatorships could and did achieve rapid economic growth when they followed the "right" policies considered essential at the time, without their having pursued political reforms, been transparent or accountable to the elected representatives of the people in Parliament, or tolerated the existence of a vibrant civil society that participated in public affairs and challenged public authorities.

The following summary of the performance of the Haitian economy from the 1970s to 1990, drawn in large part from Bank reports, tells the story. When "Baby Doc" Jean-Claude Duvalier inherited the "presidency-for-life" from his father in 1971, the USA, the Bank, the IMF, and the Inter-American Development Bank (IDB) committed themselves to supporting the regime. The young dictator was determined to preserve the corrupt practices and repressive apparatuses of the predatory state system his father had instituted (Dupuy 1989: 155–85). Though it never broached the subject of political reforms, that is, democratization, and human rights violations, that is, repression and murder, the Bank repeatedly admonished the government to undertake budgetary reforms to curb "waste and expenditure that would not stand scrutiny," and "unidentified recurrent expenditure, especially 'Special Obligations' and 'sans justification' budget lines," and to use the misused and misappropriated funds for development (World Bank 1987: xv).

The regime, however, was committed to the free market system. Haiti was seen as an "open" economy with a fully convertible currency and no controls on foreign capital flows and foreign exchange. Moreover, the regime was receptive to the development strategy recommended by the USA and the Bank, and willing to offer all the necessary advantages to foreign, mainly US, investors. In short, the regime created a climate the Bank thought favored economic growth and social development. In 1981, Ernest Preeg, US Ambassador to Haiti from 1981 to 1983, boasted "the stage was set for what was to be the most active period of collaboration between [the] two governments in at least twenty-five years" (Preeg 1985: 22).

The advantages that especially attracted foreign investors to Haiti consisted primarily of an abundant supply of unskilled and cheap, but "dexterous, and relatively non-militant" labor; the close proximity to the US market; no foreign exchange controls, and free circulation of the US dollar; the absence of government interference; the exemptions on income and profit taxes; the tax exemptions on imported raw materials, machinery, or other assets used in the operation of the assembly industries; and the exemptions on the export of the assembled products (World Bank 1976: ii, 11; 1978: 21, 35). The rationale given by the development agencies and the government for keeping wages low was that even though the wage gap between Haitian workers and workers elsewhere in the region may be high enough to offset productivity, transportation, tariff, and other costs, "they may not be able to offset the bureaucratic and political risks in Haiti which [were] still perceived as formidable. Thus assembly industry may be lost if wages [rose] to higher levels, [even if they remained] below those of relevant international competitors" (Grunwald, Delatour, and Voltaire 1984: 237–38; also in Dupuy 1989: 177). The Bank is still making the same argument today.

In other words, unless workers' demands for higher wages and better working conditions were suppressed and the government made all the concessions demanded of it, foreign investors would simply move their operations elsewhere. As the Bank itself recognized implicitly in its analysis of the current phase of globalization, with an abundant and untapped supply of cheap labor in the "loser" countries of the periphery, capital from the core countries has a great deal of leverage to compel governments desperate for foreign investments to offer the maximum advantage to the latter.

With significant infusion of foreign financial and technical assistance for public-sector and infrastructure expenditures and foreign investments in the sub-contracting export assembly industries, the Haitian economy experienced rapid economic growth between 1970 and 1977. Real GDP grew at an annual rate of 4.1 percent during that period, compared to the 1960s when the economy stagnated. The assembly industry, construction, and public utilities emerged as the most dynamic sectors. Substantial increases in coffee prices during that time also benefited Haitian coffee exports and contributed to the GDP growth as well. Overall, however, the agricultural sector, which employed about 74 percent of the labor force during that period, remained weak. Even though domestic crop production increased at an annual average rate of 2.2 percent during the period, this was not enough to meet the growing demand for food and to increase exports. Consequently food imports rose significantly during that period and worsened Haiti's foreign trade balance. Haiti's total exports paid for only 75 percent of imports. Industrial growth averaged 7 percent per year during that period—compared to an average of 0.6 percent per year during the 1960s—and contributed about 13 percent to GDP in 1977 (World Bank 1978: i–iii, 9–10). By the end of the 1970s, assembly exports accounted for about 25 percent of all the income generated in the manufacturing sector and about the same proportion of Haiti's export earnings; and it employed 80 percent of the industrial workforce. Eighty percent of the industrial labor force, however, represented only about 7 percent of the total labor force (Dupuy 1989: 175; World Bank 1978: ii). Today, the apparel industry accounts for nearly 90 percent of Haiti's exports and 20 percent of its GDP. The 23 apparel industries employ a total of 25,000 workers, which represent 58 percent of the industrial labor force, but only 0.5 percent of the total labor force (Bell 2013; CIA 2013). With a current official unemployment rate of 41 percent, the apparel industry is not the panacea the Bank had hoped it would be.

Despite the optimistic predictions of the proponents of the export assembly strategy, it had a short-lived "golden age" of expansion between 1970 and the early 1980s, and began to decline after 1984 (Dupuy 1997: 27). The Bank itself gave most of the reasons why. In addition to not solving the unemployment crisis, the assembly industry had at best a neutral effect on income distribution, but a negative effect on the balance of goods and services because it encouraged more imports of consumer goods. The industry also contributed little to government revenues because of the tax exemptions on profits and other fiscal incentives, which, along with the subsidized costs of public services and utilities, represented a transfer to the foreign investors and the Haitian entrepreneurs who subcontracted with them for the operation of the assembly industries. Other than construction and services (transportation and catering services), the assembly industry did not contribute to the expansion of other industrial sectors because it imported its raw materials and other industrial inputs rather than relying on domestic supplies; and its products were not used by other Haitian industries but exported to the USA. The processing industry is entirely dependent on the US market for its products—because it relies on contracts from US firms—thus when the limits on US import quotas are met, or if demand decreases, the industry cannot expand its production.

Because the assembly industry relies almost exclusively on unskilled and cheap labor, it neither stimulates the growth of a skilled industrial labor force nor attracts more advanced capital-intensive industries, thereby preventing the transfer of technologies and the development of new industrial sectors. Moreover, the assembly industry drains more foreign exchange than it brings in. It does this in two ways. First, except for the Haitian factory owners most of the profits of the foreign investors are not reinvested in that sector, and the absence of expanded investment opportunities leads Haitian entrepreneurs—involved in the assembly industries and other sectors of the economy—to invest their savings outside of Haiti, most often in the USA. Second, the import of consumer and producers' goods (intermediate and capital goods) surpasses the total exports of the modern industrial sector, thereby draining foreign exchange from the economy.

In light of its own analysis, then, the Bank could not but conclude that the "impact that industry—[both the foreign- and Haitian-owned assembly industries]—has had on the development of the economy as a whole has remained limited. Even [in the years when the expansion of the assembly industry] was particularly marked, little of this dynamism trickled down to other sectors" (World Bank 1978: ii–iii, 3, 21–25). The Bank reached this conclusion before the assembly industry went into decline after 1984 and would never again reach the level of employment of the 1970s.

This fact, and the Bank's own assessment of the negative effects of the processing industry on the overall economy notwithstanding, it continued to advocate the export assembly strategy until such time that Haiti could develop its agriculture, expand its infrastructure, educate its labor force, and diversify its industrial infrastructure. However, as the experience of the period under consideration as well as the Bank's own data showed, the Bank's optimism was ill-founded. Despite the importance of agriculture to the economy, it received an average of 9.7 percent of public investments between 1972 and 1976; education received 5.2 percent; and health received 6.7 percent (World

Bank 1985: 164). In other words, as the Bank was fully aware, the dictatorship and the tiny wealthy Haitian elite it was fully supporting had a long tradition of enriching themselves by appropriating all they could from the population while providing few essential services and failing to create the conditions for sustainable human development in return. By 1976, the Bank recognized that Haiti's income distribution had become extremely skewed. Seventy-five percent of the population lived in conditions of absolute poverty. The average per capita national income was about US $190, but more than 60 percent of the population received an annual income of around $60. At the upper end of the income distribution curve, however, about 5 percent of the population appropriated more than 50 percent of the national income, and the average per capita income of the highest income bracket comprising less than 1 percent of the population was 176 times as high as the lowest bracket comprising about 61 percent of the population (World Bank 1978: vi). In 2012 its GDP per capita income had risen to $1,300 and it ranked 208 out of 229 countries in the world, below all the countries of the Caribbean, Central, and South America. Eighty percent of the population of 10 million people lived below the poverty level, and 54 percent in absolute poverty; life expectancy at birth was 63 years (61 for men, 64 for women); and 53 percent (aged 15 and over) were literate. Haiti is also one of the most unequal societies in the world. In 2001 the top 10 percent of the population possessed 47.7 percent of total income and the bottom 10 percent possessed 0.7 percent, making it the seventh country in the world (out of 136 measured) with the highest income inequality (Ministère de la Planification et de la Coopération Externe n.d.: 10; Dupuy 2010; CIA 2013).

The industrial sector was not the only sector of the economy that failed to generate sustainable development in response to the Bank's export-oriented strategy. Its liberalization policies had equally devastating effects on Haitian agriculture. In 1985 the agricultural sector employed about 65 percent of the active population and accounted for about 35 percent of GDP (World Bank 1991a: 35). Today 38 percent are occupied in agriculture, and it contributes 25 percent of GDP (CIA 2013). Between 1986 and 1988, the governments (three military and one quasi civilian) that succeeded the 29-year old Duvalier dictatorship (1957–86) implemented a series of reforms that dealt with fiscal management and taxes, import and export tariffs, public spending, the public enterprises, price fixing and price controls, free market competition, and inducements to investments. At the same time that government spending was reduced, taxes on basic consumer goods were lowered, as were their prices. Income taxes were modified; import taxes were replaced with ad valorem taxes; quantitative restrictions on most imports were eliminated; and subsidies to and protection of domestic import-substitution industries were limited to encourage free market prices and competition. Taxes on the export of coffee and other agricultural products were gradually lowered or completely eliminated. And two unprofitable industrial public enterprises were closed and others were streamlined (World Bank 1991a: 4).

As a result of these measures, the economy showed signs of modest growth in real GDP; internal and external imbalances were reduced, as was inflation, and employment rates grew at 1.6 percent per year. However, by mid-1987 the economy had experienced a downturn and continued to deteriorate until 1990 (World Bank 1991a: ii–iii). Despite evidence to the contrary, the Bank believed that the reforms being pursued by the military dictatorships would have led to higher GDP growth rates in all sectors, including agriculture, had it not been for the negative effects of the political unrest and contraband imports on domestic agricultural prices (World Bank 1991a: 4, 32–33). The "political unrest" the Bank alluded to but did not identify was in fact the popular democratic movement the military tried to suppress between 1986 and 1990 that culminated in the election of Jean-Bertrand Aristide to the presidency in November 1990.

By blaming these "historical events" for aborting the beneficial effects of the reforms of 1986–87, the Bank seemed to suggest that the democracy movement was unfortunate since it prevented the military governments from providing "a reasonable framework for economic development" (World Bank 1991a: 34). Thus, even though the Bank had developed the concept of "good governance" in its 1989 report *From Crisis to Sustainable Growth—Sub-Saharan Africa: A Long Term Perspective*, and linked it to its concerns with institutional reforms and public sector management in the 1980s (World Bank 2000: 15), it was not yet ready to argue in 1991 that the post-Duvalier military dictatorships in Haiti were incompatible with sound economic policies.

If the Bank avoided linking "good governance" with democracy and sound economic policies in the late 1980s in Haiti, it also disregarded other evidence that the trade and other reforms adopted by the military regimes had devastating effects on Haitian agriculture and did not lead to a rebounding of the export processing industry. There is no doubt that the illicit trade in consumer goods in which government and military officials participated hurt domestic food production. But the lack of government support for the agricultural sector (infrastructure development, technical support, credit facilities, etc.) and the lowering or removal of the protective tariffs that accompanied the first set of structural adjustment reforms implemented in 1986 were also detrimental. Haitian rice farmers, for example, were especially hard hit by the trade liberalization measures. The Haitian market soon became flooded with subsidized "Miami rice" that sold for less than the rice produced in Haiti. As a result, household rice consumption doubled and domestic rice production fell steadily to the point that by 1995 Haitian farmers produced only about 50 percent of domestic needs. Rice imported from the USA made up the difference. In 1984, Haiti imported 5,000 metric tons (MT) of rice from the USA, but by 1995 the level reached nearly 200,000 MT, thereby making Haiti the highest per capita consumer of rice in the western hemisphere. Equally significant was the fact that a single US rice corporation, in partnership with a Haitian subsidiary, had a monopoly on rice imports (Richardson 1997: 5–6; McGowan 1997: 24–25).

Other domestic food crops suffered the same fate as rice. As other imports became known, mostly via food aid from the USA, and sold for less than those produced locally, such as corn and other cereals, tubers, and vegetables, they altered the tastes and consumption patterns of Haitian consumers to the detriment of domestic producers of these crops. At the same time, a policy urged by USAID and adopted by the Duvalier regime in the early 1980s in response to the African Swine-Fever that entered Haiti from the Dominican Republic virtually wiped out the domestic pig population in Haiti. With funds from US agricultural interest groups, the Haitian government slaughtered more than one million Haitian pigs valued at US $600 million, thereby dealing a heavy blow to Haitian farmers who historically relied on their pigs as a form of savings. The attempt to substitute US-imported pigs to replace the Haitian pig population failed because the former were not suited for conditions in Haiti.[4] Consequently hundreds of thousands of small Haitian farmers lost their source of income and were uprooted. The consequence of these policies, combined with the erosion of the soil, gradually transformed Haiti into a net importer of foodstuffs and led to a growing food insecurity for the vast majority (57 to 80 percent of the population) that is estimated to be living below the poverty level. Whereas Haiti was nearly self-sufficient in food production in the 1960s and imported about 19 percent of its food needs in the 1970s, in 1981 it imported 23 percent and 42 percent in 1993. Today Haiti imports 60 percent of all its food, 80 percent of its rice from the USA, and is the third largest importer of foodstuffs from the USA in the Caribbean (Richardson 1997: 3–5; *Caribbean Report* 2003: 3; Bell 2010; O'Connor 2013; Cohen 2013: 598).

The point of this summary, then, is that until 1990, and disregarding evidence to the contrary, the Bank believed that the Duvalier and post-Duvalier military dictatorships were capable of pursuing the "right" policies and reforms that opened the Haitian economy to foreign investments and markets, stimulated the private sector, and led to real GDP growth, all without having to democratize. According to the Bank, it was, in fact, the unfortunate "series of political crises" that erupted in mid-1987 that interrupted the path to recovery being pursued by the military dictatorship of General Henri Namphy. As such, it is fair to conclude, as Gerard Schmitz did, that at least until 1990, the "key thing [for the Bank] to ask of developing countries was not whether they were democracies or autocracies, but whether they had the governing will and wherewithal to create the 'appropriate policy framework' required to achieve efficient markets and the successful implementation of donor and creditor-mandated economic liberalization programs" (Schmitz 1995: 69).

The World Bank and the transition to democracy

The Bank initially welcomed the election of Aristide to the presidency in November 1990, seeing it as a "window of opportunity" that could allow the country to "move towards sustained social and economic progress." But that would be the case, the Bank argued, only if the government pursued the "right" policies, which, by 1991, the Bank had called the "market-friendly approach to development" in keeping with the prescriptions of the "Washington Consensus" (World Bank 1991b: 1). For low-income "developing" countries like Haiti, the Bank argued, the state must play a complementary role for the private sector by providing a "stable macroeconomic environment," and be open to trade and market competition, both domestically and internationally. Because the domestic market is too small, the economy must be export-oriented and opened to foreign investments. This argument was simply a rehash of previous Bank recommendations, with the only difference that now the target was the state itself and not just the policies it adopted. The objective was to reduce as much as possible the role or intervention of the state in the economy and maximize that of the private sector by adopting the standard structural adjustment program. Henceforth, the issue of what to do with the public-sector enterprises became a central focus of the recommended reforms. The Bank recommended that some of the nine main public-sector enterprises[5] could be privatized or opened to private participation by selling stocks or shares, whereas others could be streamlined and provided with a better regulatory framework to maintain their efficiency (World Bank 1991a: 11–13, 20–23).

Aristide had been elected on a populist and left-of-center platform, however, and to maintain the support of his mass base he espoused an anti-capitalist rhetoric and promised to eradicate past injustices, dismantle the predatory and repressive apparatuses of the Duvalierist state, and prioritize the interests of the impoverished masses. At the same time, in an effort not to alienate the business class whose investments he needed to encourage, Aristide promised to safeguard their property and enter into a partnership with them, but his dual and contradictory discourse succeeded only in alienating the Haitian bourgeoisie. The USA labelled Aristide a "radical firebrand," and the Duvalierists, who tried but failed to prevent him from taking power in February 1991, vowed to overthrow him (Dupuy 1997: 71–76). Once he assumed power in February 1991, however, Aristide pursued an economic program in line with much of the Bank's and the IMF's structural adjustment policies and reached agreement with them shortly before the Haitian military overthrew him in September 1991.

When the US-led multinational force returned Aristide to office in October 1994 the Bank and the other IFIs adopted a tougher attitude toward him.[6] As one of the conditions of his return, Aristide was compelled to accept the Emergency Economic Recovery Program (EERP) devised in Washington by a multinational task force of the IDB, the World Bank, the IMF, and USAID. The stipulations of the EERP, which became incorporated in the Haitian government's Strategy of Social and Economic Reconstruction, contained all the elements of the structural adjustment program. However, it went further than the Bank's recommendations to the Haitian government in 1991 by emphasizing the immediate or partial sale of several public enterprises. Rather than referring to this policy as the privatization of the public enterprises, the government preferred to call it their "modernization" or "democratization" to placate the opponents of the policy (Ministère de la Planification et de la Coopération Externe 1994: 6).

Foreign governmental and non-governmental organizations that are not accountable to the people of Haiti through their elected representatives in parliament devised the reforms that became accepted by Aristide's government in 1994. A new parliament and president were elected in 1995,[7] but they inherited the externally imposed policies which they were expected to implement in return for the release of foreign aid and loans. Here, then, was the new paradox that confronted the democratically elected governments of Aristide in 1991/ 1994, René Préval in 1996, and Aristide again in 2000 (and Préval again in 2006 and Michel Martelly in 2011). At the same time that Haiti was embarking on a precarious transition to democracy, its governments were being made more responsive and accountable to international institutions rather than to the people. Tying the release of foreign aid to the implementation of Bank and IMF policies, then, not only represented a radical break with the Bank's dealings with the dictatorships, but contradicted its equation of democracy with a government that is accountable to the people and encourages a civil society that can "challenge public authorities to enhance their performance and responsiveness to the citizenry" (Schmitz 1995: 70). Indeed, the Bank was well aware that a vibrant civil society could be an obstacle to the adoption of its policies if a government was more responsive to the former than to the Bank.

The Bank, then, faced a serious dilemma as it tried to link good governance and liberal democracy with the pursuit of the free market ideology of the "Washington Consensus." As Schmitz argues, if, as a result of widespread popular opposition and anti-government protests against the adjustment policies in the peripheral countries,

> governments with domestic democratic legitimacy were to begin to repudiate, rather than enforce, the Bank's development model, the unintended consequences of the "crisis of governance" would indeed hit home! The contrast between democracy's appeal and its unreliability (for elite-approved purposes) spells looming trouble for the notion that "good governance"—on terms decided by governing elites in the North for their counterparts in the South—is just the rescue operation that is needed to sustain the dominant economic development model and the "orderly" integration of developing economies into the global capitalist political economy.
>
> (Schmitz 1995: 70, 72)

This is exactly the situation the Bank and the IMF faced in Haiti. Aristide claimed in an interview he had with Catherine Orenstein after he left office in 1996 that

> the neo-liberal economic program will not solve our economic reality. Globalization and neo-liberalization promise solutions for the poor, but I

don't see that happening anywhere in the world ... The poor are becoming poorer, and Haiti is the poorest country of the Western world. Economically speaking, neo-liberalism is a kind of colonialism.

(Orenstein 1998: 16)

Yet, when the USA returned him to office in 1994 he went ahead with implementing the neoliberal and privatization policies mandated by the IFIs and stipulated in the government's Strategy of Social and Economic Reconstruction. But when these policies met with strong popular opposition in 1995, rather than taking responsibility for them, Aristide blamed and publicly distanced himself from his Prime Minister, Smarck Michel, who was forced to resign. Aristide then replaced Michel with Claudette Werleigh, who was in Michel's cabinet and belonged to the faction in parliament opposed to the neoliberal reforms. Werleigh immediately suspended further implementation of the reforms, especially those concerning the sale of the major public enterprises. The IFIs responded by halting the delivery of aid moneys to the government until it resumed the reforms (Dupuy 1997: 171; James 2002).

In the same interview mentioned above, Aristide admitted that as a poor country Haiti had no choice but to negotiate with the international financial institutions and the USA as the largest aid donors, and "evaluate what we can accept and what we cannot." But that argument is disingenuous. With Haiti dependent on foreign aid for 65 percent of its operating budget, Aristide knew that the IFIs were not negotiating with him but simply dictating their terms. The Bank conceded that in Haiti a "broad spectrum of grassroots organizations and members of parliament," as well as others "are ideologically opposed to structural adjustment," and sectors of the "economic elite who [benefit] from the lack of appropriate government structures and control (e.g., through large scale tax evasion)" remain "skeptical of the role of donors in the reform process." Consequently, these groups needed "to be convinced of the benefits of economic reform and a revised role of the state" (World Bank 1996: 5–6). The method the Bank and the IMF would use to "convince" opponents of their policies in Haiti, however, would not be through the give and take of negotiations but by blackmailing them.

As the "Report of Congressional Staff Delegation to Haiti" made clear, continued financial support from the IFIs was contingent on the implementation of the neoliberal policies (Scheunemann *et al.* 1996). As the newly elected Haitian parliament was scheduled to debate the government's economic program for ratification in May 1996, the Managing Director of the IMF, Michael Camdessus, traveled to Haiti to sign the agreement reached between the government and the IMF, and to remind the parliamentarians of their responsibility: "President Préval made [the program] his responsibility," Camdessus declared, and "I have no doubt that the Haitian people as well as the parliament will do the same ... Should the Haitian people through their representatives reject this program, it will have to accept responsibility for that [decision] ... [because this would represent] not only a rejection of the assistance it desperately needs, but also, of the entire policy of the international community and of President Préval for Haiti." To reinforce his point, Camdessus warned that while the US $1.2 billion in foreign aid that the IFIs promised to Haiti was guaranteed this would not be forever because there were many other demands and "there is a crisis in international assistance" (*Haiti en Marche* 1996). Despite mounting popular opposition, the members of parliament got the message and voted for the government's privatization and administrative reform program in September 1996. The IMF subsequently released $226 million in foreign aid (Taft-Morales 2002: 2).

The political climate worsened in 1996 when a major split occurred within the broad Lavalas Political Platform coalition in power since Aristide's return in 1994. Tensions between the Organisation Politique Lavalas (OPL—Lavalas Political Organization) and Aristide's faction increased and reached the point of rupture in November 1996. The dispute had more to do with the creation of a democratically structured political party, which Aristide opposed, than with serious ideological differences around the structural adjustment policies. Aristide left the coalition and formed his own *Fanmi Lavalas* (FL—Lavalas Family) political party. It became immediately apparent that the OPL would have difficulty maintaining its majority in parliament. The April 1997 elections bore this out. The OPL[8] claimed that the Conseil Électoral Provisoire (CEP—Provisional Electoral Council) had rigged the elections in favor of Aristide's FL candidates; it demanded the creation of a new CEP and boycotted the second round, which President Préval ultimately cancelled. The Clinton Administration, which initially considered the elections "free and fair," changed its mind when it realized that the FL had fared well in the first round and was poised to win enough seats in the second round to have veto power in parliament. In that event it was feared that the FL could block the further implementation of the structural adjustment reforms supported by the OPL and Prime Minister Rosny Smart. The issue for the USA, it must be noted, has never been whether a government was elected in free and fair elections, but rather whether that government was willing to defend its policies. Prime Minister Smarth resigned in June 1997 over the election results and the stalled privatization reforms.

Since President Préval had cancelled the second round, the OPL, which by then had changed its name to Organisation du Peuple en Lutte (still OPL—Organization of the People in Struggle), retained a slight majority in parliament and blocked several attempts to replace Prime Minister Smarth. In January 1999 President Préval refused to renew parliament's term that had expired, and ruled by decree until the end of his five-year term in February 2001. The IFIs had suspended the further release of the monies earmarked for Haiti pending the resolution of this crisis with the election of a new parliament and president in 2000 (Dupuy 2003: 4).

The parliamentary and presidential elections of 2000, however, not only failed to resolve the political crisis; they deepened it. With Aristide assured of winning the presidential election in November, the candidates for his FL party swept the May parliamentary elections as well. As a result, the OPL became a minority party. Soon after the elections however, the OPL and other parties formed a new coalition called the Convergence Démocratique (CD—Democratic Convergence)[9] to oppose Aristide and immediately won the support of the USA. The CD declared the entire elections to have been fraudulent; however, if its exaggerated and unsubstantiated allegations lacked credibility, it was not so easy to dismiss the charges made by the Organization of American States (OAS) of irregularities and other malpractices in the electoral process. The OAS noted several problems in some local and municipal contests, but it validated them none the less. It also validated the results of the elections for the Chamber of Deputies, the lower house of parliament, where Aristide's FL eventually won 72 of 83 seats in the second round. On the other hand, the OAS challenged the illegal method the CEP used to calculate the returns in the senatorial polling that granted a first round victory to eight FL candidates who in fact had received less than the 50 percent + 1 majority necessary to avoid a second round. Unchallenged, that outcome would have given the FL 18 of the 19 seats contested out of the 27 seats in the Senate, thereby granting Aristide's party overwhelming control of both houses of parliament. The OAS insisted on a recount and a second round for the eight seats awarded to FL in the Senate, but the CEP refused. The OAS in turn refused to monitor the second round elections in July as well as the presidential election in November. Subsequently the USA and the IFIs suspended nearly US $600 million in foreign aid and debt relief to Haiti.

The primary reason the USA and the OAS did not allow the CEP to get away with the malpractices in the 2000 elections was because Aristide's party won them and would have had overwhelming control of both houses of parliament, and also because there was by then an opposition the USA supported.[10] The important point then, is this. As a result of elections they did not like, both in 1997 and in 2000, the USA, the EU, and the IFIs suspended loans and foreign aid to Haiti. Thus, the suspension of aid was political in the strict sense of the term, based as it was on those entities' disapproval of the political party and president who came to power after these elections. The aid embargo had nothing to do with the Aristide government's rejection of the structural adjustment reforms or "poor governance," since it was denied aid before it became the official government in February 2001. Moreover, even assuming that Aristide and his party in parliament opposed the reforms, it does not follow that they lacked democratic legitimacy as a result. That there came to be a "crisis of governance" during Aristide's second term[11] is beside the point and after the fact in any case.

To make the point differently, consider the attitude of the USA and the IFIs in 1997 when Préval was in power and the parliament was dominated by the OPL. As I already mentioned (see Note 8), the OPL gained a majority in parliament through fraudulent elections in 1995 but the USA and the UN still accepted the results because the OPL and Préval supported the structural adjustment reforms. The USA and the IFIs offered financial aid to the Préval government until the parliamentary elections of 1997 changed the balance of power in favor of Aristide's Lavalas party. Moreover, even though the USA and the IFIs considered the Préval government legitimate, charges of corruption, abuse of power, and human rights violations abounded, as the Bank noted in its 1998 report. These facts, then, challenged the Bank's equation of "good governance" with democratic legitimacy, and both with economic growth. At issue was whether a government subjected to the dictates of the Bank supported, or could be trusted to implement, the reforms of the "second generation" Washington Consensus, whatever their consequences might be for the country to adopt them. Stated differently, the Bank was not concerned with how a government won elections or governed once in power; it cared only about the implementation of its mandated reforms.

Despite the aid embargo against his new government, Aristide did not thwart the "liberalization" of the economy demanded by the Bank and the IMF. As the former and late Minister of Planning and External Cooperation, Marc Bazin,[12] pointed out in his reply to the Bank in 2001, Haiti had one of the more open and liberal economies in Latin America. The average basic tariff was 5 percent, and zero for more than half of the 1,600 tariff positions. The exchange rate system remains flexible and the rate of exchange between the national currency (the gourde) and the US dollar fluctuates freely according to market conditions; and the foreign debt in relation to the GDP is relatively low. As Bazin concluded,

> the liberalization effort has taken place virtually without a decent level of external aid and Haiti has paid a very high price for its foray into globalization, given, in particular, the inadequacy of human and physical resources, as reflected in particular in higher unemployment, reduced purchasing power, greater inequalities, and low per capita food production.
> (Bazin 2001: 70–71)

Neither the Aristide government nor the Bank and the other IFIs proposed any solution other than to pursue the same failed policies of the past. Still believing that Haiti's cheap labor was its best asset, the Bank sought to expand the export manufacturing industry by linking it with its counterpart in the neighboring Dominican Republic. The World Bank's International Finance Corporation (IFC) approved a US $20 million loan to help build the Codevi industrial free trade zone on a 780-square meter area near the border with the Dominican Republic as the first of 14 projected free trade zones that began to operate in 2003.

The Bank and Dominican manufacturers saw the free trade zones in Haiti as a very attractive proposition. They allowed them to tap into the much cheaper wages of Haitian workers who received (in 2002) a mere US $1.25 a day in contrast to the $13 a day paid to Dominican workers. Because the Dominican producers tended to exceed their import quotas into the USA, and Haitian apparel manufacturers did not, locating the free trade zones on the Haitian side of the border allowed the former to continue to export their products to the USA but labelled "made in Haiti" (James 2002; Volk 2002; Bretton Woods Project 2003; Wells 2010).

While clearly advantageous to the investors who benefited from financial assistance from the Bank, relatively cheap infrastructure, tax exemptions, no restrictions on the repatriation of profits, and the cheapest labor costs in the Caribbean, the free trade zones were disastrous for the peasant farmers in the border region of the Maribahoux Plain in the northeast of Haiti, one of the most fertile agricultural regions of the country. The farmers who owned or leased the land in the area were left out of the negotiations held behind closed doors between Aristide and the Dominican manufacturer Grupo M, and were not told about their eviction until construction of the plant began in April 2002. In 2003, after strong protest from the evicted farmers and people from the town of Ouanaminthe, Grupo M offered a package of "social compensations" to the farmers. However, no definitive list of the number of farmers evicted had been published, and at any rate neither the compensation offered nor the prospects of working in the assembly industries would enable them to earn as much as they had done before they lost their farms. It is estimated that the loss of some 1,200 acres of farm land to the free trade zone cost farmers between US $1 million and $2.4 million; and production and earning levels could have been even higher if the government had provided farmers with better irrigation and access to credit and other technical support. Moreover, far from creating enough jobs for the population of the affected area, the new free trade zones will fuel rural-to-urban migration like the one in Port-au-Prince did, and encourage more Haitian migration to the Dominican Republic and elsewhere (James 2002; Bretton Woods Project 2003; WikiLeaks 2005).

The Bank's participation in the financing of the free trade zone, then, made it clear that it had no qualms about working with Aristide when he was willing to evict farmers from their land and guarantee the supply of a cheap labor force and other incentives to foreign and Haitian investors. But it would not authorize loans to that government directly because of its "poor governance." Still, Aristide was determined to win the Bank's confidence and support, even if that meant selling out the people he claimed to be "connected ... and in deep communion with ... to always know what they want me to do and to do that" (Orenstein 1998: 16). In June 2003 Aristide signed an agreement with the IMF that obligated Haiti to cut deficit spending, reduce inflation, clear external payment arrears, and monitor spending in public-sector enterprises (International Monetary Fund 2003). This agreement was a precondition for an approximately US $200 million loan from the IDB, which the government concluded in July after it nearly depleted its foreign reserves to pay $35 million in arrears to that bank.

This recent IDB loan, however, did not signal an end to the aid embargo against Aristide. According to IDB President Enrique Iglesias, the resumption of cooperation with the government was linked to concrete political reforms and was "an integral part of the strategy of the international community"

(*AlterPresse* 2003). And the strategy of the international community has been clear from the start: to compel compliance with the dictates of the "reformed" Washington Consensus. That, as I have shown, is the real meaning of "good governance." For Aristide, however, his compliance did not suffice for the international community (the USA, Canada, and France), which responded by supporting the organized opposition and the rebel soldiers of the former Haitian army who toppled and exiled him in 2004, earning him the distinction of being the first democratically elected Haitian head of state to be overthrown twice.

Notes

1   In 2002 the US State Department estimated that about 8 percent of all cocaine entering the USA from South America passed through Haiti (Taft-Morales 2002). Domestic usage of cocaine is very low, but the effects of the clandestine trafficking were evident in increasing violent crimes and killings by armed gangs involved in the drug trade, the corruption of police and government officials, money laundering, and the luxurious lifestyle of traffickers (Arthur 2001: 42–43). In its 2013 *World Factbook*, the Central Intelligence Agency noted that Colombian narcotic traffickers favor Haiti for their illicit transactions and transshipment of cocaine en route to the USA and Europe (CIA 2013).

2   The term "Washington Consensus" was coined by John Williamson in 1989 to refer to the set of "liberalizing policy reforms" that the Washington-based institutions—the World Bank, the IMF, and the Inter-American Development Bank—were "addressing" to the countries of Latin America (Williamson 1990).

3   These conflicts include the election and overthrow of Aristide in 1991; the repression unleashed by the military junta that toppled Aristide and ruled Haiti from 1991 to 1994; the removal of the junta by the US-led multinational force that returned Aristide to office in 1994; and the re-election of Aristide in 2000 and his second overthrow and exile in 2004.

4   Mostly US pigs could not adapt to what Haitian farmers fed them.

5   These included: Ciment d'Haiti (a cement company), Minoterie d'Haiti (a flour mill), Télécommunications d'Haiti (telephone company), Centrale Autonome d'Eau Potable and Société Nationale d'Eau Potable (water companies), Électricité d'Haiti (electricity company), Authorité Portuaire Nationale (port authority), Banque Nationale de Crédit (BNC—National Bank of Credit), and Banque Populaire Haitienne (BPH—Haitian Popular Bank).

6   The reasons for this are the following. In 1990 Aristide came to office with massive popular support. The USA could not deny the legitimacy of his victory and hence recognized that to undermine or antagonize him overtly could have led to severe social unrest, as was shown by the swift popular reaction to an attempted *coup d'état* against him in January 1991. By 1994, however, conditions had changed dramatically. Three years of repression under the military junta had decimated the popular organizations that supported Aristide and resisted the military, and Aristide was now beholden to the USA for returning him to office. He was therefore weaker politically and hence could be pressured more to abide by US directives (Dupuy 1997: 137–66).

7   International monitors reported widespread fraud in the 1995 parliamentary elections, and despite a boycott of the second round by many opposition parties, the USA and the UN accepted these elections as valid. To reject the elections would have been a major embarrassment and setback for the Clinton Administration,

which reluctantly returned Aristide to office for the remainder of his five-year term despite strong opposition from Republicans in Congress. Moreover, the USA did not believe that the parties or groups that opposed the broad coalition known as the Lavalas Political Platform headed by Aristide were viable enough to warrant its support.

8 It is interesting to note, however, that in 1995 the parties opposed to the broad Lavalas coalition of which the OPL was then a dominant faction, charged that the then CEP had rigged the elections in favor of the OPL which gained a majority in parliament. The opposition boycotted the second round as well.

9 Convergence was a coalition of 22 or so parties and groups of diverse and seemingly incompatible ideologies, ranging from neo-Duvalierist, centrist, religious, and social democratic, to former members of the Lavalas coalition and close allies of Aristide.

10 To underline the double standard, consider the example of Peru, which also held presidential elections in May 2000. The OAS also observed and detected widespread fraud in that election, which denied an outright victory to opposition candidate Alejandro Toledo against incumbent President Alberto Fujimori. As in Haiti, the OAS refused to monitor the second round in Peru. But unlike in Haiti, the USA and the OAS accepted the results and approved Fujimori as the winner. The difference between Peru and Haiti is that in Peru there was a president with autocratic tendencies who supported the US free trade policies and war on drugs, whereas in Haiti there was a president with autocratic tendencies whom the USA disliked and distrusted. The former could get away with fraud; the latter did not have a chance. The political paralysis caused by the dispute over the May 2000 senatorial elections remained unresolved, and foreign aid continued to be suspended.

11 Since his overthrow in 1991 Aristide's aim had been to win and maintain power by weakening his opponents as much as possible. Also fearing a return of the Haitian military he disbanded in 1995, or an independent police force that could act against him, Aristide sought to monopolize the means of violence as well. To that end, he decided to politicize and control the police force, and maintain a popular base of support he could call on when necessary to intimidate his opponents. As such, he failed to take an unconditional stance against acts of violence carried out in his name by his popular supporters and armed gangs against his opponents. His government interfered with judicial authorities and the police to investigate, arrest, and prosecute the perpetrators of acts of violence and human rights violations. Aristide, in other words, feared a genuine democracy and independent branches of government that exercised checks and balances on his authority. Governing without an effective opposition and checks and balances, however, opened the door to abuses of power and widespread corruption by government officials, and facilitated the emergence of rival factions and power struggles within the governing party itself. Under such conditions, responsible, accountable, and effective government became impossible. Thus, despite his promise to "democratize democracy," and to bring transparency, honesty, and an end to impunity, his government continued the predatory practices of his predecessors and could be best characterized as a hybrid regime with characteristic features of authoritarianism and democracy (Dupuy 2002).

12 Bazin, also a former Bank official, was a presidential candidate supported by the USA in the election of 1990 that Aristide won. He also served as de facto prime minister from June 1992 to June 1993 under the military junta that had overthrown Aristide.

6   Class, power, sovereignty

Haiti before and after the earthquake

In this essay I argue that one needs to distinguish between sovereignty and democracy, and ask whether it is possible to achieve either or both in peripheral capitalist societies like Haiti. If by sovereignty is meant the right of a government to rule over and decide the internal affairs of its territory or nation-state, and if democracy means the right of the people really to decide the agenda of their government, then I will argue that the logic of capitalism undermines both, for two reasons. First, insofar as capitalism is not confined within nation-states but is a world-economy, it requires that the stronger or dominant states compel weaker and poorer states to conform to the rules and processes of production, circulation, and accumulation of capital on a world scale. And second, capitalism cannot allow the right of the people to determine a democratic agenda to interfere with the right of private property in the means of production and hence with the processes of accumulation by both domestic and foreign capital. Achieving sovereignty, then, would require extending and deepening democratic control over the domestic agenda and therefore undermining the dominance and rule of capital, foreign and domestic.

The Interim Haiti Recovery Commission and the post-earthquake agenda for Haiti

On March 2010 then Prime Minister Jean-Max Bellerive appeared in front of the Haitian Senate to present his government's post-earthquake (January 2010) recovery plan known as the Action Plan for the Reconstruction and National Development of Haiti. The Action Plan had been drafted by the Haitian government and the representatives from the major donor countries, especially the USA, Canada, and France, as well as those from the international financial institutions (IFIs)—principally the World Bank, the International Monetary Fund, and the Inter-American Development Bank (Government of Haiti 2010). The Action Plan called for the creation of an Interim Haiti Recovery Commission (IHRC) charged with deciding on and implementing the programs and projects for the reconstruction of Haiti. The IHRC comprised 26 voting members drawn equally from the foreign community and Haiti, and co-chaired by former US President Bill Clinton and Prime Minister Bellerive.

The idea of the IHRC had been formulated by the US State Department, and it called for transferring the Haitian government's decision-making powers to that body. As its "Concept Note" stipulated, the IHRC would have the power to

> solicit and draw up projects that fit within the priorities of the Development Plan and decide on the eligibility of external submissions ... to award land title of dispute-free Government land, set and approve priorities and projects for development, receive and disburse funding for projects, and grant licenses and concessions for the operation of vital economic assets such as ports, airports, hospitals and power stations.
>
> (Mills 2010)

These functions were to be transferred back to the Haitian government once the IHRC's mandate expired in October 2011, 18 months after the Haitian Parliament ratified it in April 2010.

In the meantime, it was clear that the IHRC placed the Haitian government under the tutelage of a decision-making body conceived and imposed on Haiti by foreign powers. This was so because despite the appearance of equality between the foreign and Haitian members of the IHRC, the former, whose governments, especially the USA, controlled all the financing made all the key decisions. Haitian members of the IHRC complained publicly that they were shut out of the decisions of the Commission, and organizations representing wide cross-sections of Haitian society protested their exclusion and decried the Haitian government's surrender of its sovereignty to the international community (*Diario Libre* 2010). The IHRC, a former consultant admitted,

> was not intended to work as a structure or entity for Haiti or Haitians. It was simply designed as a vehicle for donors to funnel multi-nationals' and NGOs' project contracts. Project plans were initiated by the institutions that have always run Haiti: the Inter-American Development Bank, the World Bank, the UN, USAID and individual donor countries that had pledged enough to secure a seat on the IHRC board. That meant there could, by definition, be no effective realisation of the IHRC's declared main aim of assessing reconstruction needs and responding to them in a systematic, coordinated manner.
>
> (cited in Haiti Support Group 2012: 1)

When questioned by members of the Haitian Senate if Haiti had in fact surrendered its sovereignty to the IHRC, Bellerive responded candidly: "I hope you sense the dependency in this document. If you don't sense it, you should tear it up. I am optimistic that ... [soon] we will be autonomous in our decisions. But right now I have to assume, as prime minister, that we are not" (cited in Kaste 2010). This rare admission by a high-ranking public official expresses succinctly the dilemma that Haiti faced in rebuilding its shattered economy in the wake of the massive destruction caused by the January 12, 2010 earthquake. Recent estimates put the number of dead between 200,000 and 300,000, including more than 16,000 civil servants; more than 300,000 injured; and more than 1.5 million homeless people, 170,000 of whom were still living in makeshift shelters in hundreds of camps (in December 2013).[1] The value of the damage was estimated at US $7.8 billion dollars (Charbonneau 2010; International Crisis Group 2010; Maguire and Nesvaderani 2011; *Caribbean Journal* 2013; Charles 2013; Johnston and Main 2013). To make matters worse, a cholera epidemic, introduced by a contingent of UN Nepalese troops assigned to the UN Mission in Haiti (French acronym MINUSTAH), swept Haiti in October 2010 and as of February 2013 had claimed more than 8,000 deaths (Katz 2013).

Many sectors of Haitian society took a more critical stance. A statement issued by 40 civil society organizations on the anniversary of the donors' conference on the "reconstruction of Haiti" in New York in March 2010 put it thus:

> Haitian society continues to be enclosed in the same traps of exclusion, dependency, misunderstanding of our abilities, our resources, our identity ... The structures of the system of domination and dependence have been reproduced and reinforced with the setting up of a strategic plan combining the MINUSTAH, the IHRC, and the major International non-governmental organizations. Henceforth, these authorities, and in particular the IHRC, are shaping the destiny of our country and are making all the decisions in our stead.
>
> (*AlterPresse* 2011c)

The members of the Haitian senate who questioned Prime Minister Bellerive did not challenge him when he said that Haiti would become sovereign again in its decision-making once the mission of the IHRC ended. The obvious question would be what the PM meant by sovereignty, and how a country like Haiti that is so heavily dependent on the international community for financial assistance, foreign investments in key sectors of its economy, and the continued presence of a UN peacekeeping force, could be sovereign in its decision-making. For if by sovereignty we mean the right and the ability of a people and their government to determine their agenda, then both this right and this ability are undermined when the state is subordinated to the dictates of foreign governments and international financial institutions, and/or the interests of powerful private foreign and domestic actors who are not accountable to the people or their government.

Let me elaborate. To me, sovereignty is a relational concept that refers first and foremost to the ability of a people to decide and control the public agenda either directly through its active participation in the management of public affairs, or, as has become the norm under liberal capitalist democracies, by electing representatives to public office to legislate and manage the public agenda. Even in the case of liberal democracy, however, it is possible for the people to safeguard their sovereignty by retaining and exercising their right to hold their representatives accountable, by immediate recall, and/or by popular referenda, and/or by voting them out of office.

However, as Marx argued, the separation between the state and civil society under capitalism makes it possible for citizens to have rights and pursue their self-interests. Among such rights is the right to private property, including and especially property in the means of production, without which the accumulation and concentration of capital in the hands of the few resulting from the competition among their owners would not be possible (Marx 1975: 251). Property ownership, however, is an essential but insufficient condition for the accumulation of capital. The other part of the equation is the need for and supply of workers whose labor generates surplus value or profits for the owners through the production of commodities. The relationship between the buyers and sellers of labor is inherently conflictive, as the objective of the capitalist is to extract as much surplus value (profit) from the laborers without raising their wages, while the latter seek to increase their wages without working longer hours or producing more commodities in less time (Marx 1977: 320–29, 643–72).

Long before Marx, however, Adam Smith had reached the same conclusion. The interests of the masters, or owners of stock, as he called the capitalists, and those of the laborers "are by no means the same" he argued. "The workmen desire to get as much, the masters to give as little as possible. The former are disposed to combine [i.e., form unions] to raise, the latter in order to lower the wages of labour." It "is not, however, difficult to foresee which of the two parties must, upon all ordinary occasions, have the advantage in the dispute, and force the other into a compliance with their terms." This is because the "masters, being fewer in number, can combine much more easily ... can hold out much longer [whereas] many workmen could not subsist a week, few could subsist a month, and scarce a year without employment." And, equally as important, the masters have the law (or government) on their side while at the same time it works to prevent "[raising] the price of work" and to suppress the "combinations of the workmen" (Smith 1993: 64–65). Nothing fundamental has changed in the relations between labor and capital since Smith wrote those words in 1776.

Those facts granted the bourgeoisie or capitalist class the power greatly to influence government policy because the viability and wealth of the state itself came to depend on the accumulation of capital, that is, the profitability and viability of private enterprise. This is especially so in a liberal democracy where the legitimacy of and electoral support for elected governments depend on the performance of the economy in general and of the private sector in particular. Thus, expanding Smith's point, governments are constrained simultaneously to pursue policies that are favorable to the development and success of private enterprise and corporate power as well as suppress or deter the popular demands for policies that minimize the adverse effects of the market on the welfare of the people and maximize social and political equality. In other words, liberal democracy must disempower the people if it is to serve the interests of private or corporate capital. There is an inverse ratio, then, between the power of private or corporate capital and the power of the people, or between capitalism and democracy (Wood 1995: 235).

Put differently, the more the dominant capitalist class is able to wield its economic power to determine the agenda and shape public policy, the more the sovereignty of the people to form a government of, for, and by the people is undermined. And for the people to be able to determine the agenda, they must have the guarantees of basic political liberties (freedom of speech and of assembly, personal security and equal protection under the law; freedom from arbitrary arrest, inhumane, or degrading treatment); and the necessary material or economic (income security, adequate housing, food, clothing, healthcare, and transportation) and social (access to education, information, communication) resources to prevent them from falling into conditions of *nautonomy*. Under such conditions, David Held argues,

> a common structure of political action is not possible, and democracy becomes a privileged domain operating in favor of those with significant resources. In such circumstances, people can be formally free and equal, but they will not enjoy rights which shape and facilitate a common structure of political action and safeguard their capacities.
>
> (Held 1995: 171–72)

Or, as Immanuel Wallerstein also put it, democracy "is about equality ... [And] without equality in all arenas of social life, there is no possible equality in any arena of social life, only the mirage of it. Liberty does not exist where equality is absent, since the powerful will always tend to prevail in an inegalitarian system" (Wallerstein 2003: 166).

If we now consider that we are dealing with a world-capitalist economy rather than a single nation-state, the question of sovereignty becomes even more complicated. The capitalist world-economy is characterized by a hierarchical division of labor among a relatively small number of highly developed or core economies with powerful states and capitalist classes at one end, a much larger number of highly underdeveloped peripheral economies with weak states and capitalist classes at the other end, and an expanding but still smaller number of semi-developed or semi-peripheral economies with relatively strong regional states and capitalist classes in between. As Wallerstein argues, the semi-periphery performs more of a political than an economic role by making the world-system less polarized and thus more politically stable than it otherwise would be (Wallerstein 1979: 18–23). From this it follows that just as in a capitalist economy in general there is an inverse ratio between the power of private or corporate capital and that of the people as I indicated above, so too, is there an inverse ratio between the power of a highly developed core state and its capitalist class and that of an underdeveloped and weak peripheral state and its capitalist class. This is so because the rulers of the core economies don't act to facilitate the accumulation of capital within their own nation-states only, but globally as much as possible to promote the interests of their state vis-à-vis other states. By contrast, the ability of weaker states to withstand external pressure and determine their own domestic policies depends largely on their internal characteristics, the balance of power among the state, the dominant and subordinate classes, and the relative strength of their dominant classes and the state vis-à-vis the state or states that exercise(s) greatest influence on them (Dupuy 2007: 8–10).

The early 1970s represented an important turning point in the relations between core and peripheral capitalist economies, for it was then that the developed core countries led by the USA undertook a process of restructuring the relations between capital and labor in the world-economy as a whole. Basically, this restructuring was the result of the emergence, around 1973, of what David Harvey called a regime of "flexible accumulation" that displaced the previous "Fordist" (factory) mode of labor organization. Essentially this new regime of accumulation consisted of a general offensive by the state on behalf of capital against labor through state policies that led to growing inequalities and deteriorating working and living conditions for labor in the developed as well as in the underdeveloped economies. Everywhere, though to varying degrees and at different times, states have been under increasing pressure to reduce public expenditures, especially social but not corporate welfare allocations, do away with policies of full employment, deregulate their economies, and privatize public enterprises. "Flexible accumulation" also involved the greater mobility of capital, of migrant labor, the transformation of work and labor processes, occupations and management, and attacks against labor unions; the emergence of new markets, new technologies and commercial innovations, new and faster means of communication, new financial services, and important shifts in the structuring of uneven development between economic sectors within and between countries and geographic regions (Harvey 1989; Castells 1996; Amin 2000).

In the 1980s the World Bank and the International Monetary Fund pushed to implement the new offensive of the core countries—especially the USA— packaged under the "Washington Consensus" by exploiting the huge debts accumulated by the underdeveloped countries to "reform," or more accurately restructure their economies to facilitate what Harvey also called the processes of "accumulation by dispossession" (Harvey 2005: 178–79).[2] This essentially consisted of compelling the underdeveloped economies to be more open to the free market and free trade policies of the core countries, and to the takeover of their assets by foreign capital. Concretely this meant that, after the collapse of the Soviet bloc and the end of the Cold War in the late 1980s, underdeveloped countries would be even more reliant on investments from and access to the markets of developed capitalist countries. These poorer countries would be less able to withstand their demand for reforms that are more "market-friendly" and facilitate the processes of capital accumulation, and thus would be less responsive to popular demands for greater distribution of wealth, income, and resources.

It is in this context that we can return to and understand better the question of sovereignty raised by Prime Minister Bellerive and the relative incapacity of the Haitian state to exercise it vis-à-vis the major powers like the USA and the international financial institutions (IFIs) that shape its domestic economic policies. As I have shown elsewhere (see Chapter 5), the restructuring of the capital-labor relations and the new process of capital accumulation it generated began in 1971 after Jean-Claude Duvalier inherited power from his father who had ruled the country since 1957. The son's regime formed a new alliance with the Haitian bourgeoisie and foreign capital. In return for military and economic aid from the USA and other advanced countries (notably Canada and France), the Duvalier regime turned over the formulation of economic policy for Haiti to the IFIs. The Haitian business class accepted its role as a subordinate partner to foreign capital and the conditions imposed by foreign investors in the export assembly industries. The IFIs henceforth pursued a twofold strategy that succeeded, on the one hand, in turning Haiti into a supplier of the cheapest labor in the western hemisphere for the export assembly industries, and, on the other hand, one of the largest importers of US foods in the Caribbean Basin.[3] These outcomes were achieved through a series of structural adjustment policies that maintained wages low, dismantled all obstacles to free trade, removed tariffs and quantitative restrictions on imports, offered tax incentives to the manufacturing industries on their profits and exports, privatized public enterprises, reduced public-sector employment, and curbed social spending to reduce fiscal deficits.

The Haitian government's post-earthquake reconstruction plan adopted the recommendations spelled out in a report written by Paul Collier (a former World Bank official and now Professor of Economics at the University of Oxford) after hurricane Gustav hit Haiti in 2008. Titled "Haiti: From Natural Catastrophe to Economic Security: A Report for the Secretary-General of the United Nations," Collier's report laid out the same dual strategies advocated by the IFIs and the USA since the 1970s that I summarized above and examined more fully in Chapter 5. The only difference was that it called for expanding the export zones for garment production beyond the two that currently exist in order to create clusters of such industries, and similar zones for the production and export of selected agricultural crops such as mangoes. For Collier the reason for this dual strategy was straightforward. To be competitive, Haiti needed to take advantage of the Haitian-Hemispheric Opportunity through Partnership Encouragement Act of 2008 (HOPE II) enacted by the US Congress that granted Haiti and the Dominican Republic duty-free access to the USA for up to 70 million square meter equivalents (SME) each of knit and woven apparel in addition to other goods such as brassieres, luggage, and sleepwear. As it was in the 1970s, the key to Haiti's competitiveness, Collier stressed, was its abundant and low-wage, but high quality labor force which rivaled that of the People's Republic of China (Collier 2009).

Establishing these zones of garment production and the jobs they would create, he argued, was also necessary to reduce the percentage of the population that lived off the land, encouraged labor-intensive crops, and decreased agricultural output. Haitian agriculture could then switch to more land-intensive production amenable to more inputs and greater output. In addition to increasing food production for the national market, Haiti needed to establish zones for the production of export crops such as mangoes. Mangoes are important not only because they are a valuable crop, but because the trees are large enough to have a substantial root network that would thus decrease soil erosion and contribute to the process of reforestation (Collier 2009). What Collier did not say but was implicit in his argument, the success of this strategy of more land-intensive production amenable to more inputs and greater outputs would require the further dispossession of farmers from their small farms and create larger farms oriented more toward export rather than the domestic market. In addition to dispossessing farmers and creating a larger pool of low-wage workers for the assembly industries, this would also increase Haiti's dependence on food imports and labor migration.

That same year, the consulting firm Nathan Associates wrote a report, "Bringing HOPE to Haiti's Apparel Industry" at the request of the Commission Tripartite de Mise en Oeuvre de la Loi HOPE (CTMO-HOPE) in Haiti and sponsored by the World Bank (Nathan Associates Inc. 2009). As with Collier's, the HOPE report stresses the advantages the HOPE II Act and the Caribbean Basin Trade Partnership Act (CBTPA) gave Haiti to use fabrics made of US yarn produced in other countries to manufacture apparel and still qualify for duty-free benefits in the USA (Nathan Associates Inc. 2009: xi). This means that Haiti's only input to apparel production is its labor, since it neither produces the raw materials (i.e., fiber and yarn) nor the technology and the machinery used in garment production. As the report puts it, "Aside from the generous terms of access to the U.S. market under HOPE II, Haiti's labor is its biggest asset—in terms of cost and quality … While not the lowest worldwide [Haiti's low minimum wage is] competitive with regional and global benchmarks." Still, Haiti ranks 22 out of the 25 top apparel suppliers to the USA, with China leading the pack (Nathan Associates Inc. 2009: xii, 8).

However, unlike the Collier report, the HOPE report points out Haiti's weakness in the chain of apparel producers. Given the global division of labor between capital-intensive textile and labor-intensive apparel production, countries like Haiti that engage primarily in the latter are not likely to replicate the success of "early industrializers, such as South Korea" that initially relied on such labor-intensive industries (Nathan Associates Inc. 2009: 4). In Haiti, garment production is limited to cutting, finishing, and assembly of garments rather than the entire "value-chain" of production that include fiber production, spinning, weaving, knitting, wet processing, apparel design, sampling, shipping, inventory management, and retailing (ibid.). Since the apparel industry was established in Haiti in the 1970s it has never made the transition from the assembly stage to these other and higher-skilled based and value-adding stages. And there is no indication that the current efforts to expand production involve moving beyond basic low-wage, labor-intensive assembly manufacturing since, as the experience of the last four decades has shown, the interests of both the foreign and Haitian investors in that industry are to take advantage of Haiti's low-cost labor rather than investing in the long-term diversification and development of the economy.

As co-chair of the IHRC, the actions of former President Clinton were also revealing about the real objectives of foreign capital in Haiti. In testifying before the US Senate Committee on Foreign Relations on March 10, 2010, Clinton admitted that since 1981 the USA has been pursuing a policy of

> selling food to poor countries to relieve them of the burden of producing their own food so they can leap directly into the industrial era. It has not worked. It may have been good for some of my farmers in Arkansas, but it has not worked. It was a mistake I was party to. I am not pointing a finger at anybody. I did that. I have to live every day with the consequences of the lost capacity to produce a rice crop in Haiti to feed those people because of what I did.
>
> (United States Senate Committee on Foreign Relations 2010)

He went on to say in a subsequent interview that these trade liberalization policies

> have failed everywhere they've been tried … [Y]ou just can't take the food chain out of production … and go straight into an industrial era … It also undermines a lot of the culture, the fabric of life, the sense of self-determination. And we made this devil's bargain on rice [but] it wasn't the right thing to do. We should have continued to … help them be self-sufficient in agriculture.
>
> (cited in Ives 2010)

The "lost capacity to produce a rice crop" Clinton is referring to resulted from the reduction of import tariffs on rice in Haiti from 50 to 3 percent in 1995—compared to 20–25 percent in the rest of the Caribbean—as part of the structural adjustment and trade policies the USA, the International Monetary Fund, and the World Bank compelled former President Aristide to accept when the USA returned him to Haiti in 1994 to complete the remaining 18 months in his first term. Consequently Haiti went from self-sufficiency in rice production to importing 80 percent of its rice and became the fifth largest importer of subsidized US rice in the world (O'Connor 2013). Clinton also endorsed the Collier report: "A lot of what we're doing now [in Haiti]," he said, "is thinking about how can we get the coffee production up, how we can get ... the mango production up ... the avocados, and lots of other things" (cited in Ives 2010). And he called on the US Congress to lift the "ceiling [on textile and apparel exports] ... so that then we can get bigger investments here [in Haiti]." Congress did exactly that in May 2010 when it enacted the Haiti Economic Lift Program (HELP) Act, which nearly tripled the production quotas and waived tariffs on knit and woven fabrics imported from Haiti (Palmer 2010).

Neither Clinton, the Collier Report nor the Action Plan explained how Haiti was to regain self-sufficiency in rice or food production generally when none of them called for repealing the trade liberalization policies Clinton decried in his March 10 testimony. And no Haitian head of state since Aristide implemented them is contemplating doing so. On the contrary. Newly elected President Michel Martelly rejected calls to raise tariffs to protect Haitian rice growers on the grounds that doing so would hurt the average Haitian consumer who lives on US $2 a day, with 10 percent eating one meal a day and half eating only two. Instead, the government claims it wants to change Haitians' eating habits—less rice and more other locally grown crops such as yams, sweet potatoes, cassava, and maize which used to be predominant in the diet—and make Haitian agriculture more efficient. According to *The Economist* (2013a), however, even doubling Haiti's rice production in three years, as the government says it wants to do, would produce barely half the rice consumed, and transforming Haitian agriculture to reach self-sufficiency would take decades at best.

That argument, however, defies both logic and fact. First, where is the logic in the argument that Haiti should not subsidize its rice production to protect rice growers against risks and keep prices low enough for average consumers to purchase it, but instead should rely on imported US rice whose low prices are made possible by the massive subsidies from the US government? As the president and CEO of Producers Rice Mill, the second largest recipient of direct subsidies from the US government in Arkansas, stated,

> If you take away these direct payments and the domestic market does not make up the difference, odds are farmers are going to grow more beans and corns. What remaining rice is grown will obviously be at a higher price, and we're going to be less competitive in the world market. Over the long haul, if we're less competitive that means less exports.
>
> (cited in O'Connor 2013)

Second, as has been done successfully in other countries where rice farmers cultivate small holdings, Haitian rice production could be made more efficient by introducing better methods of production, such as what is known as the "System of Rice Intensification" (SRI), which reduces water requirements and the need for seeds, synthetic fertilizers, pesticides, herbicides, and labor. Third, a report from the Haitian government acknowledged that the trade liberalization policies of the past 25 years have been detrimental to the growth of rice production and Haitian agriculture in general; that under the Treaty of Chaguaramas Haiti could renegotiate the exemptions it obtained from the Caribbean Community (CARICOM); that the 3 percent tariff for Haitian rice in contrast to the 20 percent imposed by the Dominican Republic is illogical and unworkable; and that the trade liberalization imposed on Haiti is inconsistent with the promotion of job creation and poverty reduction (Wilcock and Jean-Pierre 2012: 44, 58). Fourth, and perhaps more revealing of the contradictions of the government's argument, the Secretary of State for Fiscal Reform declared recently that Haiti would raise tariffs on certain food imports like wheat flour, corn, beans, and rum because they "are harmful to national production." Raising tariffs on rice imports, however, is not being considered because production levels are not sufficient to meet local demand (*The Gleaner* 2013). But the reason for this is precisely because tariffs on subsidized rice imports were lowered.

In politics, however, class interests trump logic. Rice imports are very profitable for US producers as well as for the few Haitian firms that have a "virtual monopoly [on its imports and] exert considerable influence on tariff policy and food policy more generally" (Wilcock and Jean-Pierre 2012: 40). Thus, the reasons why the USA continues to push trade liberalization and why the Haitian government does not challenge these policies have more to do with the unequal power relations between the two countries and who benefits from them rather than with the inefficiencies of Haitian rice production. That the IFIs and heads of state disregard the evidence of their failed strategies and continue to advocate them should not be surprising. Rhetoric aside, their objective is not to promote meaningful and sustainable development in Haiti but to create conditions for the maximization of profits for foreign firms, investors, and exporters, and their Haitian business partners.

As it is with rice, so it is with garment production. In October 2012 Clinton and his wife Hillary, then US Secretary of State, along with President Martelly and other diplomats, celebrated the opening of the giant Caracol industrial park in northeast Haiti. Referring to the number of jobs the South Korean Sae-A Trading clothing manufacturer promised, Bill Clinton said "I know a couple places in America that would commit mayhem to get 20,000 jobs today" (cited in Sontag 2012).[4] That claim is doubtful. Even though Haiti's total value in garment exports to the USA increased 22 percent in 2009 subsequent to the enactment of the HOPE II Act, Haiti still has a long way to go to reach the quota set by that Act, and even more so for the higher quotas set by the HELP Act of 2010 (Nathan Associates Inc. 2009: 19).

One year after it opened in 2012, the Caracol plant employed only 1,388 people (as of March 2013). Together, the 23 plants that are operating in Haiti, ten of which are owned by Dominican, South Korean, and US investors, employ a total of about 26,000 people, or 0.5 percent of the working-age population. The foreign companies employ 59.5 percent of the workforce, with South Koreans employing 27 percent and Dominicans 21.4 percent. These firms produce for a wide range of customers, among them The Gap, J.C.

Penny, Wal-Mart, Kmart, Jos. A. Bank, and Levi's. And there is no doubt that investing in Haiti is profitable. As with the Codevi plant that was built in 2003 in the northeast town of Ouanaminthe across the border from the Dominican Republic, the Caracol plant was built with financial assistance from the Inter-American Development Bank, the US and Haitian governments, tax exemptions and duty-free access to the US market, a new port and power plant, an abundance of cheap labor, and a fully outfitted residence for the expatriates who work for the firm. The foreign-owned companies also benefit from 100 percent exemptions on import and export taxes, 100 percent repatriation of their capital and profits, exemptions on their corporate taxes for 15 years and renewable for an additional 15 years, and pay no personal income taxes. It should not be surprising, then, that after accounting for the factories' total wage bill, rent, electricity, and other overhead costs per unit of production, they earn an average profit rate of 22 percent (Nathan Associates Inc. 2009: xii, 29, 28, 31, 42; Bell 2013).

As David Wilson put it succinctly, the whole plan to expand the garment industry in Haiti was a "race to the bottom. [It wasn't] really about creating jobs; [it was] about relocating them ... [W]hen the professors and politicians [said] they will help Haitian workers by giving them jobs, what they really [meant was] that they [planned] to take the jobs away from Dominican, Mexican, and Central American workers—and pay the Haitians even less for doing the same work" (Wilson 2010). The workers, 68 percent of whom are women, are paid the minimum wage of 200 HTG (Haitian Gourde; US $4.75) per day, and after spending 61 HTGs on transportation and 81 HTG on the mid-day meal each day, that left them 57 HTG (about $1.36) a day on average for all other expenses such as food, clothing, electricity, school fees, etc. (Sontag 2012; Ayiti Kale Je/Haiti Grassroots Watch 2013).

Moreover, as with the Codevi plant that took 486 hectares (1,200 acres) of fertile land from farmers, 366 farmers were evicted from the 250 hectares (618 acres) for the Caracol plant. Those 366 farmers provided for 2,500 members of their families, and another 750 agricultural workers earned their livelihoods from the plots they farmed for parts of the year. Each farmer was paid US $1,450 per hectare for the cash revenue they lost and an additional $1,000 per hectare for the food the family would have eaten from their own plots. But the eviction of the farmers meant the loss of 1,400 metric tons (MT) of agricultural products or 2,800 MT of food (100,000 bushels of dried beans) a year produced for the Haitian market (Ayiti Kale Je/Haiti Grassroots Watch 2013).

Let us then be clear about what the IFIs and the USA mean by the "free market." It is not about creating jobs for Haitians or making Haiti "self-sufficient in agriculture." It is about subsidizing US rice (and other food) exporters so they can sell their foods cheaper and drive Haitian farmers out of business, and subsidizing foreign investors to give them access to the cheapest labor force in the Caribbean and Central America to maximize their profits. That same logic can be seen also in the limited reconstruction work the IHRC got done before parliament voted in October 2011 not to renew its mandate (Haiti Support Group 2012). Many countries had pledged some US $10 billion, including $1.1 billion in debt relief at a donors' conference in New York in 2011 to help rebuild Haiti. Some $6 billion of the total pledged was to be disbursed over the next five years, which, when divided among 10 million Haitians came to $185 per capita per year (*The Economist* 2011).

The US government pledged US $3.6 billion in aid, and $2.5 billion had been disbursed by the USAID as of September 2012. Of the $1.15 billion it awarded, some $607.8 million were in the form of grants to international organizations, and $540 million to contractors, the vast majority of which went to firms inside the beltway in Washington, DC, in Maryland and Virginia. Only 0.7 percent of that money went to Haitian firms and NGOs. At least 40 percent of aid monies went to pay the salaries, insurance, cars, rent and other miscellaneous expenses for the foreigners who came to work in Haiti. In short, although these foreign contractors employed Haitian workers mostly on a cash-for-work basis, the bulk of the money and profits went to foreign aid workers and US firms who then reinvested their profits in the USA rather than in Haiti where the spillover effects could have spread to other sectors and promoted longer-term development (*The Economist* 2011; Mendoza 2010; Katz 2013a; 2013b: 204; Johnston and Main 2013). But, as I mentioned above, to do so would be contrary to the objectives of foreign capital and foreign aid.

Thousands of foreign or international non-governmental organizations (INGOs) are also operating in Haiti with private and foreign aid monies amounting to hundreds of millions of dollars to provide services including healthcare, schools, lodging, drinking water, sanitation, psychological counseling, and distributing food aid (71 percent of which comes from the USA). These INGOs provide employment for hundreds of thousands, including the foreign staff, many of whom went to Haiti after the earthquake and knew little to nothing about the country and its culture. To be sure, the presence of so many INGOs in Haiti is a direct result of the Haitian state's failure to meet the needs of, and provide basic services to the majority of Haitians, both rural and urban. Only about 28 percent of Haitians have access to healthcare, 54 percent to potable water, and 30 percent to sanitation. Consequently, INGOs have grown to fill the gap, and there are more of them per capita in Haiti than in any other country in the world. They provide 70 percent of healthcare in rural areas and 80 percent of public services (Buss 2008; FAO 2008). However, at the same time that the state has failed in its responsibilities to meet the needs of its citizens, foreign bilateral and multilateral aid donors, in keeping with the neoliberal regime of privatizing public services and reducing social spending, have reinforced the weakness and incapacity of the state by bypassing it and funding the INGOs directly (*The Economist* 2011).

Many popular and grassroots organizations issued calls for dissolving the IHRC, the departure of MINUSTAH and the INGOs, and rescinding all the policies and practices that deepen Haiti's underdevelopment and poverty. Instead, they argued, priority should be placed on rebuilding and expanding

Haiti's infrastructure, communication, transportation, public schools, public health, and public housing; promoting Haiti's food security and sovereignty by launching an agrarian reform and subsidizing production for the local market; subsidizing the development of industries that use domestic inputs to produce consumer and durable goods; protecting the rights of workers to form trade unions and to strike, and providing a living wage to all workers, including those in the export assembly industries (*AlterPresse* 2011c, 2011d). Most of these demands had been part of the broad mass movement that resisted the attempts by the military rulers who governed Haiti from 1986 to 1990 to reinstate a dictatorship and forced the organization of elections in 1990 that brought Aristide to power.

However, since the crushing of the popular movement after Aristide's overthrow in September 1991, the grassroots and popular organizations that continue to advocate for a progressive, social democratic alternative to neoliberalism have not yet become a force to be reckoned with. This is why the Préval government and the IHRC could ignore their voices and marginalize them in devising the post-earthquake reconstruction agenda I outlined above. That is why also the international community did not fear that a progressive, left-of-center candidate would emerge in the parliamentary and presidential elections of November 2010 to challenge the status quo. Despite the lack of progress in post-earthquake reconstruction, and large parts of the capital city of Port-au-Prince still in rubble, the US government pressured a reluctant President Préval to move ahead with the presidential and parliamentary elections that were to be held in 2010. With the threat of withholding reconstruction money unless the elections were held, Préval agreed to schedule them for November (Katz 2013b: 200).

Of the 19 candidates who stood for president, only three had a serious chance of winning, either in the first round with an outright majority or, as it turned out, in a second round where the top two vote-getters would participate. The three contenders were Jude Célestin, the chosen successor and candidate of President Préval's ruling Unity party; Mirlande Manigat, a Senator, constitutional law professor, former First Lady, and General Secretary of the right-of-center Christian democratic party Rally of Progressive National Democrats; and the right-of-center populist and popular singer Michel Martelly of the Peasant Answer party. For Célestin, who presented himself as the candidate of stability and continuity, there could not have been a worse moment to hold elections. Préval's abdication of his responsibilities in dealing with the aftermath of the earthquake to his prime minister and the IHRC turned the population against him and his government, especially the poor and the displaced living in the refugee camps who had voted for him in the 2006 election.

That is why, in return for their votes in the upcoming elections, the government reportedly offered to sell plots of land for US $10 to supporters of Préval's party for which they received fake titles to build their houses on a 1,100-hectare (2,718 acres) land area outside of Port-au-Prince that was billed as a "model camp" for those displaced by the earthquake, but turned instead into a huge slum housing between 65,000 and 100,000 people. Some 10,000 people live in the planned camp; the rest are squatters (Ayiti Kale Je/Haiti Grassroots Watch 2013b). Given that Préval had appointed the members of the Conseil Électoral Provisoire (CEP—Provisional Electoral Council) in charge of organizing and running the elections, it was expected that they would ensure either an outright victory for Célestin or that he would go to the second round.

As things turned out, and based on a low voter turn-out of around 23 percent, the CEP declared that Célestin came in second with 22.5 percent of the vote, behind Manigat's 31.4 percent but ahead of Martelly's 21.5 percent (Weisbrot and Johnston 2011). Therefore, according to the electoral law, only Manigat and Célestin as the top two vote getters were qualified to go to the second round. The problem for Célestin, however, was that the election was marred by massive fraud, voter intimidation, and other technical irregularities, facts that immediately gave rise to widespread demands for the election to be annulled and redone. Indeed, 14 of the 19 presidential candidates, including Manigat and Martelly, called for annulling the elections. But these two quickly reversed themselves once Manigat saw that she came in first and Martelly realized that he could go to the second round if Célestin was forced out of the contest. Martelly quickly mobilized his followers who took to the streets to demand a vote recount and threatened more unrest if the CEP did not reverse its decision. Pressured by the international community, Préval and the CEP agreed to have an Organization of American States (OAS) Expert Verification Mission do a recount of the votes for the three contenders.

The OAS Mission found that Martelly came in second place ahead of Célestin, and recommended that the latter be removed from the race. With signs that Célestin would not back down voluntarily, the international community, notably the USA, began to pressure Préval and the CEP to accept the recommendation of the OAS. In January 2011, Susan Rice, US Ambassador to the UN, stated bluntly at a UN Security Council session on the electoral crisis in Haiti that the USA and the international community would suspend their reconstruction aid if the government did not do so. Outraged by what they saw as a blatant affront to Haiti's sovereignty, 12 of the 19 presidential candidates who had previously called for the elections to be annulled issued a statement of support for Célestin to remain in the race even though the leadership of his own party had already asked him to drop out (*AlterPresse* 2011a). It is worth noting, however, that neither Manigat nor Martelly joined the group of 12 candidates in condemning the blatant interference of the international community led by the USA in the election process because obviously one of them would become the next president of Haiti and would need their support.

That outcry led US Secretary of State Hillary Clinton to backtrack and announce that aid to Haiti would not be cut off. However, the State Department continued to pressure Préval by revoking the US visas of several high-level government officials; and both Susan Rice at the UN and Secretary of State Clinton in her meeting with Préval on January 31 raised the issue of Préval's mandate that technically was due to end on February 7, 2011 as required by the Haitian Constitution. But because Préval had not assumed power for his second term until May 2006 due to postponements of the presidential elections for that year, Parliament passed an emergency law to extend his term until May 2011. By raising this issue, the USA offered Préval a quid pro quo: you drop Célestin, we let you stay in office until May. Préval himself claimed in Raoul Peck's documentary *Assistance mortelle* (Fatal Assistance) that Edmond Mulet, former head of the MINUSTAH in Haiti, called him on the day of the November 2011 election to say: "Mr. President, this is a political problem. We need to get you on a plane and evacuate you." Mulet denied the claim (cited in Porter 2013; also in CEPR 2013; *Haïti en Marche* 2013). Contradicting Mulet, however, Ricardo Seitenfus, a former OAS special representative to Haiti who had been removed from his post after criticizing the failure of international aid in Haiti and subsequently decorated by President Préval, told BBC Brasil in January 2011 that he had "heard and was appalled" when Mulet and other representatives of the "friends of Haiti" donor countries "suggested that President René Préval should leave the country and we should think of an airplane for that" (CEPR 2013; *Le Nouvelliste* 2011; *Le Temps* 2010). What's more, Raoul Peck confirmed what Mulet said to Préval in an interview with the Haitian daily *Le Nouvelliste* (2013).

In early February 2011 Célestin withdrew from the race. But, a former chairman of the Electoral Council of 1993 who reviewed the recount conducted by the OAS Verification Mission found that its analysis was invalid and therefore did not infirm the original tabulation of the 2010 CEP. Another independent review by the Center for Economic and Policy Research (CEPR) in Washington, DC, also found the OAS recount to be flawed methodologically and statistically, and concluded "The Mission's analysis does not provide any basis—statistical or otherwise—for changing the result of the first round of the presidential election" (Weisbrot and Johnston 2011: 4).

One may well ask why US relations with Préval, whom a US Embassy cable from Haiti once referred to as the "indispensable man in Haiti" (WikiLeaks 2009a), soured to the point that the USA imperiously considered removing him from office and did not support the candidate of his ruling party. In my view, the motive was clearly political. As a US Embassy cable indicated, the USA wanted to make sure Préval was not able to engineer the election of a parliament or a president he could influence after his presidential term ended in 2011 (WikiLeaks 2009b). But why worry about Préval? As many other Embassy cables have shown, the reason had to do with his defiance of the USA by joining Petrocaribe (the Caribbean oil alliance created by the late Venezuela President Hugo Chávez) soon after his inauguration to buy subsidized oil from Venezuela by paying 60 percent of the cost upfront and the remaining balance over 25 years at 1 percent interest. The deal would save

Haiti US $100 million a year from the delayed payments. Despite strong-arm pressure from the USA and resistance from the two main US oil companies operating in Haiti, ExxonMobil and Chevron, the Haitian government did not back down. Rather, a representative of the government said that Haiti would not be "held hostage to 'capitalist attitudes' toward Petrocaribe and if the GOH could not find a compromise with [the] oil companies, [they] may have to leave Haiti" (Wikileaks 2007a). A deal was finally reached in 2008 whereby the Venezuelan state oil company PDVSA agreed to sell oil to the government of Haiti, which in turn would sell it to oil traders and the companies in Haiti for distribution. Chevron also agreed to ship the refined oil in its tankers. Exxon/Mobil decided to leave Haiti. Haiti began to receive oil from Venezuela in March 2008, and even the US Chargé d'Affaires in Haiti conceded that "Petrocaribe's generous financing terms make it a deal the GOH cannot refuse" (WikiLeaks 2006d, 2007a, 2008, 2009a).[5]

Préval was not only defiant on the oil deal with Venezuela. He also rebuffed the USA when it asked him to vote against the Cuban Embargo Resolution at the United Nations in 2007. Préval maintained that Haiti had good relations with Cuba, which provided significant aid to Haiti, especially in the area of healthcare, and also that Haiti typically supported the decisions of the Latin American and Caribbean Group of Countries (GRULAC) of which Cuba is a member. He also resisted US pressure for Haiti not to vote with CARICOM in support of Venezuela's bid for a seat on the United Nations Security Council, and to vote in favor of Guatemala instead. But more than going against US interests on these two issues, Préval hosted President Hugo Chávez in a visit to Haiti in March 2007, and decided to attend the summit meeting of the Bolivarian Alliance for the Americas (ALBA) in April. In a clear illustration of its imperial arrogance toward and frustration with Préval, the US Ambassador to Haiti emphasized that "We should convey our discontent with Preval's actions at the highest possible level" for attending the summit, a meeting she thought was "a fora (sic) [for] Chavez [to vilify] Haiti's most important and reliable bi-lateral partner," especially after Préval had already given him "a platform to attack the United States" during his visit (WikiLeaks 2006b, 2006c, 2007b, 2007c, 2007d).

These cables make it clear that the USA considers Haiti its vassal state and expects its subjects to behave accordingly. Préval did not show enough deference and thought he could play it both ways, as one of the cables pointed out. But, though they contemplated it, they could not remove him from office by capitalizing on an organized opposition that wanted to topple him, as they were able to do with Aristide in 2004. However, they could make sure he would no longer have any political influence after his term ended. Therefore, Célestin had to go.

Martelly went on to win the March 20 run-off, and as a result he is more beholden to the USA than his predecessor who had won his reelection in 2006 without its support. Even before his election, Martelly, who had ties to the defunct Haitian military that toppled Aristide in 1991, had endeared himself as a pro-business right-winger to the Center for Strategic and International Studies in Washington, DC. He also hired a former campaign advisor to Senator John McCain (Republican, Arizona) and a Spanish agency with ties to the right-wing Spanish Popular party to reshape his image from popular singer to someone who would fight corruption and change the modus operandi in Port-au-Prince (Caroit 2011; Reitman 2011). Soon after taking office Martelly declared his intention to restore the old repressive army that Aristide had disbanded in 1995, a move that met with both domestic and international opposition. The USA, the European Union, and Brazil made it clear they would not fund it and proposed instead to beef up the Haitian National Police. Martelly adopted a defiant stance at first, but so far has not moved aggressively to do so because of strong opposition from his foreign backers and within Haiti. None the less, after evicting and arresting former soldiers who had occupied two army bases in May 2012, Martelly has rekindled fears recently that he intends to keep his campaign pledge to reinstate the army by sending a small contingent of some 41 military engineers to be trained in Ecuador (Daniel 2011; Taft-Morales 2013; *The Economist* 2013b).

On the day of his inauguration, May 14, 2011, Martelly declared that Haiti was "open for business," and nominated his first of three prime ministers, Daniel Rouzier, a friend and businessman from the tiny but wealthy Haitian bourgeoisie. Rouzier, whose nomination parliament would eventually block, openly criticized the IHRC for its dysfunctionality, leading the new president's office to backtrack and say that the new administration was open to continuing discussions on how to make it more efficient. In July Martelly asked for a one-year extension of the IHRC, but parliament rejected that request and voted instead to terminate it. However, as Janet Reitman points out, the message Martelly was sending was clear: "The US government and private-sector interests had found a friendly ally in the new Haitian president" (Reitman 2011: 17). When he accompanied the Clintons for the opening of the Caracol plant in October, he boasted "this was the kind of investment model we need from Haiti's friends … [and which will] allow Haitians to regain their pride" (Charles 2011b).

In addition to seeking more investments in apparel manufacturing, the new government has been luring foreign and domestic investors to revitalize the tourist industry with fiscal incentives similar to those offered to the apparel industry—tax, import, and other exemptions—to build the infrastructure for the industry—hotels, roads, ports, airports, additional cruise stops—in both the northern and southern parts of the country (*Haïti Libre* 2011a). Moreover, with the recently discovered gold and copper deposits spread over one third of the northern mountain range, about 15 percent of the country's territory, and worth an estimated US $20 billion, US and Canadian firms and their Haitian partners have spent some $30 million in the past years on exploratory drilling. However, in February 2013, citing the trauma Haiti experienced with aluminum and copper mining in past decades (1950s and 1960s) and the environmental risks involved in these activities, the Haitian

Senate passed a resolution to suspend all initiatives to extract minerals in Haiti without consulting parliament (Ayiti Kale Je/Haiti Grassroots Watch 2012: Parts 1, 2, 4; Ali 2013; *Haïti Libre* 2013a).

In the meantime, the World Bank is working with the Haitian government to draft a new mining law to replace the 1976 law and improve the frameworks for mining, including the royalty rates that would be paid to the government, environmental safeguards, and protections for the people in the region who would be affected. They are also working to sway a skeptical parliament, but this would not be difficult given that for that body's key players patronage can easily trump principles. However, since a third of the 30-member senate seats are vacant, another dozen are scheduled to expire this year, and no date for new parliamentary elections has not yet been set (as of early December 2013), the chances of passing such a law anytime soon are slim (*The Sentinel* Staff 2013).

Moreover, based on the evidence from the past in strip-mining and from the ongoing experience with the garment industry, sectors of Haitian civil society and others, such as Oxfam America, are skeptical that the mining companies (domestic and foreign), the Haitian government, and institutions like the World Bank would prioritize the interests of the Haitian people in general, the tens of thousands of farmers who would be expropriated from the mining areas in particular, and Haiti's already fragile environment over the profits of the private investors (domestic and foreign) and the windfalls government officials would reap in the form of royalties (Ayiti Kale Je/Haiti Grassroots Watch 2012: Parts 1, 2, 3, and 4; *Haïti Libre* 2013b).[6] As a member of Oxfam America put it,

> As one of the last unexplored places on earth with billions worth of minerals in the northeastern part of the country, mining could be a major opportunity for Haiti to stand on its own two feet. But as we've seen in a number of other countries, mineral wealth can also be a curse.
>
> (*Haïti Libre* 2013b)

The majority of Haitians are poor and exploited, and, except when they are needed to cast ballots, are excluded politically. Although they are formally free and equal, the majority of the people lack the most basic social and economic resources to enable them to participate fully and equally in the political process and shape the public agenda. In other words, they live in conditions of *nautonomy*. They want to change the social order that has never served their interests, yet they have come to expect nothing from it even after they fought for and won the right to vote for those who occupy the seats of power. That is because those who win elections and form governments are beholden and more responsive to the interests of Haiti's small but wealthy and influential upper class, and especially the foreign actors with whom they are allied, neither of whom is accountable to the people. Put differently, the formal trappings of democracy in Haiti notwithstanding, the government has been hijacked by and essentially functions as the privileged domain of the wealthy and powerful classes by negotiating on their behalf with the international actors who ultimately hold veto power over the state and its agenda. Former Prime Minister Bellerive's dream of making Haiti sovereign again, then, will have to wait another day.

Notes

1 As Trenton Daniel points out: "Many Haitians left the camps not because new housing became available but because they received rental subsidies or were evicted by landowners" (Daniel 2013).
2 See also Chapter 5 for a discussion of these issues.
3 In addition to the USA, Haiti has become a major market for food and other agricultural exports from the Dominican Republic and is now its second commercial partner after the USA (Deshommes 2013).
4 See Deborah Sontag's report on Sae-A's alleged mistreatment, violation, and suppression of workers' rights in Guatemala and Nicaragua before it closed its operations in the former country and moved to Haiti (2012).
5 See a detailed summary analysis of the US Embassy cables on this issue by Coughlin and Ives (2011).
6 Recently several peasant organizations in Haiti's northeast have denounced what they claim are attempts by the Martelly government to evict them from their lands forcefully for the benefit of foreign multinational companies involved in the gold and silver mining prospects (*AlterPresse* 2013)

Bibliography

Ali, Saleem. "Haiti's Mineral Misfortune: Deliverance from Destitution?" *National Geographic*, June 15, 2013. http://newswatch.nationalgeographic.com/2013/06/15/haitis-mineral-fortune/.

Allen, Theodore W. *The Invention of the White Race*. London: Verso, 1994.

AlterPresse. "BID/Haiti: reprise de la coopération," July 28, 2003. www.alterpresse.org/spip.php?article628#.UdHVn-vBz_w.

—— "Haïti-Élections: Statu quo," January 28, 2011a. www.alterpresse.org/spip.php?article10584#.UcEZdevBz_w.

—— "Haïti-Élections: Le groupe des 12, à la fois contre le retrait de Célestin et pour l'annulation du scrutin," January 28, 2011b. www.alterpresse.org/spip.php?article10589#.UcEbCOvBz_w.

—— "Haiti-Reconstruction: Environ quarante organisations réclament la disparition de la CIRH," March 31, 2011c. www.alterpresse.org/spip.php?article10850.

—— "Haiti-Reconstruction: Des réseaux d'associations appellent à ne pas renouveler le mandat de la CIRH," April 20, 2011d. www.alterpresse.org/spip.php?article10930#.UcMHROvBz_w.

—— "Haïti-Minustah: Des manifestants continuent de réclamer le départ de la MINUSTAH, désormais 'indésirable, intolérable,'" September 23, 2011e. www.alterpresse.org/spip.php?article11605#.UcMD – vBz_w.

—— "Haïti-Premier ministre: Séance de ratification de la désignation de Lamothe attendue à la chambre des députés," May 3, 2012. www.alterpresse.org/spip.php?article12795.

—— "Haïti-agriculture: Le gouvernement accusé d'accaparer les terres agricoles des paysans dans le Nord et Nord-Est," December 10, 2013. http://www.alterpresse.org/spip.php?article15644#.UqivOutRcto

Amin, Samir. "Capitalism, Imperialism, Globalization." In Ronald H. Chilcote, ed., *The Political Economy of Imperialism: Critical Appraisals*, 157–68. Lanham, MD: Rowman and Littlefield, Publishers, 2000.

Appiah, Anthony. "The Uncompleted Argument: Du Bois and the Illusion of Race." In Henry Louis Gates, Jr., ed., *'Race,' Writing, and Difference*, 21–37. Chicago, IL: The University of Chicago Press, 1986.

Ardouin, Beaubrun. *Études sur l'histoire d'Haïti*. 11 vols. Paris, 1853–60. Reprint Port-au-Prince: F. Dalencourt, 1958.

Arendt, Hannah. *The Origins of Totalitarianism*. New York and London: Harcourt Brace Jovanovich, 1973.

—— "Race-Thinking Before Racism." *The Review of Politics* 6:1 (January 1944): 36–73.

Aristide, Jean-Bertrand. *In the Parish of the Poor: Writings from Haiti.* Translated and edited by Amy Wilentz. Maryknoll, NY: Orbis, 1990.

—— *Tout Moun se Moun/Tout Homme est un Homme.* Paris: Éditions du Seuil, 1992.

Arthur, Charles. "Raising the Stakes: Haiti Between Mayhem and Decertification." *NACLA Report on the Americas* XXXV:1 (July/August 2001): 42–43.

Ayiti Kale Je/Haiti Grassroots Watch. "Haïti – Ouverte aux affaires/Haiti – Open for Business," November 29, 2011a. http://haitigrassrootswatch.squarespace.com/journa l/2011/11/29/haiti-ouverte-aux-affaires-haiti-open-for-business.html.

—— "Anti-Union, Pro-'Race to the Bottom'," 2011b. http://haitigrassrootswatch. squarespace.com/11_2_eng.

—— "Gold Rush in Haiti: Who Will Get Rich?" Part 1, May 30, 2012a. http://haitigr assrootswatch.squarespace.com/18_01_ENG.

—— "What's in Haiti's Hills?," Part 2, May 30, 2012b. http://haitigrassrootswatch.squ arespace.com/18_02_ENG.

—— "Haiti Lags in the 'Royalties Race'," Part 3, May 30, 2012c. http://haitigrassroots watch.squarespace.com/18_03_ENG.

—— "Haiti's Mines 'Open for Business'," Part 4, May 30, 2012d. http://haitigrassroots watch.squarespace.com/18_04_ENG.

—— "The Caracol Industrial Park: Worth the Risk?" March 7, 2013a. www.ayitikaleje.org/ haiti-grassroots-watch-engli/2013/3/7/the-caracol-industrial-park-worth-the-risk.html.

—— "Reconstruction's Massive Slum Will Cost 'Hundreds of Millions'," June 17, 2013b. http://haitigrassrootswatch.squarespace.com/haiti-grassroots-watch-engli/2013/6/17/recon structions-massive-slum-will-cost-hundreds-of-millions.html.

Balibar, Etienne. *The Philosophy of Marx.* London and New York: Verso, 2007.

—— "The Nation Form: History and Ideology." In Etienne Balibar and Immanuel Wal- lerstein, *Race, Nation, Class: Ambiguous Identities,* 86–106. London and New York: Verso, 1991.

Ballard, John R. *Upholding Democracy: The United States Military Campaign Against Haiti.* Westport, CT: Praeger, 1998.

Bazin, Marc. "Government Comments (B): English Version." Republic of Haiti, Ministry of Planning and External Cooperation (September 26, 2001).

—— Attachment 2, World Bank, "Haiti: Country Assistance Evaluation," Report No. 23637 Washington, DC: The World Bank (February 12, 2002): 65–77.

Bell, Beverly. "'Miami Rice': The Business of Disaster in Haiti." *Grassroots International,* December 9, 2010. www.grassrootsonline.org/news/articles/miami-rice-business-disas ter-haiti.

—— "Jobs and Justice: Raising the Floor on Worker Rights and Wages in Haiti." *The Huffington Post,* May 24, 2013. www.huffingtonpost.com/beverly-bell/haiti-jobs_b_3 327314.html.

Bell, Beverly and Alexis Ekert. "A Hard Day's Labor for $4.26: The Offshore Assembly Industry in Haiti." *Other Worlds,* April 25, 2013. www.otherworldsarepossible.org/ another-haiti-possible/hard-day-s-labor-476-offshore-assembly-industry-haiti.

Bell, Madison Smartt. *Toussaint Louverture: A Biography.* New York: Pantheon Books, 2007.

Bellegarde, Dantès. *L'occupation américaine d'Haïti et ses conséquences morales et économiques.* Port-au-Prince: Chéraquit, 1929.

—— *La nation haïtienne.* Paris: J. De Gigord, 1938.

Blancpain, François. *Un siècle de relations financières entre Haïti et la France (1825– 1922).* Paris: L'Harmattan, 2001.

Blancpain, François, and Marcel Dorigny. "Restitution de la dette de l'Indépendance?" Annexe 2. In Régis Debray, *Haïti et la France: Rapport à Dominique de Villepin, ministre des affaires étrangères*, 101–4. Paris: La Table Ronde, 2004.

Boulle, Pierre H. "Race: The Evolution of an Idea." In Sue Peabody and Tyler Stovall, eds, *The Color of Liberty: Histories of Race in France*, 11–27. Durham, NC and London: Duke University Press, 2003.

Bretton Woods Project. "IFC Decision Pending on Controversial Free Trade Zone." Bretton Woods Project, 2003. www.brettonwoodsproject.org/2003/09/art-18671.

Buss, Terry F., with Adam Gardner. *Haiti in the Balance: Why Foreign Aid Has Failed and What We Can Do About It*. Washington, DC: Brookings Institution Press, 2008.

Cabon, Adolphe. *Histoire d'Haïti*. 4 vols. Paris: Congrégation des Frères de Saint-Jacques, 1929.

Carey, Henry F. "Foreign Aid, Democratization and Haiti's Provisional Electoral Council, 1987–2002." *Wadabagei: A Journal on the Caribbean and its Diaspora* 5: 2 (Summer 2002): 1–47.

Caribbean Journal. "Haiti: Number of People Living in Tent Camps Down 79 Percent Since 2010." *The Caribbean Journal*, April 16, 2013. www.caribjournal.com/2013/04/16/haiti-number-of-people-living-in-tent-camps-down-79-percent-since-2010/.

Caribbean Report. "US Exports of Foodstuffs to the Caribbean." *Latin American Newsletters*, RC-03-03, April 1, 2003.

Caroit, Jean-Michel. "Le chanteur Michel Martelly est élu président d'Haïti." *Le Monde*, April 5, 2011. www.lemonde.fr/ameriques/article/2011/04/05/le-chanteur-michel-martelly-est-elu-president-d-haiti_1503220_3222.html.

Castells, Manuel. *The Rise of the Network Society, Volume 1: The Information Age: Economy, Society and Culture*. Malden, MA: Blackwell Publishers, 1996.

Central Intelligence Agency (CIA). *The World Factbook, Central America and the Caribbean: Haiti*, May 15, 2013. www.cia.gov/library/publications/the-world-factbook/geos/ha.html.

Center for Economic and Policy Research (CEPR). "Haiti's Former President Préval Has Credible Charges that UN Tried to Remove Him." Center for Economic and Policy Research, May 13, 2013. www.cepr.net/index.php/blogs/relief-and-reconstruction-watch/haitis-former-president-preval-has-credible-charges-that-un-tried-to-remove-him.

Césaire, Aimé. *Lettre à Maurice Thorez* (Letter to Maurice Thorez). Paris: Éditions Présence africaine, 1957.

—— *Toussaint Louverture: La Révolution française et le problème colonial*. Paris: Livre Club Diderot, 1960.

—— *Discourse on Colonialism*. Translated from the French by Joan Pinkham. New York: Monthly Review Press, 1972.

—— *The Original 1939 Notebook of a Return to the Native Land*, bilingual edition. Translated and edited by A. James Arnold and Clayton Eshleman. Middletown, CT: Wesleyan University Press, 2013.

Charbonneau, Louis. "Haiti Can Get 8 Percent GDP Rise in Next 5 Years, IMF Says." *Reuters*, March 31, 2010. www.reuters.com/article/2010/03/31/us-haiti-un-imf-idUSTRE62U4P320100331.

Charles, Carolle. "Transnationalism in the Construction of Haitian Migrants' Racial Categories of Identity in New York City." In Nina Glick Schiller, Linda Basch, Cristina Blanc Stanton, eds, *Towards a Transnational Perspective on Migration: Race, Class, Ethnicity and Nationalism Reconsidered*, 101–23. New York: The New York Academy of Sciences, 1992.

Charles, Jacqueline. "Clinton Urges Adopting OAS Report for Haiti Elections." *The Miami Herald*, January 31, 2011a.

―― "Charity Fatigue has Haitian Officials Calling for More Investments." *The Miami Herald*, November 30, 2011b.

―― "Haiti Sees Big Drop in Quake Homeless," *The Miami Herald*, July 8, 2013. www.miamiherald.com/2013/07/05/3486879/haitis-quake-homeless-sees-big.html.

Charles, Jacqueline, and Trenton Daniel. "Haiti Faces Overhaul of Election System." *The Miami Herald*, February 3, 2011.

Chavla, Leah. "Bill Clinton's Heavy Hand on Haiti's Vulnerable Agricultural Economy: The American Rice Scandal." *The Council on Hemispheric Affairs' Washington Report on the Hemisphere*, April 13, 2010. www.coha.org/haiti-research-file-neoliberalism%E2%80%99s-heavy-hand-on-haiti%E2%80%99s-vulnerable-agricultural-economy-the-american-rice-scandal/.

Cohen, Marc J. "Diri Nasyonal ou Diri Miami? Food, agriculture and US–Haiti relations." *Food Security* 5:4 (August 2013): 597–606.

Cole, Hubert. *Christophe, King of Haiti*. New York: The Viking Press, 1967.

Collier, Paul. "Haiti: From Natural Catastrophe to Economic Security: A Report for the Secretary General of the United Nations." Oxford: University of Oxford Department of Economics, 2009.

Coughlin, Dan and Kim Ives. "WikiLeaks Haiti: The Petrocaribe Files." *The Nation*, June 1, 2011. www.thenation.com/article/161056/wikileaks-haiti-petrocaribe-files?page=full.

Cournand, Antoine de (Abbé). "Requête présentée à nosseigneurs de l'Assemblée Nationale en faveur des gens de couleur de l'île de Saint-Domingue, 1790." In *La Révolution française et l'abolition de l'esclavage. Vol 4: Traite des noirs et esclavage*. Paris: Éditions d'Histoire Sociale, 1968.

Cox, Oliver C. *Caste, Class, and Race: A Study in Social Dynamics*. New York: Monthly Review Press, 1970.

Daniel, Trenton. "Haiti's Plan to Rebuild Army Meets Opposition." *The Miami Herald*, September 29, 2011.

Davis, David Brion. *Inhuman Bondage: The Rise and Fall of Slavery in the New World*. Oxford and New York: Oxford University Press, 2006.

―― *The Problem of Slavery in the Age of Revolution 1770–1823*. Ithaca, NY and London: Cornell University Press, 1975.

Debien, Gabriel. "Gens de couleur et colons de St. Domingue." *Revue d'histoire de l'Amérique Française*, 4:2 (1950): 211–32.

―― "Plantations et esclaves á Saint-Domingue: Sucrerie Conineau, 1750–77." *Notes d'histoire coloniale* 66 (1962): 7–84.

Debien, Gabriel, Fouchard, Jean and Menier, Marie-Antoinette. "Toussaint Louverture avant 1789: légendes et réalités". *Conjonction, Revue Franco Haïtienne* 134 (1977): 65–80.

Depestre, René. "An Interview with Aimé Césaire." In Aimé Césaire, *Discourse on Colonialism*, translated from the French by Joan Pinkham, 63–79. New York: Monthly Review Press, 1972.

―― *Bonjour et Adieu à la Négritude*. Paris: Éditions Robert Laffont, 1980.

Deshommes, Fritz. "Haïti-Rép. Dominicaine: Aux origines de la domination commerciale dominicaine," *AlterPresse*, November 29, 2013. http://www.alterpresse.org/spip.php?article15578#.UqiWmutRcto.

Diario Libre. "Reproches gobierno de Haití matizan reunión de la CIRH," December 15, 2010. www.diariolibre.com/noticias/2010/12/15/i272455_reproches-govierno-haiti-matizn-reunion-cirh.html.

Doucet, Isabeau. "Made in Haiti, Dumped in Haiti," *The Dominion*, July 12, 2013. http://dominion.mediacoop.ca/story/made-haiti-dumped-haiti/17482.

Du Bois, W. E. B. *The Souls of Black Folks*. New York: Penguin, 1989.

Dubois, Laurent. *Avengers of the New World: The Story of the Haitian Revolution*. Cambridge, MA: Harvard University Press, 2004.

Dupuy, Alex. "Conceptualizing the Duvalier Dictatorship." *Latin American Perspectives* 15: 4 (1988): 105–14.

—— *Haiti in the World Economy: Class, Race, and Underdevelopment Since 1700*. Boulder, CO: Westview Press, 1989.

—— "Toussaint Louverture and the Haitian Revolution: A Reassessment of C.L.R. James' Interpretation." In Selwin R. Cudjoe and William E. Cain, eds, *C.L.R. James: His Intellectual Legacy*, 106–17. Amherst, MA: University of Massachusetts Press, 1995.

—— *Haiti in the New World Order: The Limits of the Democratic Revolution*. Boulder, CO: Westview Press, 1997.

—— "Haiti: Social Crisis and Population Displacement." United Nations High Commissioner for Refugees, Emergency and Security Service, WRITENET Paper Series No. 18/2001. Geneva, Switzerland: UNHCR, March 2002. www.refworld. org/publisher,WRITENET,COUNTRYREP,HTI,3d8f11fe4,0.html.

—— "Who is Afraid of Democracy in Haiti? A Critical Reflection." *Haiti Papers*, 7 (June 2003): 1–12.

—— "Globalization, the World Bank, and the Haitian Economy." In Franklin W. Knight and Teresita Martinez-Vergne, eds, *Contemporary Caribbean Cultures and Societies in a Global Context*, 43–70. Chapel Hill: The University of North Carolina Press, 2005.

—— "Haiti Election 2006: A Pyrrhic Victory for René Préval?" *Latin American Perspectives*, 148:33:3 (May 2006): 132–41.

—— *The Prophet and Power: Jean-Bertrand Aristide, the International Community, and Haiti*. Lanham, MD: Rowman and Littlefield Publishers, 2007.

—— "Disaster Capitalism to the Rescue: The International Community and Haiti after the Earthquake." *NACLA Report on the Americas* (July/August 2010): 14–19.

—— "Class, Power, Sovereignty: Haiti before and after the Earthquake." In Linden Lewis, ed., *Caribbean Sovereignty, Development and Democracy in an Age of Globalization*, 17–34. New York: Routledge, 2012.

Easterly, William. "The Lost Decade: Developing Countries' Stagnation in Spite of Policy Reform 1980–98." *Journal of Economic Growth* 6 (June 2001): 135–57.

Easterly, William, Michael Kremer, Lant Pritchett, and Lawrence Summers. "Good Policy or Good Luck? Country Growth Performance and Temporary Shocks." *Journal of Monetary Economics* 32:3 (December 1993): 459–83.

Economist Intelligence Unit. "Country Profile: Haiti, 2000–2001." London: Economist Intelligence Unit, 2000.

Evans, Peter. "The Eclipse of the State? Reflections on Stateness in the Era of Globalization." *World Politics* 50 (1997): 62–87.

Fajnzylber, Pablo and J. Humberto López, eds. *Migration and Development: Lessons from Latin America*. Washington, DC: The World Bank, 2008.

Fanon, Frantz. *Black Skin, White Masks*. Translated by Charles Lam Markmann. New York: Grove Press, Inc., 1967.

—— *The Wretched of the Earth*. Translated by Richard Philcox with commentary by Jean-Paul Sartre and Homi K. Bhabha. New York: Grove Press, 2004.

Fatton, Robert, Jr. *Haiti's Predatory Republic: The Unending Transition to Democracy.* Boulder, CO: Lynne Rienner, 2002.

—— "Michel-Rolph Trouillot's State Against Nation: A Critique of the Totalitarian Paradigm." *small axe* 42 (November 2013): 203–12.

Ferguson, James. *Papa Doc, Baby Doc: Haiti and the Duvaliers.* Oxford: Basil Blackwell, 1987.

Fick, Carolyn. *The Making of Haiti: The Saint-Domingue Revolution from Below.* Knoxville, TN: University of Tennessee Press, 1990.

—— "The French Revolution in Saint-Domingue: A Triumph or a Failure?" In David Barry Gaspar and David Patrick Geggus, eds, *A Turbulent Time: The French Revolution and the Greater Caribbean*, 51–75. Bloomington and Indianapolis: Indiana University Press, 1997.

Fields, Barbara Jeanne. "Slavery, Race and Ideology in the United States of America." *New Left Review*, 181 (May/June 1990): 95–118.

Fletcher, Pascal. "Improved US Terms for Haiti Textile Imports Sought." *Reuters*, March 22, 2010. www.reuters.com/article/2010/03/22/idUSN22237675.

Food and Agricultural Organization (FAO). "Country Profiles: Rural Poverty in Haiti." 2008. www.ruralpovertyportal.org/web/guest/country/home/tags/haiti.

Foucault, Michel. *La volonté de savoir*. Paris: Gallimard, 1976.

—— *The History of Sexuality Vol. I: An Introduction*. Translated from the French by Robert Hurley. New York: Vintage Books, 1980.

—— *Il faut défendre la société: Cours au Collège de France, 1976.* Paris: Gallimard/Seuil, 1997.

—— *Society Must Be Defended: Lectures at the Collège de France*. Translated from the French by David Macey. London: Penguin Books, 2004.

Fox-Genovese, Elizabeth. "Antebellum Southern Households: A New Perspective on a Familiar Question." *Review* 7:2 (Fall 1983): 215–53.

Frank, Andre Gunder. *Capitalism and Underdevelopment in Latin America*. New York: Monthly Review Press, 1969.

Gaillard, Roger. *Les Blancs débarquent*, 7 vols. Port-au-Prince: Imprimerie Le Natal, 1973–85.

Garrigus, John D. *Before Haiti: Race and Citizenship in French Saint-Domingue*. New York and Houndmills: Palgrave Macmillan, 2006.

—— "Saint-Domingue's Free People of Color and the Tools of Revolution." In David Patrick Geggus and Norman Fiering, eds, *The World of the Haitian Revolution*, 49–64. Bloomington and Indianapolis: Indiana University Press, 2009.

Geggus, David Patrick. *Haitian Revolutionary Studies*. Bloomington and Indianapolis: Indiana University Press, 2002.

Genovese, Eugene D. *The Political Economy of Slavery: Studies in the Economy and Society of the Slave South*. New York: Vintage Books, 1967.

Gisler, Antoine. *L'esclavage aux Antilles françaises, XVIIe–XIXe siècles*. Fribourg, Suisse: Presses Universitaires Fribourg, 1965.

Government of Haiti. *Action Plan for the Reconstruction and Development of Haiti*. Port-au-Prince: Government of the Republic of Haiti, 2010.

Greene, Anne. *The Catholic Church in Haiti: Political and Social Change*. East Lansing: Michigan State University Press, 1993.

Grunwald, Joseph, Leslie Delatour and Karl Voltaire. "Offshore Assembly in Haiti." In Charles R. Foster and Albert Valdman, eds, *Haiti—Today and Tomorrow*, 231–52. Lanham, MD: University Press of America, 1984.

Haïti en Marche. "Visite houleuse du PDG du FMI au Parlement." May 29–4 June 1996.
—— "Les députés émettent de fortes réserves." XXV:2 (June 22–28 2011a).
—— "Réponse du Groupe des 16 à l'ex-Premier-Ministre désigné." XXV:29 (August 10–16 2011b).
—— "Le duel Mulet-Préval," XXVII:18 (May 22–28 2013).
Haïti Libre. "Tour d'horizon sur le développement touristique en Haïti," September 11, 2011a. www.haitilibre.com/article-4211-haiti-tourisme-tour-d-horizon-sur-le-deve loppement-touristique-en-haiti.html.
—— "Haiti ne peut pas continuer à faire la diplomatie comme avant," November 12, 2011b. www.haitilibre.com/article-4233-haiti-politique-haiti-ne-peut-pas-continuer-a-faire-de-la-diplomatie-comme-avant.html.
—— "Le Sénat vote la suspension des Permis Miniers en Haïti," February 21, 2013a. www.haitilibre.com/article-7929-haiti-economie-le-senat-vote-la-suspension-des-per mis-miniers-en-haiti.html.
—— "Ressources minières, bénédiction ou malédiction?" June 5, 2013b. www.haitilibre. com/article-8724-haiti-economie-ressources-minieres-benediction-ou-malediction.html.
Haiti Support Group. *Haiti Briefing*, No. 69, January 2012. www.haitisupportgroup. org/index.php?option=com_rsfiles&view=files&layout=download&path=Haiti_Brie fing_69.pdf& Itemid=255.
Hall, Douglas. "Slaves and Slavery in the British West Indies." *Social and Economic Studies* 11 (1962): 305–18.
Hannaford, Ivan. *Race: The History of an Idea in the West*. Washington, DC: The Woodrow Wilson Center Press, 1996.
Harvey, David. *The Condition of Postmodernity: An Enquiry into the Origins of Cultural Change*. Oxford: Blackwell Publishers, 1989.
—— *A Brief History of Neoliberalism*. Oxford and New York: Oxford University Press, 2005.
Hector, Carry. "Fascisme et sous-développement: le cas d'Haïti." *Nouvelle Optique*, 5 (January–March 1972): 39–72.
Held, David. *Democracy and the Global Order*. Stanford, CA: Stanford University Press, 1995.
Hume, David. *Essays and Treatises on Several Subjects*. 2 vols. Dublin: J. Williams, 1742.
International Crisis Group. "Haiti's Stabilisation and Reconstruction After Quake." *Latin American/Caribbean Report* No. 32, March 31, 2010.
International Monetary Fund. "Haiti: Staff-Monitored Program." *IMF Country Report* No. 03/260, August 2003.
nternational Office of Migration. *World Migration*. http://www.iom.int/cms/en/sites/ iom/home/about-migration/world-migration.html
Ives, Kim. "International Donor's Conference at the UN: For $10 Billion of Promises, Haiti Surrenders Its Sovereignty." *Haïti Liberté*, 3:37 (March 31–6 April 2010).
James, C. L. R. *The Black Jacobins: Toussaint L'Ouverture and the San Domingo Revolution*. 2nd edn. New York: Vintage, 1963 [1938].
James, Clara. "Haiti Free Trade Zone: Aristide's 'Different' Capitalism is the Same Old Story." *Dollars and Sense* (November/December 2002): 20–23.
James, Erika Caple. (2010) *Democratic Insecurities: Violence, Trauma, and Intervention in Haiti*. Berkeley: University of California Press.
Janvier, Louis-Joseph. *Les Affaires d'Haïti (1883–1884)*. Paris: Marpon et Flammarion, 1885.

Jefferson, Thomas. "Notes on the State of Virginia." In Thomas Jefferson, *Writings*, 123–325. New York: Library Classics of the United States, Inc., 1984.

Joachim, Benoit. "L'indemnité coloniale de Saint-Domingue et la question des rapatriés." *Revue Historique* (October–December 1971): 359–76.

Johnston, Jake and Alexander Main. "Breaking Open the Black Box: Increasing Aid Transparency and Accountability in Haiti." Center for Economic and Policy Research, April 2013.

Kant, Immanuel. *Essays and Treatises on Moral, Political, Religious and Various Philosophical Subjects*, Vol. 2. London: William Richardson, 1799.

Kaste, Martin. "After Quake in Haiti, Who's Boss?" *National Public Radio*, Morning Edition, March 31, 2010. www.npr.org/templates/story/story.php?storyId=125328026.

Katz, Jonathan M. "Humanitarian Malfeasance: The United Nations is responsible for killing more than 8,000 Haitians since 2010. And it's not even willing to say it's sorry." *Slate.com*, February 25, 2013a. www.slate.com/articles/news_and_politics/foreigners/2013/02/ban_ki_moon_rejects_haitian_cholera_claims_the_united_nations_brought_a.single.html.

—— *The Big Truck that Went By: How the World Came to Save Haiti and Left Behind a Disaster*. New York: Palgrave Macmillan 2013b.

Labelle, Micheline. *Idéologie de couleur et classes sociales en Haïti*. Montréal: Les Presses de l'Université de Montréal, 1978.

Lacroix, François-Joseph-Pamphile. *Mémoires pour servir à l'histoire de la révolution de Saint-Domingue*. 2 vols. Paris: Pillet Ainé, 1820.

Latin American Caribbean and Central America Report (LACCR). "Haiti: Martelly Government Gets Up and Running," November 2012.

Le Noir de Rouvray, Laurent-François. *Une Correspondance familiale au temps des troubles de Saint-Domingue: lettres du Marquis et de la Marquise de Rouvray à leur fille, Saint-Domingue-États-Unis, 1791–1796*. Edited by M. E. McIntosh and B. C. Weber. Paris: Société de l'Histoire des Colonies Françaises de Librairie Larose, 1959.

Le Nouvelliste. "Ricardo Seitenfus décoré par René Préval," March 2, 2011. http://lenouvelliste.com/article4.php?newsid=89855.

—— "Pour Peck, Mulet ment," June 14, 2013. www.lenouvelliste.com/article4.php?newsid=117819.

Léon, Pierre. *Marchands et spéculateurs dauphinois dans le monde antillais du XVIII siècle*. Paris, 1963.

Le Temps. "Le représentant de l'OEA rappelé au Brésil," December 22, 2010. www.letemps.ch/Page/Uuid/747b22be-0d4a-11e0-8878-76b803449127/Le_repr%C3%A9sentant_de_lOEA_rappel%C3%A9_au_Br%C3%A9sil#.UmVJGVOHk1I and http://lenouvelliste.com/article4.php?newsid=87115.

Lewis, Gordon K. *Main Currents in Caribbean Thought: The Historical Evolution of Caribbean Society in its Ideological Aspects, 1492–1900*. Baltimore, MD: The Johns Hopkins University Press, 1983.

Leyburn, James G. *The Haitian People*. New Haven, CT: Yale University Press, 1941.

Loury, Glenn C. *The Anatomy of Racial Inequality*. Cambridge, MA: Harvard University Press, 2002.

Madiou, Thomas. *Histoire d'Haïti*, Vol. VI. Port-au-Prince: Henri Deschamps, 1988.

—— *Histoire d'Haïti*, Vol. II. Port-au-Prince: Éditions Henri Deschamps, 1989.

Maguire, Robert, and Tara Nesvaderani. "What is in Haiti's Future?" *Peace Brief*, 84, March 7, 2011. Washington, DC: United States Institute of Peace.

Manigat, Leslie. *La politique agraire du gouvernement d'Alexandre Pétion*. Port-au-Prince: Imprimerie La Falange, 1962.

—— *Éthnicité, nationalisme et politique: Le cas d'Haïti*. New York: Les Éditions Connaissance d'Haïti, 1975.

Martinez, Gil. "De l'ambiguité du nationalisme bourgeois en Haiti." *Nouvelle Optique*, 9 (January–March 1973):1–32.

Marx, Karl. "Confidential Communication (Excerpt)." In Karl Marx and Frederick Engels, *On Colonialism: Articles from the New York Tribune and Other Writings*, 260–61. New York: International Publishers, 1972.

—— *Grundrisse: Foundations of the Critique of Political Economy* (Rough Draft). Translated with a Foreword by Martin Nicolaus. Middlesex: Penguin Books Ltd. London: New Left Review, 1973.

—— *Economic and Philosophic Manuscripts of 1844*. In Karl Marx and Frederick Engels, *Collected Works, Vol. 3 Marx and Engels: 1843–44*, 229–346. New York: International Publishers, 1975.

—— *The Poverty of Philosophy*. In Karl Marx and Frederick Engels, *Collected Works, Vol. 6 Marx and Engels: 1845–48*, 105–212. New York: International Publishers, 1976.

—— *Capital: A Critique of Political Economy: Volume One*. Translated by Ben Fowkes. New York: Vintage Books/Random House, 1977.

—— "Marx to Pavel Vasilyevich Annenkov. 28 December 1846." In Karl Marx and Friedrich Engels, *Collected Works, Vol. 38: Letters 1844–51*, 95–105. London: Lawrence & Wishart with Electric Book, 1982.

Marx, Karl, and Frederick Engels. *The Civil War in the United States*. New York: International Publishers, 1971.

—— *Manifesto of the Communist Party*. In Karl Marx and Frederick Engels, *Collected Works, Vol. 6 Marx and Engels: 1845–48*, 477–519. New York: International Publishers, 1976.

Maurel, Blanche, and Étienne Taillemite. "Biography." In Médéric-Louis-Élie Moreau de Saint-Méry, *Description topographique, physique, civile, politique, et historique de la Partie Française de l'Isle de Saint-Domingue*, 3 vols. Nouvelle édition by Blanche Maurel and Étienne Taillemite, VII–XXX. Paris: Société de l'Histoire des Colonies Françaises et Librairie Larose, 1797/1958.

Mbeki, Thabo. "Address by the President of South Africa, Thabo Mbeki, at the Celebrations of the Bicentenary of the Independence of Haiti." Port-au-Prince, Haiti: January 1, 2004.

McGowan, Lisa. "Democracy Undermined, Economic Justice Denied: Structural Adjustment and the Aid Juggernaut in Haiti." Washington, DC: The Development GAP, January 1997.

McGuigan, Claire. *Agricultural Liberalisation in Haiti*. London: Christian Aid, 2006.

Meiksins Woods, Ellen. "Capitalist Change and Generational Shifts." *Monthly Review* 50:5 (October 1998): 1–10.

Mendoza, Martha. "Haiti Flight Log Details Early Chaos." *Associated Press*, February 18, 2010.

Millet, Kethly. *Les paysans haïtiens et l'occupation américaine, 1915–1930*. Québec: Collectif Paroles, 1978.

Mills, Cheryl. "Concept Note: Haiti Development Authority." Unpublished Document. Washington, DC: United States Department of State, February 4, 2010.

Ministère de la Planification et de la Coopération Externe, *Bilan Commun de Pays pour Haïti*. Port-au-Prince: République d'Haïti, n.d.

—— *Strategy of Social and Economic Reconstruction.* Port-au-Prince: République d'Haïti, 1994.

Mintz, Sidney. *Caribbean Transformations.* Chicago, IL: Aldine Publishing Co., 1974.

Montesquieu, Charles de Secondat, Baron de. *De l'Esprit des lois.* 2 vols. Introduction by Robert Derathé. Paris: Éditions Garnier Frères, 1973.

Moral, Paul. *Le Paysan haïtien: étude sur la vie rurale en Haïti.* Paris: G.P. Maisonneuve, 1961.

Moreau de Saint-Méry, Médéric-Louis-Élie. *Description topographique, physique, civile, politique et historique de la Partie Française de l'Isle de Saint-Domingue.* Nouvelle édition par Blanche Maurel et Étienne Taillemite, 3 Vols. Paris: Société de l'Histoire des Colonies Françaises et Librairie Larose, 1958.

Naim, Moises. "Fads and Fashion in Economic Reforms: Washington Consensus or Washington Confusion?" *Third World Quarterly* 21:3 (2000): 505–28.

Nathan Associates Inc. *Bringing HOPE to Haiti's Apparel Industry: Improving Competitiveness through Factory-level Value-chain Analysis.* November 2009. www.nathaninc.com/resources/bringing-hope-haiti%E2%80%99s-apparel-industry.

Nemours, Alfred. *Histoire militaire de la guerre d'Indépendance de Saint-Domingue.* 2 vols. Paris: Berger-Levrault, 1925.

Nicholls, David. *From Dessalines to Duvalier: Race, Colour and National Independence in Haiti.* London and New York: Cambridge University Press, 1979.

Nicholson, Philip Y. *Who Do We Think We Are?: Race and Nation in the Modern World.* New York: M.E. Sharpe, Inc., 1999.

O'Connor, Maura R. "Subsidizing Starvation: How American Tax Dollars are keeping Arkansas Rice Growers Fat and Starving Millions of Haitians." *Foreign Policy,* June 9, 2013. www.foreignpolicy.com/articles/2013/01/11/subsidizing_starvation?page=full&wp_login_redirect=0.

Orenstein, Catherine. "An Interview with Jean-Bertrand Aristide." *Tikkun* 13:3 (May/June 1998). www.tikkun.org/article.php/may1998_orenstein.

Palmer, Doug. "US House Approves Trade Bill to Help Haiti." *Reuters,* May 5, 2010.

Paquin, Lyonel. *The Haitians: Class and Color Politics.* Brooklyn, NY: Multi-Type, 1983.

Paul, Edmond. *Les causes de nos malheurs: appel au people.* Kingston: George Henderson & Co., 1882. Reprint Port-au-Prince: Les Éditions Fardin, 1976.

Péan, Leslie. *Haïti: Économie politique de la corruption: De Saint-Domingue à Haïti, 1791–1870.* Paris: Maisonneuve & Larose, 2000.

—— *Haïti: Économie politique de la corruption: L'État marron (1870–1915).* Tome II. Paris: Maisonneuve & Larose, 2005.

—— *Haïti: Économie politique de la corruption: Le saccage.* Tome III. Paris: Maisonneuve & Larose, 2006.

——. *Haïti: Économie politique de la corruption: L'ensauvagement macoute et ses conséquences 1957–1990.* Tome IV. Paris: Maisonneuve & Larose, 2007.

Pierre-Charles, Gérard. *L'Économie haïtienne et sa voie de développement.* Paris: Éditions G.P. Maisonneuve & Larose, 1967.

Pluchon, Pierre. *Toussaint L'Ouverture: de l'esclavage au pouvoir.* Paris: Éditions de l'École, 1979.

Pomeau, René. "Introduction." In Voltaire, *Essai sur le moeurs et l'esprit des nations.* i–lxxxii. Paris: Éditions Garnier Frères, 1963.

Porter, Catherine. "Haiti's René Préval Says UN Tried to Remove Him." *Toronto Star,* May 13, 2013. www.thestar.com/news/world/2013/05/13/haitis_ren_prval_says_un_tried_to_remove_him.html.

Post, Ken. *Arise Ye Starvelings: The Jamaican Labour Rebellion of 1938 and its Aftermath.* The Hague: Martinus Nijoff, 1978.

Preeg, Ernest H. *Haiti and the CBI: A Time of Change and Opportunity.* Miami, FL: Institute of Interamerican Studies, Graduate School of International Studies, University of Miami, 1985.

Price-Mars, Jean. *Lettre ouverte au Dr. René Piquion: le préjugé de couleur est-il la question sociale?* 2nd edn. Port-au-Prince: Les Éditions des Antilles, 1967.

Przeworski, Adam. *Capitalism and Social Democracy.* Cambridge: Cambridge University Press, 1985.

Raphael, Ray. *A People's History of the American Revolution: How Common People Shaped the Fight for Independence.* New York: Harper Collins, 2002.

Raymond, Julien. "Mémoire sur les causes des troubles et des désastres de la colonie de Saint-Domingue, 1793." Paris: Archives Nationales, Marines et Colonies, Série ADVII–27. 1793.

Reitman, Janet. "How the World Failed Haiti." *Rolling Stone,* August 6, 2011. www.rollingstone.com/politics/news/how-the-world-failed-haiti-20110804.

Renda, Mary A. *Taking Haiti: Military Occupation and the Culture of US Imperialism.* Chapel Hill: The University of North Carolina Press, 2001.

Rich, Bruce. *Mortgaging the Earth: The World Bank, Environmental Impoverishment, and the Crisis of Development.* Boston, MA: Beacon Press, 1994.

Richardson, Laurie. "Feeding Dependency, Starving Democracy: USAID Policies in Haiti." Grassroots International. Boston: Grassroots International, 1997. www.grassrootsonline.org/sites/default/files/Feeding-Dependency-Starving-Democracy.pdf.

Robinson, Randall. "Honor Haiti, Honor Ourselves, Forget Haiti, Forget Ourselves." *CounterPunch,* January 1, 2004.

Rodrik, Dani. *The Globalization Paradox: Democracy and the Future of the World Economy.* New York: W.W. Norton & Company, 2011.

Roediger, David R. *The Wages of Whiteness: Race and the Making of the American Working Class.* London and New York: Verso, 1991.

Rogers, Dominique. "De l'origine du préjugé de couleur en Haïti." In Marcel Dorigny, ed., *Haïti: première république noire,* 83–101. Paris: Publications de la Société Française d'Histoire d'Outre-Mer, 2003.

Rousseau, Jean-Jacques. *Discours sur l'origine et les fondements de l'inégalité parmi les hommes.* Paris: A Londres, 1782.

Rueschemeyer, Dietrich, and Peter Evans. "The State and Economic Transformation: Toward an Analysis of the Conditions Underlying Effective Intervention." In Peter Evans, Dietrich Rueschemeyer, and Theda Skocpol, eds, *Bringing the State Back In.* Cambridge: Cambridge University Press, 1985.

Saint-Louis, Vertus. "Relations internationales et classe politique en Haïti (1789–1814)." In Marcel Dorigny, ed., *Haïti: première république noire,* 154–175. Paris: Publications de la Société Française d'Histoire d'Outre-Mer et Association pour l'Étude de la Colonisation Europeenne, 2003.

Sannon, H. Pauléus. *Histoire de Toussaint L'Ouverture.* 3 vols. Port-au-Prince: Imprimerie A. Héraux, 1933.

Sartre, Jean-Paul. "Preface." In Frantz Fanon, *The Wretched of the Earth.* Translated from the French by Richard Philcox with commentary by Jean-Paul Sartre and Homi K. Bhabha, xliii–lxii. New York: Grove Press, 2004.

Sauer, Carl Ortwin. *The Early Spanish Main.* Berkeley: The University of California Press, 1969.

Scheunemann, Randy, Charles Flickner, Christopher Walker and Roger Noriega. "Report of Congressional Staff Delegation to Haiti," Congressional Record – Senate, Measure Placed on the Calendar – S. 1028, Haiti Policy, April 19, 1996. www.gpo. gov/fdsys/pkg/CREC-1996-04-19/pdf/CREC-1996-04-19-pt1-PgS3742-2.pdf.

Schmidt, Hans. *The United States Occupation of Haiti, 1915–1934*. New Brunswick, NJ: Rutgers University Press, 1971.

Schmitz, Gerald J. "Democratization and Demystification: Deconstructing 'Governance' as Development Paradigm." In David B. Moore and Gerald J. Schmitz, eds, *Debating Development Discourse: Institutional and Popular Perspectives*, 54–90. London: MacMillan Press Ltd; and New York: St. Martin's Press, Inc., 1995.

Schoelcher, Victor. *Vie de Toussaint L'Ouverture*. 2nd edn. Paris: Paul Ollendorff, 1889.

Sepinwall, Alyssa Goldstein. "The Specter of Saint-Domingue: American and French Reactions to the Haitian Revolution." In David Patrick Geggus and Norman Fiering, eds, *The World of the Haitian Revolution*, 317–38. Bloomington and Indianapolis: Indiana University Press, 2009.

Shacochis, Bob. *The Immaculate Invasion*. New York: Viking/Penguin, 1999.

Smith, Adam. *An Inquiry into the Nature and Causes of the Wealth of Nations: A Selected Edition*. Oxford and New York: Oxford University Press, 1998.

Smith, Matthew J. *Red and Black in Haiti: Radicalism, Conflict, and Political Change, 1934–1957*. Chapel Hill: University of North Carolina Press, 2009.

Soederberg, Susanne. "The Emperor's New Suit: The New International Financial Architecture as a Reinvention of the Washington Consensus." *Global Governance* 7 (2001): 453–67.

Sontag, Deborah. "Earthquake Relief Where Haiti Wasn't Broken." *The New York Times*, July 5, 2012. www.nytimes.com/2012/07/06/world/americas/earthquake-relief-where-haiti-wasnt-broken.html?ref=deborahsontag.

Stiglitz, Joseph E. *Globalization and Its Discontents*. New York: W.W. Norton & Company, 2002.

Taft-Morales, Maureen. "Haiti: Issues for Congress." *CRS Issue Brief*. Washington, DC: Congressional Research Service, December 19, 2002.

—— "Haiti Under President Martelly: Current Conditions and Congressional Concerns." Washington, DC: Congressional Research Service, May 10, 2013. www.fas. org/sgp/crs/row/R42559.pdf.

The Economist. "Rebuilding Haiti: The Long, Hard Haul." March 17, 2011. www. economist.com/node/18390114.

—— "Feeding Haiti: The Government Tries to Load Up the Plates for the Poorest People in the Americas." June 22, 2013a. www.economist.com/news/americas/21579 875-government-tries-load-up-plates-poorest-people-americas-new-menu.

—— "Haiti's Army: Who Needs Them?" October 19, 2013b. www.economist.com/news/ americas/21588085-michel-martelly-pushes-ahead-reviving-army-who-needs-them.

The Gleaner. "Haiti Moving to Protect Local Enterprises." August 27, 2013. http:// jamaica-gleaner.com/gleaner/20130827/business/business2.html.

The Sentinel Staff. "World Bank Says it's Helping Haiti Draft Mining Laws." *The Sentinel*, May 19, 2013. www.sentinel.ht/politics/articles/international/4301-world-bank-says-its-helping-haiti-draft-mining-laws.

Thornton, John. *Africa and Africans in the Making of the Atlantic World, 1400–1800*. Second Edition. New York: Cambridge University Press, 1998.

Trenton, Daniel. "USAID now focusing on housing finance in Haiti," *Associated Press*, December 10, 2013. http://abcnews.go.com/International/wireStory/usaid-now-focusing-housing-finance-haiti-21153719

Trouillot, Michel-Rolph. "Motion in the System: Coffee, Color, and Slavery in Eighteenth-Century Saint-Domingue." *Review* 3 (Winter 1982): 331–88.

—— *Nation, State, and Society in Haiti: 1804–1984*. Washington, DC: The Woodrow Wilson International Center for Scholars, 1985.

—— *Les racines historiques de l'État duvalierien*. Port-au-Prince: Henri Deschamps, 1986.

—— *Haiti: State Against Nation*. New York: Monthly Review Press, 1990.

—— *Silencing the Past: Power and the Production of History*. Boston, MA: Beacon Press, 1995.

Turnier, Alain. *La Société des Baïonnettes*. Port-au-Prince: Imprimerie Le Natal, 1985.

—— *Quand la nation demande des comptes*. Port-au-Prince: Imprimerie Le Natal, 1989.

United States Senate Committee on Foreign Relations. "Building on Success: New Directions on Global Health." US Senate Committee on Foreign Relations Hearing, March 10, 2010. www.foreign.senate.gov/hearings/building-on-success-new-directions-in-global-health.

Volk, Alex. "Made in Haiti: Discontent with New Free Trade Zone." *Washington Report on the Hemisphere* 22:15 Washington, DC: Council on Hemispheric Affairs, August 2002, 3–5.

Voltaire, François-Marie Arouet. *Essai sur les moeurs et l'esprit des nations*. Edited with an Introduction and Notes by René Pomeau. Paris: Éditions Garnier Frères, 1963.

Wallerstein, Immanuel. "The Rise and Future Demise of the World Capitalist System: Concepts for Comparative Analysis." In Immanuel Wallerstein, *The Capitalist World-economy: Essays*, 1–36. Cambridge: Cambridge University Press, 1979.

—— *Historical Capitalism with Capitalist Civilization*. London and New York: Verso 1996.

—— *The Decline of American Power: The U.S. in a Chaotic World*. New York: The New Press, 2003.

—— *European Universalism: The Rhetoric of Power*. New York: The New Press, 2006.

Wallez, Jean-Baptiste Guidlain. *Précis historique des négociations entre la France et Saint-Domingue*. Paris: Imprimerie de Goetschy, 1826.

Walsh, John Patrick. "Césaire Reads Toussaint Louverture: The Haitian Revolution and the Problem of Departmentalization." *small axe: a Caribbean journal of criticism*, 34 (March 2011): 110–24.

Waters, Mary C. *Ethnic Options: Choosing Identities in America*. Berkeley: University of California Press, 1990.

Weisbrot, Mark, and Jake Johnston. "Analysis of the OAS Mission's Draft Report on Haiti's Election." Washington, DC: Center for Economic and Policy Research, January 2011.

Wells, Jennifer. "Haiti's Garment Industry Hanging by a Thread." *Toronto Star*, October 16, 2010. www.thestar.com/news/world/2010/10/16/haitis_garment_industry_hanging_by_a_thread.html.

WikiLeaks. "Grupo M Update: Source of the Problem." Embassy, Port-au-Prince, June 16, 2005. http://wikileaks.org/cable/2005/06/05PORTAUPRINCE1666.html.

—— "Préval Will Sign Petrocribe Deal on May 15." Embassy Port-au-Prince, 06Portau-Prince758, April 28, 2006a. http://wikileaks.org/cable/2006/04/06portauprince758.html.

—— "Préval Tries to Dodge Issue of Venezuela and UNSC Seat." Embassy Port-au-Prince, 06PortauPrince1258, July 12, 2006b. http://wikileaks.org/cable/2006/07/06portauprince1258.html.

—— "Préval Says CARICOM Will Support Venezuela for UNSC Seat." Embassy Port-au-Prince, 06PortauPrince1379, July 31, 2006c. http://wikileaks.org/cable/2006/07/06portauprince1379.html.

—— "GOH Intends to Meet 100% Fuel Demand with Petrocaribe," Embassy Port-au-Prince, 06PortauPrince1905, October 4, 2006d. http://wikileaks.org/cable/2006/10/06portauprince1905.html.

—— "GOH on Petrocaribe: Stoking the Fires." Embassy Port-au-Prince, 07PortauPrince78, January 18, 2007a. http://wikileaks.org/cable/2007/01/07portauprince78.html.

—— "Préval: Chavez Visit a Mess." Embassy Port-au-Prince, 07PortauPrince522, March 16, 2007b. http://wikileaks.org/cable/2007/03/07portauprince522.html.

—— "Préval Going to ALBA Summit: Returning with a Check?" Embassy Port-au-Prince, 07PortauPrince781, April 26, 2007c. http://wikileaks.org/cable/2007/04/07portauprince781.html.

—— "Haiti Likely to Support Cuba Embargo Resolution." Embassy Port-au-Prince, 07PortauPrince1743, October 30, 2007d. http://wikileaks.org/cable/2007/10/07portauprince1743.html.

—— "Chevron Signs Petrocaribe Deal with GOH." Embassy Port-au-Prince, 08PortauPrince234, February 15, 2008. http://wikileaks.org/cable/2008/02/08portauprince234.html.

—— "Deconstructing Préval." Embassy Port-au-Prince, 09PortauPrince575, June 16, 2009a. http://wikileaks.org/cable/2009/06portauprince575.html.

—— "Préval Consolidating Power." Embassy Port-au-Prince, 09PortauPrince575, October 26, 2009b. http://wikileaks.org/cable/2009/10/09portauprince895.html.

—— "Haiti Pleased with Petrocaribe and Summit." Embassy Port-au-Prince, 09PortauPrince591, June 19, 2009c. http://wikileaks.org/cable/2009/06/09PortauPrince591.html.

Wilcock, David C., and Franco Jean-Pierre. "Haiti Rice Value Chain Assessment: Rapid Diagnosis and Implications for Program Design." *Oxfam America Research Backgrounder Series 2012*. www.oxfamamerica.org/publications/haiti-rice-value-chain-research.

Williams, Eric. *From Columbus to Castro: The History of the Caribbean, 1492–1969*. New York: Harper and Row, 1970.

Wilson, David. "'Rebuilding Haiti': The Sweatshop Hoax." 2010. http://mrzine.monthlyreview.org/2010/wilson040310.html.

Williamson, John. "What Washington Means by Policy Reform." In John Williamson, ed., *Latin American Adjustment: How Much Has Happened?*, 7–19. Washington, DC: Institute for International Economics, 1990.

Wood, Ellen Meiksins. *Democracy Against Capitalism*. Cambridge: Cambridge University Press, 1995.

World Bank. *Current Economic Position and Prospects of Haiti*, Report No. 410-HA. Washington, DC: The World Bank, April 1974.

—— *Current Economic Position and Prospects of Haiti, Volume 1: Main Report*, Report No. 1243-HA. Washington, DC: The World Bank, December 1976.

—— *Current Economic Position and Prospects of Haiti, Volume 1: Main Report*, Report No. 2165-HA. Washington, DC: December 1978.

—— *Haiti: Policy Proposals for Growth*, Report No. 5601-HA. Washington, DC: The World Bank, June 1985.

—— *Haiti: Public Expenditure Review*. Washington, DC: The World Bank, January 1987.

—— *Economic Recovery in Haiti: Performance, Issues and Prospects*, Report No. 7469-HA. Washington, DC: The World Bank, December 1988.

—— *Haiti: Restoration of Growth and Development*, Report No. 9523-HA. Washington, DC: The World Bank, 1991a.

—— *World Development Report: The Challenge of Development*. Washington, DC: 1991b.

—— *Haiti: Country Assistance Strategy*, Report No. 15945-HA. Washington, DC: The World Bank, August 1996.

—— *Haiti: The Challenge of Poverty Reduction, Volume 1*, Report No. 17242-HA. Washington, DC: The World Bank, August 1998.

—— *Reforming Public Institutions and Strengthening Governance*. Washington, DC: The World Bank, 2000.

—— *Haiti: Country Assistance Evaluation*, Report No. 23637. Washington, DC: The World Bank, February 2002a.

—— *Globalization, Growth, and Poverty: Building an Inclusive World Economy*. Washington, DC: The World Bank, 2002b.

—— *The Development Impact of Workers' Remittances in Latin America, Vol. I: Main Findings*, Report No. 37026. Washington, DC: The World Bank, 2006.

Index

Action Plan for the Reconstruction and National Development 115–16

affranchis (free people of color) 50–51n6, 51n7, 54, 58, 76; in Saint-Domingue 1, 27, 28, 32n6, 38–39, 43

African "predatory states," slave trade and 22, 51n13

African psychology and culture 81

agglomeration economies, clustering of 97

agricultural land-intensive production 122

agricultural market (and employment), liberalization and effects on 103, 104–5

agricultural production, decline in 64

aid for Haiti, World Bank suspensions of 94–95

Ali, Saleem 133

Allen, Theodore W. 11

AlterPresse 91, 113, 117, 128, 129

American Federation of Labor-Congress of Industrial Organizations (AFL-CIO) Solidarity Center 69

Americas: American Revolution 1, 33, 52; capitalist slave system in 36–37; colonial expansion in 20–21; consequences of discovery of 21; cultural assimilation, limitations on 20–21; indentured servants 22; indigenous populations, genocide of 21, 22; plantations, capitalist slave system in 37; planter classes in, labor supply and 22; slavery, cash crops and necessity for 22

Amin, Samir 120

Appiah, Anthony 75

Ardouin, Beaubrun 41, 46, 51n10

Arendt, Hannah 19, 29

Aristide, Jean-Bertrand 3–4, 6, 63, 67–68, 71n12, 72n15, 74, 85–91, 93–95, 104–13, 113–14n7, 113n3, 113n6, 114n9, 114n11, 114n12, 128, 131; armed uprising against (2004) 67; break with interests of subordinate classes 87–89; class forces, changes in balance under 67; democratic discourse, Aristide and emergence of 85–86; Duvalierism, perspective on 86; landslide election victory (1990) 67, 105–6; lower classes, inclusion in political debate 85; neoliberal policies, pursuit of 3, 68; popular mandate for change, opposition to plans of 67; popular movement in support of, composition of 85; radical views on capitalism 95

aristocracy of the skin 27–28

Arouet, François-Marie 24

Arthur, Charles 113n1

Association of Haitian Industries 69

Ayiti Kale Je/Haiti Grassroots Watch 69, 70, 126, 129, 132–33

Bali 69

Balibar, Etienne 8, 10, 13

Ballard, John R. 72n18

Bazin, Marc 111

Bell, B. and Ekert, A. 69–70

Bell, Beverly 101, 105, 126

Bell, Madison Smartt 44–45

Bellegarde, Dantès 55, 71n11

Bellerive, Jean-Max 68, 115–16, 117, 121, 134

Bennett, Michèle 84

biological racism 11–12, 13, 14, 15–17, 18, 23–24, 28–29; slavery and 27–28

biopower, exercise of 16–17